THE XXL 365 AIR FRYER COOKBOOK

Delicious and Super-Easy Recipes for Every Day of
the Year incl. Sides, Breakfast, Desserts & More

MATTHEW K. ADAMS

ISBN - 9798351925127

TABLE OF CONTENTS

EXCLUSIVE BONUS

40 Weight Loss Recipes

&

14 Days Meal Plan

Scan the QR-Code and receive
the FREE download:

Introduction

First appearing in 2010, the air fryer has recently surged in popularity as a permanent feature of the family kitchen.

The air fryer is designed to cook great–tasting foods with the delicious fried flavour we love, yet with only a fraction of the oils and fats found in traditional fried foods.

Inside the pages of The XXL 365 Air Fryer Cookbook, you will discover 365 delicious, easy–to–prepare recipes for the whole family to enjoy.

Choose from a wide selection of sides, starters, snacks; hearty mains; and scrummy desserts that will have you reaching for The Air Fryer Cookbook again and again.

Cooking food with the air fryer has been associated with –
- Healthier diets containing less of the fats associated with heart disease, obesity, and other related health conditions
- Promoting weight loss as part of a reduced fat diet
- Each of the 365 recipes includes –
- a list of all the ingredients you will need
- the nutritional values of each recipe per Serving
- UK and US units of measurement

Choose a different recipe for every day of the year from our selection of tasty meat and fish dishes, vegetarian meals, and a wide variety of sweet and savoury options to suit everyone!

Happy Air Frying!

Tips and Tricks for Cooking with an Air Fryer
- Read the instruction booklet for your air fryer thoroughly before use.
- Preheat the air fryer before cooking.
- During cooking, open the air fryer periodically and give the food basket a gentle shake.
- Don't overfill the air fryer basket. Air fryers are available in a variety of sizes. Adapt your ingredients' quantities to suit your air fryer or cook in batches.
- Cooking times may vary according to the size, style, and brand of air fryer.
- Some recipes make use of the different utensils available for air fryers. Check your air fryer brand, model, and size to ensure you purchase the correct cooking accessories.

Alternatively, use ovenproof dishes that you already have, but check they fit your air fryer before starting to prepare your meal.

Note: To adapt the recipes to accommodate metric and imperial measurements quantities have been rounded up to the nearest whole or half number.

STARTERS AND SNACKS – AIRFRYER COOKBOOK

STARTERS, SNACKS AND SIDES – VEGETABLE DISHES

SWEET POTATO CHIPS

INGREDIENTS

- 1 large or 2 medium sweet potatoes
- Olive oil spray (other cooking oil sprays can be used)
- Salt (or other seasonings to taste)

METHOD

1. Preheat the air fryer to 200C//400F.
2. Peel and wash the sweet potatoes thoroughly.
3. Slice the potatoes as thinly as possible without them breaking up. A mandolin slicer is a useful tool here. You can use a knife but take care with fingers.
4. Pat the sweet potato pieces dry, then spread evenly across the air fryer basket.
5. Coat the potato pieces with the oil spray.
6. Optional: sprinkle in some salt to taste. (You can experiment with your preferred seasonings).
7. Cook for 12–15 minutes at 200C//400F.
8. Shake the basket every 5 minutes so the chips don't clump together.
   Continue cooking to your preferred taste and transfer to a cooling rack. Add additional seasonings as required and enjoy!

Nutritional Information per Serving:

SERVES –2 | CALORIES –52KCAL | PROTEIN –1.2G | CARBOHYDRATES –11.8G | FAT –01.G

CRISPY FRIED ONIONS

INGREDIENTS

- 2 large yellow onions
- 20ml of cooking oil
- Salt and pepper to taste

METHOD

1. Peel the onions and cut them into very thin round pieces with a sharp knife/
2. Preheat the air fryer to 150C//300F and spray with cooking oil.
3. Put your onion rings into a bowl and drizzle oil over them. Separate them.
4. Put the onion rings into the air fryer and cook at 150C//300F for about 10 minutes, giving them a shake to separate them about halfway through.
5. Turn the temperature down to 115C//240F and continue cooking for about 15–18 minutes.
6. Enjoy.

Nutritional Information per Serving:

SERVES –1+ | CALORIES –200KCAL | PROTEIN –15.2G | CARBOHYDRATES –43.2G | FAT –2.2.G

SALT AND VINEGAR CHICKPEAS

INGREDIENTS

- 1 x 425g//15oz can of chickpeas, drained and rinsed
- 250ml of white vinegar
- ½ teaspoon of sea salt
- 15ml of olive oil

METHOD

1. Drain and rinse the can of chickpeas. Dry thoroughly with kitchen roll.
2. Put the vinegar and dried chickpeas into a small saucepan and bring to a gentle simmer.
3. Remove the pan from the heat and steep the chickpeas in the vinegar for a further 30 minutes.
4. Drain the chickpeas removing any loose skins.
5. Preheat the air fryer to 200C//390F.
6. Spread the chickpeas evenly across the air fryer and cook for 4 minutes to dry them.
7. Add the salt and olive oil to a heated mixing boil.
8. Add the hot chickpeas to the bowl and toss to evenly coat in the salt and oil mixture.
9. Return the coated chickpeas to the air fryer and cook for a further 8 minutes, shaking the basket at intervals until crispy.
10. Add a little more seasoning to taste if required and serve immediately.

Nutritional Information per Serving:

SERVES –4 | CALORIES –430KCAL | PROTEIN –20.5G | CARBOHYDRATES –64.5G | FAT –9.9G

SWEET, SALT, OR BUTTER POPCORN

INGREDIENTS

- 75g//3oz of popcorn kernels
- ½ teaspoon of olive oil

Optional:

- ½ teaspoon salt
- 1 teaspoon sugar
- 1 tablespoon of melted butter

METHOD

1. Preheat the air fryer to 200C//400F.
2. Toss the kernels and olive oil together in a bowl. Make sure the kernels are well–coated in the oil.
3. Spread the kernels evenly across the bottom of the air fryer pan. Don't pack it too tightly as the corn needs room to pop!
4. Close the air fryer firmly! You don't want popping kernels to escape all over your kitchen.
5. Cook for about 7 minutes, giving the basket a shake every 2 minutes.
6. When you can no longer hear the corn popping, transfer to a bowl, toss with your preferred flavouring and serve immediately.

Nutritional Information per Serving:

SERVES –4 | CALORIES –89KCAL | PROTEIN –2 G | CARBOHYDRATES –13.8G | FAT –4G

CAYENNE BUFFALO CAULIFLOWER

INGREDIENTS

- 1 large head cauliflower
- 130g//4.50z of plain flour
- 1 teaspoon chicken bouillon granules
- 1/4 teaspoon cayenne pepper
- 1/4 teaspoon chilli powder
- 1/4 teaspoon of paprika
- 1/4 teaspoon of dried chilli flakes
- 225ml milk
- Cooking oil spray
- 30g//1oz butter
- 60ml cayenne hot sauce
- 2 cloves garlic, minced

METHOD

1. Cut the cauliflower into bite-size pieces, then rinse and drain.
2. Put all the dry ingredients into a large bowl, then gently whisk in the milk until you have a thick batter.
3. Spray the air fryer basket with canola oil and preheat to 200C//390F.
4. Toss the cauliflower into the batter until it is thoroughly coated.
5. Place the battered cauliflower in the air fryer basket and cook for 20 minutes at 200C//390F. Turn the cauliflower pieces after 10 minutes.
6. In a small saucepan, gently bring the butter, hot sauce, and garlic to a slow boil.
7. Once the mixture is boiling, reduce the heat, cover, and simmer for 2–3 minutes.
8. Transfer the cooked cauliflower to a large bowl and pour over the sauce.
9. Serve immediately.

Nutritional Information per Serving:

SERVES –4 | CALORIES –99KCAL | PROTEIN –3G | CARBOHYDRATES –14.8G | FAT –3.2G

TOMATOES AND HERBS IN BALSAMIC VINEGAR

INGREDIENTS

- 60ml of balsamic vinegar
- 1/2 teaspoon of sea salt
- 1/4 teaspoon of ground black pepper
- 15g//0.50z of dried oregano
- 1 teaspoon of red pepper flakes
- 2 large firm tomatoes
- Olive oil cooking spray

METHOD

1. In a shallow dish, mix the salt, pepper, oregano, and red pepper flakes into the balsamic vinegar.
2. Cut each tomato into four even pieces.
3. Preheat the air fryer to 180C//360F.
4. Dip each tomato slice into the vinegar mixture and place in a single layer in the air fryer.
5. Pour the remaining vinegar over the tomatoes.
6. Spray lightly with the olive oil.
7. Cook at 180C//360F for 5 minutes.
8. Carefully remove the tomatoes from the air fryer and serve hot.

Nutritional Information per Serving:

SERVES –4 | CALORIES –61KCAL | PROTEIN –0.7G | CARBOHYDRATES –5.8G | FAT –4.2G

HANUKKAH LATKES

INGREDIENTS

- 2–3 medium potatoes, peeled, washed and grated
- 1/2 a medium yellow onion, peeled and grated
- 2 eggs
- 30g//1oz of matzo meal (breadcrumbs or semolina make a useful alternative)
- Salt and pepper to taste
- Cooking spray
- Optional: sour cream and applesauce, for serving

METHOD

1. 1. Dry the grated onion and potatoes with a tea towel to remove the excess moisture.
2. 2. In a large bowl, mix the potato, onion, eggs, matzo meal, salt and pepper together thoroughly.
3. 3. Preheat the air fryer to 190C//375F and spray with cooking oil.
4. 4. Use a tablespoon to drop large scoops of the latke mixture into the air fryer, flattening the tops to make a patty. Spray with cooking spray.
5. 5. Cook the latkes for 8 minutes at 190C/375F. Repeat with the remaining latke mixture.
6. 6. Serve the cooked latkes with sour cream and applesauce.

Nutritional Information per Serving:

SERVES −4 | CALORIES −206KCAL | PROTEIN −3.5G | CARBOHYDRATES −19G | FAT −13G

DELICIOUSLY HEALTHY FALAFEL

INGREDIENTS

- 425g//15oz can of chickpeas
- 50g//2oz parsley
- 50g//2oz of coriander
- 30g//1oz of chopped onion
- 1/2 tablespoon of minced garlic
- 1 teaspoon of cumin
- 1 teaspoon of salt
- 1/4 teaspoon of pepper
- Optional: 1 small jalapeno chilli pepper, seeded and diced
- 1 teaspoon of baking powder
- 30g//1oz plain flour

METHOD

1. Drain the chickpeas and pat dry.
2. Use a food processor or hand blender to blend the chickpeas, parsley, coriander, onion, garlic, cumin, salt, pepper, jalapeño, and baking powder. You should have a smooth mixture.
3. In a bowl, combine the flour with the blended spices.
4. Use 2 tablespoons of mixture to make a small ball. Repeat until all the mixture is gone.
5. Preheat the air fryer to 180C//350F
6. Put the falafel balls into the air fryer
7. Cook at 180C//350F for 5−7 minutes. Turn the falafel over and cook for a further 5−7 minutes.
8. Serve hot or cold with dips, or as an accompaniment to a main meal.

Nutritional Information per Serving:

SERVES −4 (APPROXIMATELY 3 BALLS PER SERVING) | CALORIES −243KCAL | PROTEIN −12G | CARBOHYDRATES −43G | FAT −3G

STUFFED MUSHROOMS

INGREDIENTS

- 230g//8oz of button mushrooms
- 115g//4oz cream cheese, softened
- 1/2 teaspoon of garlic powder
- 1/4 teaspoon of paprika
- 1/4 teaspoon of chilli powder
- 1/4 teaspoon of sea salt
- Ground black pepper
- 60g//2oz grated cheese
- Parsley, finely chopped
- Spray cooking oil

METHOD

1. Remove the mushroom stems, chop into pieces, and put to one side.
2. Spray the mushroom cups thoroughly with cooking oil spray to prevent them drying out during cooking.
3. In a bowl, mix the cream cheese, garlic powder, paprika, chilli powder, salt, and pepper. Add the chopped mushroom stems and fold into the cream cheese mixture.
4. Preheat the air fryer to 182C//360F.
5. Stuff the mushroom cups with the cheese mixture.
6. Carefully place the stuffed mushrooms in the air fryer in a single layer. Cook in batches if required, but do not overfill the air fryer.
7. Cook at 182C//360F for 6–8 minutes. Larger mushrooms may need a little longer.
8. Sprinkle the grated cheese over the stuffed mushrooms and cook for another 1–2 minutes until the cheese melts.
9. Allow the mushrooms to cool, top with the chopped parsley, and serve.

Nutritional Information per Serving:

SERVES –MAKES 10 MUSHROOMS | CALORIES –66KCAL | PROTEIN –3G | CARBOHYDRATES –2G | FAT –5G

GARLIC MUSHROOMS

INGREDIENTS

- 230g//8oz of mushrooms
- 15–30ml of olive oil
- ½ teaspoon of garlic powder
- 1 teaspoon of Worcestershire Sauce
- Salt and pepper to taste
- Optional: lemon wedges
- 1 teaspoon of fresh parsley, chopped

METHOD

1. Cut mushrooms into large pieces (halves or quarters will do).
2. In a bowl toss your mushroom pieces with the oil, garlic powder, Worcestershire Sauce, salt, and pepper.
3. Preheat your air fryer to 200C//380F.
4. Add the mushroom mixture and cook at 200C//380F for 5–6 minutes.
5. Shake, and cook for a further 5–6 minutes.
6. Serve with a squeeze of lemon and topped with chopped parsley.

Nutritional Information per Serving:

SERVES –2 | CALORIES – 92KCAL | PROTEIN – 3G | CARBOHYDRATES – 4G | FAT – 7G

CHEESY BROCCOLI BITES

INGREDIENTS

- 280g//10oz fresh broccoli florets (not frozen as they will just go soggy)
- 60ml water
- 1 egg
- 200g//7oz of grated cheddar
- 85g//3oz of breadcrumbs
- Salt and pepper to taste

METHOD

1. In a saucepan of water, bring the broccoli to the boil and gently simmer for about 5 minutes, or until it is cooked through. It should still be quite firm, not soggy.
2. Chop the broccoli up finely, then place in a bowl.
3. Add the rest of the ingredients to the broccoli and mix thoroughly.
4. Use 2 tablespoons of the broccoli mixture to make a small ball and place on a baking tray. Repeat until all the mixture is gone.
5. Put the broccoli balls in the freezer for 30 minutes.
6. Preheat the air fryer to 180C//350F.
7. Remove the broccoli balls from the freezer and place them in the air fryer in a single layer.
8. Cook at 180C//350F for 5–10 minutes. Cook in batches that suit the size of your air fryer.
9. Eat hot or cold with your favourite dips.

Nutritional Information per Serving:

SERVES –4 (MAKES 28 BROCCOLI BITES) | CALORIES – 217KCAL | PROTEIN – 18.2G | CARBOHYDRATES – 22.8G | FAT – 6G

FRIED OLIVES

INGREDIENTS

- 1 x 280g//10oz jar stuffed green olives
- 255g//9oz of breadcrumbs
- 85g//3oz plain flour
- ½ teaspoon of garlic powder
- ½ teaspoon of paprika or chilli powder
- 3 eggs
- Olive oil cooking spray

METHOD

1. Start with 3 bowls. Crack the egg into the first bowl and whisk. Mix the flour, paprika and garlic powder in the second bowl. Put the breadcrumbs into the third bowl.
2. Drain and dry the olives and toss them in the flour.
3. Next, dip the olives in the bowl of beaten egg, coating them well.
4. Finally, turn the olives in the breadcrumb mixture so they are completely covered, then place them in a single layer onto a plate.
5. Spray the olives with the cooking oil and give the air fryer a light spritz of oil too.
6. Arrange the olives in the air fryer with plenty of space between them.
7. Preheat the air fryer to 200C//400F, then air fry them for 5 minutes.
8. Turn the olives, spray them with cooking spray, and air fry for a further 3 minutes.
9. Transfer them to a plate.
   Delicious served with a fresh oregano garnish and/or sprinkled with parmesan cheese.
   Eat with your favourite dipping sauce.

Nutritional Information per Serving:

SERVES −4 OLIVES PER SERVING | CALORIES −48KCAL | PROTEIN −1.9G | CARBOHYDRATES −7.2G | FAT −18.7G

BAKED BRIE

INGREDIENTS

- 1 sheet of prepared puff pastry
- 230g//8oz of brie cheese
- 60g//2oz fruit preserve
- 30g//1oz of mixed toasted nuts
- 1 egg
- 15ml of water
- Cooking oil spray

METHOD

1. Roll out the puff pastry sheet and put the brie in the centre.
2. Place the toasted nuts and jam on top of the brie.
3. Bring the corners of the puff pastry together over the brie and pinch the edges to seal it tightly.
4. Whisk the egg and water together in a bowl and brush the mixture over the pastry evenly.
5. Preheat the air fryer to 190C//375F, and spray with cooking oil.
6. Place the pastry−wrapped brie into the air fryer and cook at 190C//375F for 15−20 minutes, or until the pastry turns a golden brown.
7. Allow to cool for a few minutes before serving.

Nutritional Information per Serving:

SERVES −8 | CALORIES −314KCAL | PROTEIN −9.1G | CARBOHYDRATES −21.3G | FAT −21.5G

CRISPY POTATO PANCAKES

INGREDIENTS

- 455g//16oz leftover mashed potatoes cold
- 3 spring onions, sliced
- 1 teaspoon of dried oregano
- 1teaspoon of smoked paprika
- Salt and pepper
- 30g//1oz of plain flour
- 1 egg

METHOD

1. Put the mashed potato and sliced spring onions into a large bowl.
2. Add the flour, oregano, smoked paprika, salt, and pepper and mix well.
3. Whisk the egg and pour into the potato mixture. Mix thoroughly.
4. Use 2 tablespoons of potato mixture for each potato pancake and make into a burger shape.
5. Preheat the air fryer to 190C//380F and spray lightly with cooking oil.
6. Put the potato pancakes into the air fryer and cook at 190C//380F for 5 minutes.
7. Turn the potato pancakes, spritz with cooking oil, and cook for a further 5 minutes.
8. Plate your potato pancakes and serve with sour cream or your favourite dip.

Nutritional Information per Serving:

SERVES −6 | CALORIES −12KCAL | PROTEIN −1G | CARBOHYDRATES −3G | FAT −1G

COURGETTE FRITTERS

INGREDIENTS

- 3 courgettes
- 1/2 teaspoon sea salt
- 1 egg
- 60g//2oz plain flour
- 30g//1oz grated parmesan cheese
- 1/2 teaspoon of baking powder
- 1/4 teaspoon of lemon pepper
- 1/2 teaspoon of garlic powder
- 1/2 teaspoon of smoked paprika
- 1/2 teaspoon of Italian seasoning
- 2 spring onions, finely sliced
- Spray cooking oil

METHOD

1. Grate the courgettes into a bowl and stir in the salt. Leave to rest for 10 minutes.
2. Use a tea towel to squeeze any excess water out of the courgettes and return to the bowl.
3. Whisk the egg in a jug and add to the bowl along with the remaining ingredients (except the cooking oil.) Mix until combined.
4. Preheat the air fryer to 190C//380F and spray with cooking oil.
5. Use a tablespoon or ice cream scoop to add portions of the mixture to the air fryer about an inch apart. Gently flatten into burger shapes and spritz with cooking oil.
6. Cook at 190C//385F for 5–6 minutes, then flip, spritz with oil, and cook for another 5–6 minutes.
7. Continue in batches until all the batter is gone.
8. Serve warm with a dollop of sour cream and top with chopped spring onions or dill along with lemon wedges.

Nutritional Information per Serving:

SERVES –9 | CALORIES –68KCAL | PROTEIN –4G | CARBOHYDRATES –3G | FAT –5G

AVOCADO FRIES

INGREDIENTS

For the Avocado Fries:

- 2 avocados
- 1 egg, lightly beaten
- 85g//3oz breadcrumbs
- 1 and 1/4 teaspoons of lime chilli seasoning

For the Lime Dip:

- 60g//2oz fat–free of Greek yoghurt
- 45ml of light mayonnaise
- 2 teaspoons of fresh lime juice
- 1/2 teaspoon of lime chilli seasoning
- Sea salt to taste

METHOD

1. Peel the avocados, remove the stone, and cut into 16 wedges.
2. Whisk the egg in a shallow bowl.
3. In a separate bowl, combine the breadcrumbs with 1 teaspoon of the lime chilli seasoning.
4. Season the avocado wedges with the remaining 1/4 teaspoon of the lime chilli seasoning.
5. Dip each avocado piece first in the egg, and then in the breadcrumbs.
6. Preheat the air fryer to 200C//390F.
7. Spray the avocado fries with oil, transfer to the air fryer and cook for 3–4 minutes.
8. Turn the fries, spritz with oil, and cook for a further 3–4 minutes.
9. Serve hot with dipping a favourite dip.

Nutritional Information per Serving, 4 fries with sauce:

SERVES −4 | CALORIES −197KCAL | PROTEIN −7G | CARBOHYDRATES −15G | FAT −12.5G

BUTTERNUT BITES

INGREDIENTS

- 1 small butternut squash
- 30ml of olive oil
- 1/2 teaspoon of paprika
- 1/2 teaspoon of garlic powder
- Salt and pepper to taste

METHOD

1. Peel and cut the butternut squash into 1/2" cubes.
2. In a large bowl whisk the oil, paprika, garlic powder, salt, and pepper.
3. Add the cubes of squash and coat in the marinade.
4. Preheat the air fryer to 190C//380F.
5. Transfer the squash to the air fryer and cook at 190C//380°F for 10 minutes.
6. Shake and turn the squash, then continue cooking for the remaining 10–15 minutes until the squash is tender.
7. Serve warm.

Nutritional Information per Serving:

SERVES −4 | CALORIES −125KCAL | PROTEIN −1.5G | CARBOHYDRATES −16.8G | FAT −7.2G

CHEESE 'N' GARLIC CORN ON THE COB

INGREDIENTS

- 3 fresh corns on the cob
- 30g//1oz of softened butter
- 1 teaspoon of garlic powder
- Salt and black pepper to taste
- 30g//1oz grated parmesan
- 30g//1oz of fresh chopped parsley

METHOD

1. Remove the leaves and clean the cobs of corn. Cut them in half if you have a small air fryer.
2. Preheat the air fryer to 190C//380F.
3. Coat the corn thoroughly in the softened butter and season with garlic powder, salt, and pepper.
4. Put the cobs into the air fryer in a single layer with space between each one.
5. Cook at 190C//380F for 10 minutes.
6. Turn the corn and cook for a further 3–8 minutes until the corn is tender (times will depend on the size of the cobs of corn, and your air fryer model).
7. Serve warm coated in the parmesan and chopped parsley.

Nutritional Information per Serving:

SERVES −3 | CALORIES −184KCAL | PROTEIN −6G | CARBOHYDRATE −19G | FAT −1G

TORTILLA CHIPS

INGREDIENTS

- 12 corn tortillas
- 15ml of olive oil
- 2 teaspoons salt
- 15g//0.5oz of Jazzy Spice Blend (or make your own using equal parts white pepper, black pepper, garlic powder, paprika, cayenne, and onion powder)
- Optional: guacamole

METHOD

1. Brush the tortillas lightly on each side with olive oil and sprinkle with salt and the spice blend.
2. Cut each tortilla into 6 wedges.
3. Preheat the air fryer to 180C//350F.
4. Add the tortilla wedges to the air fryer in single layer batches (depending on the size of your air fryer).
5. Cook at 180C//350F for about 5 minutes until crispy and golden.
6. Serve with traditional guacamole or a dip of your choice.

Nutritional Information per Serving:

SERVES –2 | CALORIES –373KCAL | PROTEIN –8G | CARBOHYDRATES –64G | FAT –10G

SKIN—ON SQUASH CRISPS

INGREDIENTS

- 1 delicata squash (or small squash of your choice)
- 1/2 teaspoon of salt
- Olive oil cooking spray

METHOD

1. Wash the squash thoroughly and cut off the base and the stem.
2. Cut the squash in half from top to bottom and scoop out the seeds.
3. Cut the squash into half mood shape fries approximately 1/4–inch–thick.
4. Pre–heat the air fryer to 190C//375F.
5. Add the fries to the air fryer, spray with olive oil spray and sprinkle with salt.
6. Cook at 190C//375F for 5 minutes.
7. Pause the air fryer and shake well. Cook for a further 5 minutes and shake again.
8. Cook for a further 4–5 minutes, or until the fries cooked to taste.

Nutritional Information per Serving based on the delicata squash:

SERVES –2 | CALORIES –77KCAL | PROTEIN –5G | CARBOHYDRATES –19G | FAT –1G

GOATS CHEESE BITES WITH HONEY AND SPICE

INGREDIENTS

- 115g//4oz goats' cheese (not the crumbly type)
- 15g//0.5oz of finely chopped chives
- 1 egg
- 30g//1oz breadcrumbs
- Olive oil cooking spray
- 85g//3oz honey
- Tabasco sauce to taste

METHOD

1. In a bowl, gently fold together the goat's cheese and chives until they are evenly mixed.
2. Break off pieces of the mixture and roll into approximately 10 balls. Put on a tray and place in the freezer for about 45 minutes.
3. Lightly whisk the egg in one bowl and place the breadcrumbs into a second separate bowl.
4. Preheat the air fryer to 200C//400F.
5. Remove the cheese balls from the freezer and dip each one first into the egg and then into the breadcrumbs. Place immediately into the air fryer.
6. Lightly spray the cheese balls with the olive oil spray and cook at 200C//400F for about 6 minutes.
7. While the cheese balls are cooking, mix the honey and tabasco sauce.
8. Once cooked, let the cheese balls rest for 5 minutes in the air fryer before removing.
9. Put the Goats Cheese Bites on a plate, drizzle with spiced honey and serve warm.

Nutritional Information per Serving:

SERVES −10 | CALORIES −61G | PROTEIN −3.1G | CARBOHYDRATES −2.4G | FAT −4.4G

PUMPKIN SEED SNACK ATTACK

INGREDIENTS

- 255g//9oz fresh pumpkin seeds cut directly from a fresh pumpkin
- 15g//0.5oz butter, melted
- ½ teaspoon of garlic salt

METHOD

1. Wash and cut the pumpkin and remove the seeds and pulp.
2. Put into a colander or sieve and wash the pulp from the seeds. Pick off any stubborn bits with your fingers.
3. Put the seeds into a saucepan of boiling water, and simmer for 5 minutes. Drain and place the seeds in a bowl.
4. Preheat the air fryer to 180C//360F.
5. Add melted butter and garlic salt to the pumpkin seeds and stir thoroughly.
6. Pop the buttery seeds into the air fryer and cook at 180C//360F for 15 minutes.

Nutritional Information per Serving:

SERVES −4 | CALORIES −204KCAL | PROTEIN −10G | CARBOHYDRATES −3G | FAT −19G

CHEESY DIPPING STICKS

INGREDIENTS

- 8 cheese sticks
- ½ teaspoon of garlic powder
- ½ teaspoon of smoked paprika
- 1 egg
- 30g//1oz plain flour
- 60g//2oz breadcrumbs

METHOD

1. Place the cheese sticks on a tray in the freezer for 30 minutes.
2. In a bowl, whisk up the egg. In a separate bowl, combine the spices and breadcrumbs. Set the bowls to one side.
3. Put the flower in a resealable plastic food bag.
4. Take the cheese sticks from freezer and cut in half. Place the halves into the bag with the flour. Shake gently to thoroughly cover the cheese sticks with the flour.
5. Dip each cheese stick in egg wash then in the breadcrumbs so that they are thoroughly coated.
6. Return the coated cheese sticks to the freezer for a further 30 minutes.
7. Preheat the air fryer to 190C//370F.
8. Remove the cheese sticks from the freezer and cook for about 4–5 minutes at 190C//370F degrees.
9. Once cooked, turn off the heat and allow to rest in the air fryer for a few minutes. Gently reshape with a silicon kitchen utensil.
10. Remove from the air fryer and serve warm with a favourite dipping sauce.

Nutritional Information per Serving:

SERVES –8 | CALORIES –130KCAL | PROTEIN –8G | CARBOHYDRATES –9G | FAT –7G

MACARONI CHEESY BITES

INGREDIENTS

- 110g//4oz leftover chilled macaroni cheese (see mains recipe)
- 1 egg beaten
- 15ml of milk
- 130g//4.5oz golden breadcrumbs
- 1½ teaspoon of oregano
- 1 teaspoon of garlic powder
- 1 teaspoon of paprika
- 1 teaspoon of black pepper
- Cooking oil spray
- Chopped chives
- Chopped chillies
- Diced sausages

METHOD

1. Optional: combine your extra ingredients with the leftover macaroni cheese.
2. Scoop out a tablespoon of the macaroni mixture and roll in a ball. Repeat until all the mixture is gone.
3. Place the macaroni balls in the freezer for 15 minutes to firm up.
4. In a bowl, combine the golden breadcrumbs, garlic powder, paprika and dried oregano.
5. In a separate bowl, whisk the egg with the milk.
6. Preheat your air fryer to 180C//350F. Spray lightly with cooking oil.
7. Remove the macaroni balls from the freezer. Dip each one into the beaten egg, then roll in the seasoned breadcrumbs mixture until thoroughly coated.
8. Place directly into the air fryer in a single layer leaving space between each macaroni ball. You may need to cook in batches.
9. Cook for 8 minutes at 180C//350F.
10. Shake the basket gently, spray in a little more cooking oil and cook for a further 4–5 minutes.
11. Serve immediately.

Nutritional Information per Serving:

SERVES –10 | CALORIES –76KCAL | PROTEIN –3G | CARBOHYDRATES –13.6G | FAT –1.2G

ONION AND MUSHROOM SIDE

INGREDIENTS

- 2 garlic cloves, finely chopped
- 30ml of olive oil
- 4 teaspoons of freshly squeezed lemon juice
- 1 teaspoon of salt
- 1 teaspoon of Worcestershire sauce
- 450g//1lb button mushrooms, cut into halves
- 1 small onion, sliced thinly
- 15g//0.5oz of fresh chopped parsley
- 15g//0.5oz of fresh thyme leaves
- ¼ teaspoon of lemon zest

METHOD

1. Whisk the garlic, oil, lemon juice, salt, and Worcestershire together in a large bowl.
2. Preheat the air fryer to 200C//400F.
3. Toss the mushrooms and onion in the mixture until it has been completely absorbed (about 30 seconds).
4. Spoon the mushroom mixture in a single layer into the air fryer.
5. Cook at 200C//400° for 13–15 minutes, tossing at intervals.
6. When the mushrooms and onions are tender and golden, serve hot sprinkled with the lemon zest, fresh parsley, and thyme.

Nutritional Information per Serving:

SERVES –2 | CALORIES –201KCAL | PROTEIN –6G | CARBOHYDRATES –16G | FAT –14G

SWEET POTATO HASH

INGREDIENTS

- 1 large, sweet potato
- 1 yellow onion, finely chopped
- 1 red bell pepper, seeded and finely chopped
- 45ml of olive oil
- 1 and 1/2 teaspoons of smoked paprika
- 1 teaspoon of sea salt
- Freshly ground pepper to taste
- 2 spring onions, thinly sliced
- Fresh chopped dill

METHOD

1. Peel and chop the sweet potato into ½ cubes and place in a large bowl.
2. Preheat the air fryer to 200C//400F.
3. Add the onion, pepper, olive oil, paprika, salt and pepper, and toss with the potato cubes until combined.
4. Cook the mixture in batches according to the size of your air fryer.
5. Arrange the potato mixture in a single layer and cook at 200C//400F for 14 minutes, tossing at intervals.
6. Serve hot topped with spring onions and dill.

Nutritional Information per Serving:

SERVES –2 TO 4 | CALORIES –144KCAL | PROTEIN –1G | CARBOHYDRATES –11G | FAT –11G

HASH BROWNS

INGREDIENTS

- 450g//1lb russet potatoes (or 3 medium potatoes) peeled and grated
- 60ml of water
- 15ml of vegetable oil
- 3/4 teaspoon of salt

METHOD

1. Cook the potatoes in the water for a few minutes. They should be cooked through, but firm and the mixture should be slightly sticky.
2. Once cooked, allow potatoes to cool, then toss with the oil and salt.
3. Preheat the air fryer to 200C//400F.
4. Shape the hash browns into burger shapes about ¼" thick.
5. Place in the air fryer in single layered batches for 15–20 minutes at 200C//400F until the hash browns are golden brown and crispy.

Nutritional Information per Serving:

SERVES –4 | CALORIES –108KCAL | PROTEIN –1.9G | CARBOHYDRATES –17.8G | FAT –3.5G

BLOOMING ONION WITH DIPPING SAUCE

INGREDIENTS

For the Onion:

- 1 large yellow onion
- 3 eggs
- 15ml of water

- 130g//4.5oz breadcrumbs
- 2 teaspoons of paprika
- 1 teaspoon of garlic powder

- 1 teaspoon of onion powder
- 1 teaspoon of salt
- 45ml of olive oil

For the Sauce:

- 85g//3oz mayonnaise
- 30g//1oz of ketchup
- 1 teaspoon of horseradish

- ½ teaspoon of paprika
- ½ teaspoon of garlic powder
- ¼ teaspoon of dried oregano

- Salt to taste

METHOD

1. Peel the onion and cut off the onion's stem so that you have a flat section to rest the onion upon.
2. Cut down through the onion into 12–16 sections (like segments of an orange,) taking care not to cut all the way through so that the onion pieces are still attached.
3. Gently tease out onion sections, like separated petals.
4. Whisk the eggs together with the water in a bowl.
5. In a separate bowl, combine the breadcrumbs and spices.
6. Preheat the air fryer to 190C//375F.
7. Gently dip the 'petals' of the onion into the egg, then immediately dip it into the breadcrumb mixture so that they stick to the egg.
8. Drizzle oil over the onion, place in the air fryer and cook at 190C//375F for about 20–25 minutes, or until the onion is tender all the way through.
9. While waiting for the onion to cook, in another bowl, blend the remaining ingredients to make a smooth dipping sauce.
10. Serve immediately.

Nutritional Information per Serving:

SERVES –4 | CALORIES –379KCAL | PROTEIN –9.5G | CARBOHYDRATES –35.3G | FAT –23.1G

SPANISH OMLETTE

INGREDIENTS

- 500g//1.1lb of baby potatoes
- 6 eggs
- 30ml of olive oil
- Olive oil cooking spray
- Sea salt

METHOD

1. Leaving the skins on the potatoes, chop them into medium slices.
2. Preheat the air fryer to 180C//360F.
3. Toss the potatoes in a bowl with the olive oil and salt.
4. Put the potatoes in the air fryer and cook for at 180C/360F for 17–20 minutes.
5. Pause the air fryer at intervals to give the potatoes a gentle shake.
6. Break the eggs into a bowl and whisk with a little salt to taste.
7. When the potatoes have finished cooking, load into a baking pan and pour over the egg mixture making sure all the potatoes are covered.
8. Place the pan in the air fryer and cook at 160C//320F for 17 minutes.
9. Cook immediately for a further 5 minutes at the higher temperature of180C/360F to make sure the eggs are set.
10. Turn the omelette over, spritz with cooking oil and cook for another 5 minutes.
11. When cooked, remove from the air fryer, slice into wedges, and serve.

Nutritional Information per Serving:

SERVES –4 | CALORIES –104KCAL | PROTEIN –5G | CARBOHYDRATES –11G | FAT –4G

FRENCH TOAST DIPPING STICKS

INGREDIENTS

- 8 slices bread (white or brown – or mix it up!)
- 4 eggs
- 60ml of milk
- 2½ teaspoons of ground cinnamon
- 1 teaspoon of vanilla extract
- ½ teaspoon of salt

METHOD

1. Cut each slice of bread into 3–4 pieces, or 'sticks'.
2. Whisk the eggs, milk, vanilla, cinnamon, and salt in a bowl.
3. Preheat the air fryer to 190C//375F.
4. Dip the bread sticks into the egg mixture, but don't let them soak.
5. Place the egg covered bread sticks on a lined tray, or directly into the lined air fryer.
6. Cook the French Toast for 5–6 minutes at 190C//375F or until crisp and golden.
7. Serve immediately with honey, jam, or maple syrup.

Nutritional Information per Serving:

SERVES –4 | CALORIES –131KCAL | PROTEIN –5.1G | CARBOHYDRATES –14.8G | FAT –7.3G

BREAKFAST BANANA SOUFFLE

INGREDIENTS

- 2 medium bananas, peeled
- 2 eggs
- ½ teaspoon of ground cinnamon
- Olive oil cooking spray

METHOD

1. Using a hand blender, combine the peeled bananas, eggs, and cinnamon into a smooth batter.
2. Preheat the air fryer to 180C//350F.
3. Spritz the souffle ramekin dishes with olive and distribute the batter mix evenly among them.
4. Put the ramekins carefully into the air fryer and cook for 15 minutes at 180C/350F.
5. Serve immediately with vanilla ice cream.

Nutritional Information per Serving:

SERVES –2 | CALORIES –85KCAL | PROTEIN –3G | CARBOHYDRATES 14G | FAT –2G

ROASTED BEETROOT

INGREDIENTS

- 3 medium beetroots, peeled
- 15ml of olive oil
- Salt and pepper to taste
- Olive oil cooking spray

METHOD

1. Cut your peeled beetroots in wedges, fries, or cubes as preferred.
2. Preheat the air fryer to 180C//360F.
3. Put the olive oil and seasoning into a bowl and toss in the beetroot pieces. Make sure the beetroot is coated well in the oil.
4. Cook in the air fryer for 20 minutes at 180C//360F.
5. Spritz with the olive oil cooking spray, turn the air fryer up to 200C//400F and cook for a further 5 minutes.

Nutritional Information per Serving:

SERVES –3 TO 4 | CALORIES –115KCAL | PROTEIN –2G | CARBOHYDRATE –12G | FAT –7G

MIXED VEGGIE FRIES

INGREDIENTS

- 2 medium carrots, peeled, washed, and sliced
- 1 medium courgette, washed and sliced
- 200g//7oz butternut squash, peeled, washed, and sliced
- 200g//7oz sweet potato, peeled, washed, and sliced
- 1.5 teaspoons of olive oil
- 2 teaspoons of dried oregano
- 2 teaspoons of dried thyme
- Salt and pepper to taste

NB: mix and match any of the vegetables in the recipe to the quantities specified.

METHOD

1. In a bowl, mix the seasoning into the olive oil.
2. Preheat the air fryer to 180C//360F.
3. Toss in the sliced vegetables ensuring they are coated well with the seasoned oil.
4. Cook in the air fryer at 180C//360F for 20 minutes, pausing the fryer to give them a shake at intervals.
5. Optional: if you prefer your fries crispy, then cook for a further 12 minutes at the same temperature.
6. Serve with your favourite dipping sauce.

Nutritional Information per Serving:

SERVES –3 TO 4 | CALORIES –103KCAL | PROTEIN –2G | CARBOHYDRATES –21G | FAT –2G

CLASSIC CHEESY DUMPLINGS

INGREDIENTS

- 60g//2oz of shredded suet
- 100g//3.5oz of self–raising flour
- 45g//1.5oz cheddar cheese, grated
- 15g//0.5oz of fresh parsley, chopped
- Salt and pepper to taste
- 50–75ml of water to mix

METHOD

1. In a large bowl, add all the ingredients and mix thoroughly.
2. Measure 75ml of water into a jug. Add a little water to the dry mixture and begin combining the ingredients.
3. Continue adding a little water at the time to bind the mixture until you have a soft, slightly sticky dough mixture.
4. Preheat the air fryer to 160C//320F.
5. With floured hands, break pieces off the dough mixture to form golf ball sized dumplings. Put the dumplings into the air fryer with space between each one.
6. Cook for about 10 minutes at 160C//320F.
7. Serve hot in stews or casseroles.

Nutritional Information per Serving:

SERVES –3 TO 4 | CALORIES –238KCAL | PROTEIN –6G | CARBOHYDRATES –18G | FAT –15G

QUESADILLA

INGREDIENTS

For the Quesadilla Filling:

- 1 can of black beans
- 170g//6oz sweetcorn
- 255g//9oz grated cheddar cheese, frozen
- 30ml of sour cream
- 30g//1oz of garlic powder
- 15g//0.5oz of Mexican seasoning

For the Wraps:

- 8 tortilla wraps
- 1 egg, whisked with a little water
- 45g//1.5oz of salsa
- 100g//3.5oz of Mexican cheese, grated

METHOD

1. Put all the Quesadilla filling ingredients into a large bowl and mix thoroughly with a fork.
2. Load some filling over one of the tortilla wraps and sprinkle grated cheese over the top.
3. Spread salsa on one side of a second tortilla wrap and press it salsa–side down over the grated cheese on the first wrap to create a sandwich.
4. Preheat the air fryer to 180C//360F.
5. Brush egg wash over the top of the tortilla 'sandwich' and fix it with cocktail sticks to hold the Quesadilla firmly together.
6. Place it carefully into the air fryer. Cook at 180C//360F for 4 minutes.
7. Remove the cocktail sticks and carefully turn the Quesadilla over. Brush with a little extra egg wash.
8. Increase the temperature to 200C//400F and cook for another 2 minutes.
9. Repeat until the remaining tortilla wraps and fillings are all gone.
10. Slice and serve hot or cold with extra salsa on the side.

Nutritional information per Serving:

SERVES –4 | CALORIES –590KCAL | PROTEIN –28G | CARBOHYDRATES –45G | FAT –34G

CROUTONS

INGREDIENTS

- 3 small bread rolls
- 1 teaspoon of olive oil
- 1 teaspoon of garlic puree
- 1 teaspoon of dried oregano

METHOD

1. Dice the bread and put into a bowl with the olive oil.
2. Add the garlic puree and oregano. (If you prefer plain crouton then leave this step out.)
3. Use your hands to mix the bread chunks thoroughly with the seasoned olive oil.
4. Preheat the air fryer to 200C//400F.
5. Put the bread chunks into the air fryer and cook at 200C//400F for 4 minutes.
6. Serve immediately with soup or salad.
7. Optional: For hard croutons to accompany soups cook for 6 minutes.

Nutritional Information per Serving:

SERVES –4 | CALORIES –69KCAL | PROTEIN –2G | CARBOHYDRATES –11G | FAT –2G

ROASTED BELL PEPPERS

INGREDIENTS

- 3 bell peppers of different colours
- Olive oil cooking spray
- 1 teaspoon of dried thyme
- Salt and pepper to taste

METHOD

1. Remove the stalk and seeds from the peppers and wash thoroughly.
2. Cut the peppers into chunks.
3. Preheat the air fryer to 180C//360F.
4. Lightly spray the air fryer with oil and add the pepper chunks.
5. Spritz the pepper lightly with olive oil spray and sprinkle over the thyme.
6. Cook at 180C//360F for 8 minutes, pausing the fryer to give the peppers a shake at intervals. Serve while still warm.
7. Optional: For crispy pepper cook for 10 minutes. For chargrilled peppers cook for 12 minutes.

Nutritional Information per Serving:

SERVES −3 TO 4 | CALORIES −56KCAL | PROTEIN −2G | CARBOHYDRATES −11G | FAT −1G

WARM SALAD WITH CHICKPEAS, PEPPERS, AND SWEETCORN
• •

INGREDIENTS

- 600g//21oz of canned chickpeas
- 1 medium red pepper
- 200g//7oz of frozen sweetcorn kernels
- 2 crisp celery sticks
- 1 small avocado

- ¼ of a cucumber
- ½ small red onion
- 30ml of olive oil
- 1 teaspoon of wholegrain mustard
- ¼ teaspoon of garlic powder

- 1 teaspoon of dried basil
- 2 teaspoons of Mexican seasoning
- Salt and pepper to taste

METHOD

1. Preheat the air fryer to 180C//360F.
2. Remove the seeds and stem from the red pepper, wash, and chop into medium pieces. Drain and rinse the can of chickpeas, and pat dry.
3. Put the pepper and chickpeas into the air fryer with the frozen sweetcorn and sprinkle with Mexican seasoning and salt and pepper.
4. Cook for 8 minutes at 180C//360F.
5. Meanwhile, peel and slice the avocado and red onion. The red onion should be cut into thin slices, and the avocado into small chunks. Wash and dice your cucumber and celery. Put all these ingredients aside in a salad bowl.
6. In a separate bowl, mix up the olive oil, basil, wholegrain mustard, and garlic powder.
7. Pour the seasoned olive oil into the salad bowl with the onion, cucumber and celery and mix.
8. The air fryer should be finished cooking, so open it up and add the ingredients to the salad bowl. Toss lightly, but thoroughly.
9. The salad is best served immediately but can be stored in containers to eat cold later.

Nutritional Information per Serving:

SERVES −3 TO 4 | CALORIES −348KCAL | PROTEIN −16G | CARBOHYDRATES −58G | FAT −12G

ROASTED MEDITERRANEAN VEGETABLES

INGREDIENTS

- 500g//1.1lb fresh mix of Mediterranean vegetables, such as red onion, courgette, butternut squash and red peppers
- Optional: alternatively, buy a bag of prepared frozen Mediterranean vegetables
- 15ml of olive oil
- 15g//0.5oz of dried parsley
- 15g//0.5oz of dried oregano
- Salt and pepper to taste

METHOD

1. Wash, peel and chop the vegetables into medium sized chunks (or open your bag of vegetables) and place in a bowl.
2. Preheat the air fryer to 180C//360F.
3. Add the dried seasonings and olive oil to the veggie bowl and mix well until the vegetables are well coated.
4. Put the seasoned vegetables into the air fryer and cook for 12 minutes at 180C//360F.
5. Check the courgettes with a fork. It should be tender and crispy when cooked. If not quite done, then cook for a further 3 minutes.

Nutritional Information per Serving:

SERVES –3 TO 4 | CALORIES –229KCAL | PROTEIN –9G | CARBOHYDRATES –36G | FAT –8G

VEGETABLE PAKORA

INGREDIENTS

For the Batter:

- 255g//9oz gram flour
- 60g//2oz self–raising flour
- 15ml of lime juice
- A little water for mixing

For the Filling:

- 1 medium sweet potato, peeled and diced
- 150g//5oz leftover vegetables
- 1 teaspoon of garam masala
- ¼ teaspoon of chilli powder
- 1 teaspoon of tandoori powder
- Salt and pepper to taste

METHOD

1. Steam the sweet potatoes on the stove until they are soft and slightly mushy.
2. In a separate bowl, add both flours, seasoning and lime juice and mix well.
3. Add the lime juice, and gradually stir/whisk in a little water a bit at time until you have a smooth thin batter.
4. When the steamed potato is ready, mash well with the leftover vegetables to create a vegetable mash mixture.
5. Add the vegetable mash to the batter and mix well to combine.
6. Preheat the air fryer to 180C//360F.
7. Scoop out tablespoons of the Pakora mixture and shape into balls or burger shapes. They should be arranged in a single layer with space between each one.
8. Cook at 180C//360F for 20 minutes.
9. Serve with raita, Greek yoghurt, or mayonnaise.

Nutritional Information per Serving:

SERVES –4 | CALORIES –342KCAL | PROTEIN –17G | CARBOHYDRATES –57G | FAT –5G

SPINACH WITH BUTTER AND GARLIC

INGREDIENTS

- 300g//10.50z fresh washed spinach
- 30g//1oz of butter, room temperature
- 2 teaspoons of garlic powder
- Salt and pepper to taste

METHOD

1. Preheat the air fryer to 180C//360F.
2. Lightly squeeze any excess water out of the spinach and add to the air fryer. Layer the top with butter and seasoning.
3. Cook for 3 minutes at 180C//360F.
4. Stir with a fork and cook for a further 2 minutes at 180C//360F.
5. Stir and serve.

Nutritional Information per Serving:

SERVES –2 | CALORIES –80KCAL | PROTEIN –5G | CARBOHYDRATES –8G | FAT –5G

SAGE AND ONION STUFFING BALLS

INGREDIENTS

- 450g//1lb sausage meat
- 20g/0.7oz butter, firm, straight out of the fridge
- ½ white onion
- ½ bread roll
- 2 tablespoons dried sage
- Salt and pepper to taste
- Optional: extra breadcrumbs for binding

METHOD

1. Chop the bread roll into small chunks.
2. Peel and dice your onion into small pieces.
3. Chop the butter into small chunks.
4. Put all the ingredients with the seasoning in a bowl and mix to combine.
5. Take a tablespoon of mixture and make a medium sized ball, about golf ball sized. Place on a tray and repeat until all the mixture is gone.
6. Place the tray of stuffing balls in the fridge for an hour.
7. A few minutes before you begin cooking, preheat the air fryer to 180C//360F.
8. Remove the stuffing balls from the fridge, place in the air fryer, and cook for 10 minutes at 180C/360F.

Nutritional Information per Serving:

SERVES –4 (MAKES APPROXIMATELY 9–12 MEDIUM STUFFING BALLS) | CALORIES –135KCAL | PROTEIN –6G | CARBOHYDRATES –1G | FAT –12G

CRISPY KALE

INGREDIENTS

- 80g//3oz of fresh kale
- 15ml of olive oil
- Salt and pepper to taste

METHOD

1. Preheat the air fryer to 180C//360F.
2. Wash and trim the kale and place in a mixing bowl.
3. Add the salt, pepper and olive oil and toss in the kale until it is well coated with the seasoned olive oil.
4. Put the kale in the air fryer. Cook for 3 minutes at 180C//360F.
5. Turn the air fryer up to 200C//400F and cook for a further 2 minutes.
6. Serve immediately.

Nutritional Information per Serving:

SERVES −2 | CALORIES −81KCAL | PROTEIN −1G | CARBOHYDRATES −3G | FAT −7G

SNACKY AVOCADO AND EGG

INGREDIENTS

- 2 medium avocados
- 4 eggs
- A small handful of fresh parsley, finely chopped
- A small handful of fresh chives, finely chopped
- Salt and pepper

METHOD

1. Cut the avocado in half from top to bottom. Remove the stones and some of the flesh to increase the size of the holes.
2. Preheat the air fryer to 175C//340F.
3. Sprinkle the avocado halves with salt, pepper, and the fresh parsley and chives.
4. Carefully break an egg into each avocado hole where the stone was.
5. Put the avocado halves carefully into the air fryer.
6. Cook for 8 minutes at 175C//340F.
7. Sprinkle with extra salt and pepper to taste, and garnish with chives and parsley and serve.

NB: Sprinkle a little grated cheese over the top for added flavour.

Nutritional Information per Serving:

SERVES −2 | CALORIES −447KCAL | PROTEIN −15G | CARBOHYDRATES −18G | FAT −38G

VEGETABLE THAI PATTIES

INGREDIENTS

- 1 large broccoli
- 1 large cauliflower
- 6 large carrots
- A handful of peas
- 420g//15oz of cauliflower rice (or make your own by blending half a large head of cauliflower into rice−sized pieces)
- 1 large onion peeled and diced
- 1 small courgette
- 2 leeks, washed thoroughly and thinly sliced
- 1 can of coconut milk
- 60g//2oz of plain flour
- 1 cm of fresh ginger, peeled and grated
- 15g//0.5oz of garlic puree
- 15ml of olive oil
- 15g//0.5oz of Thai green curry paste
- 15g//0.5oz of ground coriander
- 15g//0.5oz of mixed spice
- 1 teaspoon of cumin
- Salt and pepper to taste

METHOD

1. First, prepare the vegetables so they are ready to use when they're needed.
2. Add the olive oil, onion, garlic and ginger to a wok, and fry until the onion is browned.
3. Steam the broccoli, cauliflower, carrots, and peas until nearly cooked – about 20 minutes.
4. Now, add the courgette and leek with the Thai green curry paste to the wok and cook on for 5 minutes on a medium heat.
5. Pour in the coconut milk and seasonings and mix well.
6. Add in the cauliflower rice and mix again. Simmer for a further 10 minutes.
7. After 10 minutes of simmering, the sauce should now be reduced by half.
8. Add in the steamed vegetables and mix thoroughly until combined.
9. Transfer the mixture to a bowl and place in the fridge for about an hour to cool and firm up.
10. The vegetable Thai patties mixture is ready to cook.
11. Preheat the air fryer to 180C//350F.
12. Use a tablespoon to scoop out spoonfuls of mixture and shape them into patties.
13. Place in the air fryer and cook at 180C//350F for about 10 minutes.
14. Serve with your favourite dipping sauce.

NB: Adjust the spicy heat of the final patties by reducing or adding to the ginger and Thai green curry paste.

Nutritional Information per Serving:

SERVES –4 | CALORIES –117KCAL | PROTEIN –2G | CARBOHYDRATES –12G | FAT –7G

CAULIFLOWER BITES WITH HONEY GLAZE

INGREDIENTS

- 1 small cauliflower
- 30g//1oz of oats
- 45g//1.5oz of plain flour
- 45g//1.5oz desiccated coconut
- 1 egg, beaten
- 30g//1oz of honey
- 1 teaspoon of garlic puree
- 30ml of soy sauce
- 1 teaspoon of mixed spice
- 1 teaspoon of dried mixed herbs
- ½ teaspoon of mustard powder
- Salt and pepper to taste.

METHOD

1. Cut the cauliflower up into small florets and set to one side.
2. Preheat the air fryer to 180C//350F.
3. Put the oats, flour, coconut, salt and pepper into a bowl and mix. Beat the egg in a separate bowl and set to one side.
4. Roll the cauliflower florets in the beaten egg, and then the oat mixture.
5. Put the florets into the air fryer and cook for 15 minutes on 180C//350F.
6. In a mixing bowl prepare the honey glaze by mixing the remaining ingredients together.
7. When it's cooked, remove the cauliflower florets carefully from the air fryer and put them into the glaze. Use tongs to turn the cauliflower so that it is thoroughly coated in the honey mixture.
8. Put the florets back in the air fryer (use a baking mat or shallow dish as it will be messy) and cook for another 5 minutes at 180C//350F.
9. Serve with crisp Iceberg lettuce and sliced ham.

Nutritional Information per Serving:

SERVES –2 TO 4 | CALORIES –134KCAL | PROTEIN –5G | CARBOHYDRATES –24G | FAT –2G

PINEAPPLE FRIES WITH HONEY GLAZE

INGREDIENTS

- 1 medium pineapple
- 15g//0.5oz of cinnamon

For the Honey Glaze:

- 85g//3oz honey
- 15g//0.5oz of light brown sugar
- 15g//0.5oz butter, softened
- Optional: ¼ teaspoon of vanilla extract

METHOD

1. Prepare the honey glaze. Combine all the ingredients for the glaze in a bowl and stir until they are all combined.
2. Cut off the top and bottom of the pineapple and remove the scaly skin.
3. Cut the pineapple fruit into slices.
4. Preheat the air fryer to 180C//360F and spray lightly with cooking oil.
5. Load the slices into the air fryer in a single layer with space between each one.
6. Gently brush the honey glaze over the pineapple pieces. It will be a bit messy so take care.
7. Air fry at 180C//360F for 8–12 minutes.
8. Sprinkle a little ground cinnamon over the pineapple in the air fryer oven, turn the air fryer up to 200C//400F, and cook for a further 5 minutes.
9. Serve immediately.

Nutritional Information per Serving:

SERVES –4 | CALORIES –118KCAL | PROTEIN –1G | CARBOHYDRATES –31G | FAT –1G

CRISPY AUBERGINE

INGREDIENTS

- 1 medium aubergine, cut into ¼ inch rounds
- 4 teaspoons sea salt
- 2 lightly beaten eggs
- 60ml milk
- 85g//3oz of Italian breadcrumbs (or make your own Italian breadcrumbs, seasoned with onion powder, garlic powder, parsley, basil, oregano, and salt and pepper to taste.)
- 30g//1oz grated parmesan cheese
- Cooking oil spray

METHOD

1. Place the aubergine rounds on a wire rack and salt thoroughly. Leave for 30–40 for the salt to absorb any excess moisture.
2. Rinse the salt from the aubergine and pat dry with kitchen roll.
3. Preheat the air fryer 190C//370F.
4. Whisk the eggs and milk together in a bowl. In a separate bowl, combine the Italian breadcrumbs and parmesan cheese.
5. Dip the aubergine rounds in the egg, and then the breadcrumbs. Make sure they are thoroughly coated with breadcrumbs.
6. Spritz the air fryer with cooking oil and place the breaded rounds into the air fryer in a single layer.
7. Cook at 190C/370F for 7 minutes. Pause the air fryer. Turn the aubergine rounds and spritz with a little more oil. Cook for another 7 minutes.
8. Remove the breaded aubergine slices, and sprinkle lightly with salt to taste.
9. Cook in batches depending on the size of your air fryer.

Nutritional Information per Serving:

SERVES −4 | CALORIES −286KCAL | PROTEIN −14G | CARBOHYDRATES −39G | FAT −9G

MOROCCAN ROAST POTATOES

INGREDIENTS

- 1kg//2lb potatoes
- Juice of 1 large lemon
- 80ml of olive oil
- 5 garlic cloves, minced
- 1 teaspoon cumin
- ½ teaspoon paprika
- ½ teaspoon turmeric
- ½ teaspoon black pepper
- 1 teaspoon of salt
- ½ teaspoon vegetable stock powder
- Optional: for a spicier taste, add 2 teaspoons of Harissa paste

METHOD

1. Peel the potatoes and cut into large chunks roughly the same size.
2. Combine the remaining ingredients in a measuring jug and whisk until blended.
3. Preheat air fryer to 200C/400F.
4. Pour the oil and spice mixture into a large bowl and carefully add the potatoes, turning until they are thoroughly coated in the mixture.
5. Put the potatoes in the air fryer. Don't overfill it; 2 layers maximum.
6. Cook at 200C//400F for about 10 minutes. Pause the air fryer, toss the potatoes, and cook for a further 10 minutes to ensure they are crispy all over.
7. Serve hot.

Nutritional Information per Serving:

SERVES −4 | CALORIES −347KCAL | PROTEIN −5G | CARBOHYDRATES −43.2G | FAT −19G

ROAST RADISHES

INGREDIENTS

- 450g//1lb fresh radishes
- 15ml of olive oil
- 1 teaspoon garlic powder
- 1/2 teaspoon salt
- 15g//0.5oz parmesan cheese, grated
- 1 teaspoon fresh parsley, finely chopped

METHOD

1. Wash and dry the radishes. Trim and cut into large chunks; halves or quarters, depending on how large the radishes are.
2. Preheat air fryer to 200C//400F.
3. In a large bowl, mix the oil, garlic powder and salt.
4. Add the radish chunks and turn to coat thoroughly with the oil mixture.
5. Put the oiled radishes into the air fryer and cook for 12 minutes at 200C//400F. Give the radishes a shake about halfway through cooking.
6. Test them with a fork, and if they are tender, then remove from the fryer.
7. Serve sprinkled with the parmesan cheese and chopped parsley.

Nutritional Information per Serving:

SERVES −4 (1 RADISH PER SERVING) | CALORIES −57KCAL | PROTEIN −1G | CARBOHYDRATES −5G | FAT −4G

CHEESY PARMESAN CRISPS

INGREDIENTS

- 45g//1.5oz of parmesan cheese, shredded, not grated
- Dried basil (optional)

METHOD

1. Preheat the air fryer to 200C//400F.
2. Use a tablespoon to sprinkle and share the parmesan cheese among some muffin tins.
3. If you are using the seasoning, sprinkle basil over the top.
4. Put the muffin tins to the heated air fryer for about a minute until the cheese has melted.
5. Once the parmesan has melted, air fry at 190C//380F about 1−2 minutes or until crisp and golden.
6. Remove the crisps and serve. (If the crisps are stuck to the muffin tins, gently push the edge of the parmesan and they should dislodge.)

Nutritional Information per Serving:

SERVES −1 | CALORIES −98KCAL | PROTEIN −9G | CARBOHYDRATES −1G | FAT −6G

VIETNAMESE EGG LOAF

INGREDIENTS

For the Loaf:

- 15g//0.5oz oyster mushrooms
- 30g//1oz dried shiitake mushrooms
- 4 eggs
- 60ml milk
- 1 small carrot shredded or grated
- 4 garlic cloves, minced
- 70g//2.5oz of glass noodles
- 30ml of fish sauce
- ¼ teaspoon of sugar
- ¼ teaspoon of salt
- ¼ teaspoon of black pepper

For the Sauce:

- 45ml of lime juice
- 15g//0.5oz of sugar
- 30ml of water
- 30ml of Thai sweet chilli sauce
- 30ml of fish sauce
- 6 cloves of garlic, minced

METHOD

1. Soak the mushrooms in warm water for about 20 minutes.
2. Squeeze out the excess water in the shiitake mushrooms.
3. Thinly slice all the mushrooms.
4. Soak the noodles in cold water for about 15 minutes, then cut them into 2-inch pieces.
5. Crack the 4 eggs into a large bowl but remove 2 of the egg yolks only into a separate bowl and put to one side for later.
6. Add the milk to the egg mixture in the large bowl and whisk until blended.
7. Add all the remaining ingredients into the large bowl (keeping the two egg yolks to one side) and mix thoroughly.
8. Preheat the air fryer to 140C//280F.
9. Spritz a mini loaf tin with oil and pour in the egg mixture, making the surface as smooth as possible to prevent charring.
10. Place the loaf tin in the air fryer and cook at 140C//280F for 16-18 minutes until the egg is set.
11. Meanwhile, add salt to the egg yolks and mix.
12. In a separate container, add all the sauce ingredients and mix thoroughly.
13. Once cooked, remove the egg loaf from the air fryer and pour the salted egg yolk over the top, spreading it evenly.
14. Turn the temperature to 200C//400C and cook for a further 2 minutes, or until the egg yolk topping has hardened.
15. Allow to cool, then remove the egg loaf from the loaf tin and cut into ¾ inch thick slices.
16. Serve warm with the sauce spooned over the top.

Nutritional Information per Serving:

SERVES -4 | CALORIES -167KCAL | PROTEIN -8G | CARBOHYDRATES -24G | FAT -5G

ROASTED GARLIC

INGREDIENTS

- 3-4 head of garlic
- 30ml of olive oil
- Salt and pepper

METHOD

1. Preheat the air fryer to 200C//400F.
2. Cut the top off the garlic and place on a sheet of aluminium foil.
3. Drizzle with the olive oil and sprinkle with salt and pepper to taste.
4. Wrap the garlic in the aluminium foil, place in the air fryer and cook for 25–30 minutes until tender and golden brown.

Nutritional Information per Serving:

SERVES –4 | CALORIES –65KCAL | PROTEIN –1G | CARBOHYDRATES –1G | FAT –7G

GARLIC AND PARMESAN FRIES/CHIPS

INGREDIENTS

- 2 Russet potatoes, peeled and chipped
- 15ml of olive oil
- Salt to taste
- 4 cloves of garlic, peeled and minced
- 1/2 teaspoon dried parsley
- 15g//0.5oz of parmesan cheese, grated

METHOD

1. Rinse the chipped potatoes in clean cold water, drain and pat dry.
2. Preheat the air fryer to 190C//380F.
3. Toss the chipped potatoes into a large bowl with half the olive oil and salt. Make sure the chips are thoroughly coated in the oil.
4. If you prefer, line the air fryer with aluminium foil and put the potato chips onto the foil.
5. Air fry for about 15 minutes at 190C//380F. Shake the basket a couple of times during cooking.
6. When the 15 minutes is up, drizzle the chips with the remaining oil and add the garlic, parsley, and half of the parmesan cheese. Gently stir to distribute the seasonings.
7. Turn the air fryer temperature to 200C//400F and cook the chips for a further 3–4 minutes until they are nice and crispy.
8. Sprinkle with the remaining parmesan cheese and serve hot.

Nutritional Information per Serving:

SERVES –4 | CALORIES –133KCAL | PROTEIN –4G | CARBOHYDRATES –20G | FAT –5G

CANDIED WALNUTS

INGREDIENTS

- 100g//3.5oz of shelled walnut
- 30g//1oz of egg white
- 15g//0.5oz of sugar
- 1/4 teaspoon cinnamon

METHOD

1. Preheat the air fryer to 150C//300F.
2. Toss the walnuts into a bowl with the egg white making sure that the walnuts are thoroughly coated.
3. Add the sugar and cinnamon and toss the walnuts again.
4. Place the walnuts onto a sheet of aluminium foil and put in the air fryer.
5. Cook at 150C//300F for about 8 minutes.
6. Allow to cool before serving.

Nutritional Information per Serving:

SERVES –4 | CALORIES –166KCAL | PROTEIN –4.6G | CARBOHYDRATES –6.4G | FAT –15G

SWEET AND SOUR BALSAMIC BRUSSELL SPROUTS

INGREDIENTS

- 1.4kg//3lb brussels sprouts, washed, trimmed, and halved
- 30ml of olive oil
- 60ml of soy sauce or tamari
- 60ml of balsamic vinegar
- 30g//1oz of brown sugar
- ½ teaspoon of ground ginger
- ¼ teaspoon of black pepper
- 15g//0.5oz loosely packed fresh parsley leaves, finely chopped

METHOD

1. Preheat the air fryer to 230C//450F.
2. Spray cooking oil onto 2 cooking trays.
3. Spread the sprouts onto the tray in a thin single later. Spray the sprouts with cooking oil.
4. Cook in the air fryer for 25 minutes at 230C//450F until golden brown. Keep stirring and turning the sprouts throughout to ensure even cooking.
5. While the sprouts are cooking, in a saucepan heat the soy sauce, vinegar, brown sugar, ginger, and pepper to boiling.
6. Bring to a simmer and cook for 12 –15 minutes on a low heat until syrupy.
7. Remove from heat.
8. In a bowl, toss the sprouts with parsley and enough sauce to coat them and serve with the remaining sauce on the side.

Nutritional Information per Serving:

SERVES –4 | CALORIES –90KCAL | PROTEIN –4G | CARBOHYDRATES –15G | FAT –3G

BREAKFAST GRANOLA

INGREDIENTS

- 160ml of maple syrup
- 2 teaspoons of vanilla extract
- 125ml olive oil
- 1 egg white
- ½ teaspoon of salt
- 255g//9oz old–fashioned oats
- 130g//4.5oz roasted, salted almonds, coarsely chopped
- 60g//2oz sunflower seeds
- 60g//2oz almond flour
- 1 ½ teaspoons of ground cinnamon

METHOD

1. Preheat air fryer to 180C//350F.
2. Line a baking sheet with baking paper. Make sure it will fit in your air fryer.
3. In a bowl, gently whisk the maple syrup, vanilla, olive oil, egg white and 1/2 teaspoon salt until blended.
4. Combine all the dry ingredients together in a separate bowl.
5. Pour the dry ingredients into the maple syrup mixture and thoroughly mix.
6. Press the mixture onto the baking sheet and bake at 180C//350F for 25–30 minutes. Open the air fryer and turn the tray around twice during cooking, but don't stir.
7. Allow to cool for an hour, then break the mixture up into chunks.
8. Serve with milk or Greek yoghurt, and fresh fruit.
9. Can be stored for up to a week in an airtight container.

Nutritional Information per Serving:

SERVES –12 | CALORIES –335KCAL | PROTEIN –7G | CARBOHYDRATES –30G | FAT –22G

ONION RINGS

• •

INGREDIENTS

- 1 large onion, peeled
- 115g//4oz of plain flour
- 1 egg
- 15ml of milk
- 60g/2oz breadcrumbs
- Cooking oil spray
- Salt and pepper to taste

METHOD

1. Carefully cut and separate the onion slices into rings about 1.5cms thick.
2. Put half the flour (2 tablespoons) into a bowl with the salt and pepper.
3. Put the remaining flour in a bowl with the egg and milk and whisk to a smooth batter.
4. Put the breadcrumbs in a shallow bowl nearby.
5. Preheat the air fryer to 180C//350F.
6. Coat the onion rings all over in the flour, and lightly tap off any excess. Dip the floured rings into the batter, coating them thoroughly, then put them in the breadcrumbs, turning to cover fully.
7. Spritz the air fryer with the spray cooking oil and add the breaded onion rings in a single layer. Gently spray over them with a little more oil.
8. Air–fry for 10 minutes at 180C//350F, turning halfway through.
9. Serve immediately with mayonnaise.

Nutritional Information per Serving:

SERVES –2 | CALORIES –293KCAL | PROTEIN –9.3G | CARBOHYDRATES –39.2G | FAT –11.2G

ROASTED CASHEWS

• •

INGREDIENTS

- 20g//7oz raw cashew nuts without shells
- 1 teaspoon melted butter
- Salt and pepper to taste

METHOD

1. Preheat the air fryer to 180C//355F.
2. Put all the ingredients in a bowl and toss until the cashews are evenly coated with the seasoned butter.
3. Put in the air fryer and for 5 minutes at 180C//355F.
4. Pause to shake the nuts up, then cook for a further 4–5 minutes at the same temperature.

Nutritional Information per Serving:

SERVES –3 | CALORIES –369KCAL | PROTEIN –12G | CARBOHYDRATES –19G | FAT –5G

ROAST BUTTERNUT SQUASH

INGREDIENTS

- 1 small butternut squash (approx. 700g//1 ½ pounds). Check the size with your air fryer and adjust accordingly
- 15ml of olive oil
- ¼ teaspoon of cinnamon
- Salt and pepper to taste
- Optional: 15g//0.5oz of brown sugar

METHOD

1. Leave the peel on. Cut the stalk and bottom of the butternut off, then slice in half from top to bottom (cut into quarters if it won't fit into your air fryer). Scoop out the seeds and pulp.
2. Preheat the air fryer to 180C//350F.
3. Brush the raw flesh of the squash with olive oil, season with salt and pepper and sprinkle with the cinnamon.
4. Optional: sprinkle with the brown sugar now if you're using it.
5. Put the squash into the air fryer, cut side facing up (cook the two halves separately if necessary).
6. Cook at 180C//350F for 40–50 minutes or until tender.
7. Serve sliced or mashed and topped with a little butter.

Nutritional Information per Serving:

SERVES –4 TO 6 | CALORIES –127KCAL | PROTEIN –2G | CARBOHYDRATES –25G | FAT –4G

HONEY ROASTED PEANUTS

INGREDIENTS

- 240g//0.5lb shelled, raw peanuts
- 30g//1oz butter
- 45g//1.5 oz honey
- 1 teaspoon of cinnamon
- Optional: salt to taste
- Optional: sugar to taste (15-30g//0.5-1oz)

METHOD

1. Preheat the air fryer to 180C//350F.
2. In saucepan, on a low heat, melt the butter and honey together and stir to combine.
3. Add the peanuts and cinnamon. Stir to ensure the peanuts are well–coated in butter.
4. Lay a single layer of peanuts into the air fryer and cook for 8–10 minutes at 180C//350F. Shake the peanuts every few minutes during cooking.
5. Leave the peanuts to cool on a baking tray lined with foil.
6. Sprinkle the sugar and/or salt over the top to suit your taste.
7. Continue to stir the peanuts on the tray every few minutes until cool so that they don't clump together.
8. Serve, or store in an airtight container.

Nutritional Information per Serving:

SERVES –8 | CALORIES –251KCAL | PROTEIN –9G | CARBOHYDRATES –11G | FAT –21G

SKIN—ON POTATO WEDGES

INGREDIENTS

- 4 medium potatoes (red potatoes are recommended)
- Olive oil cooking spray
- Seasoning of choice
- Salt and pepper to taste

METHOD

1. Wash/scrub the potatoes and cut into wedge shapes.
2. Preheat the air fryer to 180C//350F.
3. Place in a bowl and spray with cooking oil. Add your seasonings, toss the potatoes and spray with a little more oil ensuring they are fully coated.
4. Lay the potato wedges in the air fryer in an even layer.
5. Cook at 180C//350F for about 12 minutes.
6. Serve hot with your favourite dips.
7. Makes 2 servings. Serving size 1/2 of the recipe (divide evenly into 2 portions).

Nutritional Information per Serving:

SERVES −2 | CALORIES −263KCAL | CARBOHYDRATES −57.3G | PROTEIN −5.1G | FAT −2.6G

CRUNCHY ITALIAN RAVIOLI

INGREDIENTS

- 30g//1oz grated parmesan cheese
- 100g//3.5oz breadcrumbs
- 1/2 teaspoon of dried parsley
- 1 x 255g//9oz package of refrigerated ravioli
- 2 beaten eggs
- Cooking oil spray
- Marinara sauce for dipping

METHOD

1. Mix the grated parmesan cheese, dried parsley, and breadcrumbs together in dish.
2. Put the beaten eggs in a separate dish.
3. Preheat the air fryer to 180C//350F.
4. Dip the ravioli first in the beaten egg, then in the breadcrumb mix, ensuring each piece is thoroughly coated and place the ravioli directly into the air fryer. (Line the air fryer with baking paper or foil if you think it's necessary).
5. Spray the ravioli with cooking spray.
6. Cook for about 7 minutes at 180C//350F. The breadcrumbs will turn a golden brown when cooked.
7. Optional: Serve hot with the marinara dipping sauce (or a dipping sauce of your choice.)

Nutritional Information per Serving:

SERVING SIZE −1 | CALORIES −340KCAL | FAT −11.9G | CARBOHYDRATES −41.8G | PROTEIN −15.7G

MEXICAN STREET FOOD CORN ON THE COB

INGREDIENTS

- 4 pieces of corn on the cob
- Cooking oil spray
- Salt and pepper to taste

For the Cream Sauce:

- 30ml of natural Greek yoghurt (fat–free or low fat is fine)
- 30g//1oz of mayonnaise
- 4 garlic cloves, minced
- Lemon juice
- 10g//0.35oz of fresh coriander, chopped
- 30g//1oz of soft cheese

METHOD

1. Preheat your air fryer to 200C//400F.
2. Spray the corn cobs individually with cooking oil spray and season with salt and pepper.
3. Put the corn cobs into the air fryer and cook at 200C//400F for 10 minutes.
4. Meanwhile, for the sauce, whisk together the yoghurt, mayonnaise, lemon juice, garlic, and coriander until blended. Season with salt and pepper to taste.
5. Remove the corn cobs from the air fryer. Brush with the sauce and serve sprinkled with Queso Fresco cheese.

Nutritional Information per Serving:

SERVES –4 | CALORIES –230KCAL | FAT: –7.8G | CARBOHYDRATES –37.5G | PROTEIN –7G

CHEESY POTATO SKINS

INGREDIENTS

- 4 medium potatoes (red potatoes are best for chips, wedges, and fries)
- Cooking oil spray
- Salt and pepper to taste
- 115g//4oz of cheddar cheese
- 115g//4oz sour cream
- 2 spring onions, sliced thinly

METHOD

1. Wash/scrub the potatoes thoroughly and pat dry.
2. Preheat air fryer to 200C//400F.
3. Spray potatoes with cooking oil spray and add salt and pepper to taste.
4. Cook the potatoes in the air fryer at 200C//400F for about 30–40 minutes. Test the potatoes for readiness with a fork. You should be able to push the fork easily into the potato.
5. One cooked, allow the potatoes to cool enough to handle, then cut them in half and scoop out the inside. Leave a thin layer of potato covering the inside skin.
6. Spray the potatoes again with cooking oil and lay them flat side down in the air fryer.
7. Cook at 200C//400F for an extra 5 minutes.
8. Open the air fryer enough to sprinkle the Cheddar over the top of the potato skins. Cook for a further 3 minutes until the cheese has melted.
9. Remove the potatoes from the air fryer and serve with sour cream, spring onions and black pepper.

Nutritional Information per Serving:

SERVES –4 | CALORIES –363KCAL | FAT –19.9G | CARBOHYDRATES –35.7G | PROTEIN –12G

CRISPY BABY CORN

INGREDIENTS

- 20 baby corns, washed
- 60g//2oz of ketchup
- 30g//1oz of hot and spicy sauce (e.g., sriracha sauce)
- 2 teaspoons of cooking oil
- 1/4 teaspoon of salt
- 1 teaspoon of ginger–garlic paste
- 150g//5oz of breadcrumbs

METHOD

1. Put the ketchup, sriracha sauce, oil, salt, and ginger–garlic paste in a bowl, mix well, and put to one side.
2. Line the air fryer with baking paper or aluminium foil and preheat to 175C//350F.
3. Dip the baby corn in the sauce, then immediately into the breadcrumbs, turning it so it is thoroughly coated.
4. Put the corn in the air fryer basket and cook at 175C//350F for about 10 minutes. You may need to cook in batches depending on the size of your air fryer.
5. Serve hot with your favourite dip.

Nutritional Information per Serving:

SERVES –4 | CALORIES –214KCAL | FAT –5G | CARBOHYDRATES –35.1G | PROTEIN –6.3G

CAULIFLOWER RICE BALLS

INGREDIENTS

- 1 Italian chicken sausage with the casing removed
- 130g//4.5oz of frozen cauliflower rice (or blend up your own)
- Salt to taste
- 30ml of marinara sauce
- 115g//4oz of shredded mozzarella
- 1 beaten egg
- 30g//1oz of breadcrumbs
- 15g//0.5oz of parmesan
- Olive oil cooking spray

METHOD

1. Cook the sausage in a frying pan for about 4–5 minutes until it is cooked. Stir and break up with a spoon into small pieces.
2. Add the cauliflower, salt and marinara sauce and simmer for a further 5–6 minutes until the cauliflower is cooked through.
3. Once cooked, take the pan off the heat, and stir in the mozzarella cheese.
4. Allow to cool enough to be handled before progressing to the next stage.
5. Use a tablespoon to scoop out about 50–60g of the mixture and form into a small ball. Set to one side and repeat until all the mixture is gone.
6. In one bowl, place the beaten egg.
7. Mix the breadcrumbs and parmesan together in another bowl.
8. Preheat the air fryer to 200C//400F.
9. Dip each ball into the egg, then into the crumbs ensuring they are completely covered at each stage.
10. Place on a greased baking tray and spray with cooking oil.
11. Cook at 200C//400F for about 9 minutes, remembering to pause cooking halfway to turn the balls.
12. Serve with a marinara dipping sauce.

Nutritional Information per Serving:

SERVES –1 SERVING IS 3 BALLS | CALORIES – 257KCAL | PROTEIN – 21.5G | CARBOHYDRATES – 15.6G | FAT – 11.5G

CRISPY GREEN TOMATOES

INGREDIENTS

- 4 medium green tomatoes, rinsed and sliced
- 45g//1.5oz plain flour
- 2 egg whites
- 60ml of almond milk
- 115g//4oz ground almonds
- 60g//2oz breadcrumbs
- 2 teaspoons olive oil
- 1 teaspoon paprika
- 1 clove garlic, peeled and minced
- Parmesan cheese, shredded

METHOD

1. Put the plain flour into a bowl.
2. In a second bowl, beat the almond milk and egg whites until frothy.
3. In a third bowl, mix ground almonds, breadcrumbs, olive oil, paprika and garlic.
4. Preheat the air fryer to 200C//400F.
5. Dip the slices of tomato into the flour, then into the milk, and finally into the breadcrumb mixture. At each stage ensure the tomatoes are thoroughly coated with the mixture.
6. Put the breaded tomato slices into the air fryer and cook at 200C//400F for about 6–8 minutes until crispy and golden in colour.
7. Serve hot, sprinkled with shredded parmesan cheese.

Nutritional Information per Serving:

SERVES –4 | CALORIES –330KCAL | FAT –19.1G | CARBOHYDRATES –29.4G | PROTEIN –13.9G

SAVOURY MACARONI AND CHEESE MUFFINS

INGREDIENTS

- 540g//19oz cold, leftover macaroni cheese
- 60g//2oz seasoned breadcrumbs
- 45g//1.5oz cheddar cheese, shredded (plus a little extra for topping)
- 1 egg
- Cooking oil spray

METHOD

1. Put all the ingredients into one large bowl and mix well.
2. Spray muffin tins with cooking oil spray.
3. Preheat the air fryer to 160C//320F.
4. Spoon the mixture into the muffin tins and place the muffin pan in the air fryer.
5. Cook for 5 - 8 minutes at 160C//320F until the macaroni and cheese is bubbling.
6. Pause the air fryer, top the muffins with cheese and air fry again for 2–3 minutes until the cheese is melted and golden brown.
7. Serve hot.

Nutritional Information per Serving:

SERVES –4 | CALORIES –240KCAL | FAT –11.8G | CARBOHYDRATES –23.7G | PROTEIN –9.9G

CHERRY OATMEAL BREAKFAST BAKE

INGREDIENTS

- 150g//5oz frozen dark sweet cherries
- 60g//2oz of oatmeal
- 3 eggs
- 1 teaspoon of chia seeds
- 1/4 teaspoon of salt
- 60g//2oz melted butter
- 45g//1.5oz pure maple syrup
- 30g//1oz of UK double cream//US heavy cream
- 15g//0.5oz of brown sugar
- 1 teaspoon of vanilla extract
- ½ teaspoon ground coriander
- ½ teaspoon ground cinnamon

METHOD

1. Mix the oatmeal, chia seeds, salt, and spices together in a large bowl.
2. Next, add the eggs, cream, melted butter, vanilla, and maple syrup.
3. Put the frozen cherries into the bowl with the other ingredients and mix well.
4. Preheat the air fryer to 180C//350F.
5. Divide the mixture between 4 ramekins and place in the air fryer.
6. Cook for 15 to 20 minutes at 180C//350F.
7. Remove the ramekins from the air fryer – take care, the ramekins will be hot – and allow to cool for 10 minutes before serving.
8. Drizzle with maple syrup or sprinkle icing sugar over the top and serve.

Nutritional Information per Serving:

SERVES –4 | CALORIES –303KCAL | FAT –19.0G | CARBOHYDRATES –26.4GG | PROTEIN –6.7G

OATY BREAKFAST COOKIES

INGREDIENTS

- 240g//8.5oz creamy peanut butter
- 85g//3oz honey
- 1 teaspoon of pure vanilla extract
- 2 medium ripe bananas
- 200g//7oz rolled oats
- 45g//1.5oz of dried cranberries
- 45g//1.5oz of raisins
- 70g//2.5oz of mixed nuts (if you prefer just one variety, use that)
- 1 teaspoon of salt
- 1 teaspoon of ground cinnamon
- 1 teaspoon of ground nutmeg

METHOD

1. In a large mixing bowl, combine the bananas, oats, peanut butter, honey, vanilla extract, ground cinnamon, ground nutmeg, and salt.
2. Add the nuts and dried fruits and mix thoroughly.
3. Preheat the air fryer to 170C//330F.
4. Line a tray, or the air fryer with baking paper.
5. Create cookie shapes out of balls of dough and place on the lined tray or air fryer. Cook at 170C//330F for 4–6 minutes.
6. Once cooked, allow to cool for a few minutes before removing from the air fryer let the cookies cool and harden slightly before removing them from the tray.
7. Serve and enjoy.

Nutritional Information per Serving:

SERVES –20 | CALORIES –162KCAL | FAT –9G | CARBOHYDRATES –18G | PROTEIN –5G

BROWN SUGAR GRAPEFRUIT

INGREDIENTS

- 2 grapefruit
- 30g//1oz of brown sugar

METHOD

1. Preheat the air fryer to 200C//400F.
2. Cut the grapefruit in half.
3. Rub the brown sugar on the cut of each half.
4. Put the grapefruit halves into the air fryer and cook for 5 minutes at 200C//400F.

Nutritional Information per Serving:

SERVES −4 | CALORIES −73KCAL | FAT −0G | CARBOHYDRATES −19G | PROTEIN −1G

ROAST ASPARAGUS

INGREDIENTS

- 450g//1lb trimmed asparagus
- Salt and pepper to taste
- Olive oil cooking spray

METHOD

1. Rinse the asparagus, drain, and pat dry.
2. Preheat the air fryer to 180C//360F.
3. On a plate, spray the asparagus with olive oil, add salt and pepper and turn gently to ensure it's fully coated.
4. Line the air fryer with foil or baking paper paper and put the asparagus inside in a single layer.
5. Cook at 180C//360F about 6−8 minutes until tender.

Nutritional Information per Serving:

SERVES −2 | CALORIES −54KCAL | FAT −4G | CARBOHYDRATES −4G | PROTEIN −3G

TURNIP FRIES

INGREDIENTS

- 230g//8oz turnip peeled and cut into sticks
- 1/4 teaspoon of salt
- Olive oil cooking spray
- 1/4 teaspoon of paprika
- 1/4 teaspoon of onion powder
- White pepper to taste
- Optional: cayenne pepper to taste.

METHOD

1. Put the turnip fries into a bowl and cover with the salt to draw the water out. Let it rest for about 20 minutes, then rinse and pat dry.
2. Preheat the air fryer to 190C//380F.
3. Put the turnip fries into a bowl and spray well with cooking oil. Add the rest of the ingredients and toss the turnip to ensure a good covering of the seasoned oil.
4. Spread the turnip fries in the air fryer in a single layer, not too thickly.
5. Cook at 190C//380F for 10−12 minutes until crispy and golden brown. Pause the fryer to give the fries a shake at intervals during cooking.
6. Serve immediately with a sprinkling of dried basil.

Nutritional Information per Serving:

SERVES −2 | CALORIES −69KCAL | FAT −4G | CARBOHYDRATES −8G | PROTEIN −1G

MILLET PORRIDGE AND DRIED FRUIT

INGREDIENTS

- 200g//7oz of millet
- 400ml of cold milk
- 45g//1.5oz raisins
- 45g//1.5oz gooseberries
- NB: if you don't want raisins and gooseberries, combine dried fruits of your choice.

METHOD

1. Rinse the millet thoroughly in cold water.
2. In a saucepan of water, bring the millet to the boil and drain well.
3. Divide the millet and the dried fruit between 4 ramekins and stir.
4. Preheat the air fryer to 130C//260F.
5. Share the cold milk equally between the ramekins.
6. Grease around the top of the ramekin with a little butter. Add salt to taste.
7. Put the ramekins in the air fryer and cook for 30 minutes at 130C//260F.
8. Turn the air fryer off and leave the ramekins to stand for another 10 minutes.
9. Remove from air fryer and allow to cool slightly before eating.

Nutritional Information per Serving:

SERVES −4 | CALORIES −280KCAL | FAT −2.7G | CARBOHYDRATES −52.1G | PROTEIN −12.3G

MUSHROOMS IN SOY SAUCE

INGREDIENTS

- 450g/1lb mushrooms button or cremini recommended, cut into quarters
- 15ml of soy sauce
- 15ml of sesame oil

To Garnish:

- sesame seeds
- spring onions

METHOD

1. Wash and pat dry the mushrooms. Cut into quarters.
2. Toss the mushrooms in a bowl with the sesame oil and soy sauce. Marinate for 30 minutes.
3. Preheat the air fryer to 200C//400F.
4. Add the marinated mushrooms to the air fryer and cook at 200//400F for 12–15 minutes. Pause during cooking to shake the basket a couple of times.
5. When browned and roasted through, serve immediately and garnish with the sesame seeds and sliced spring onions.

Nutritional Information per Serving:

SERVES −2 | CALORIES −59KCAL | FAT −4G | CARBOHYDRATES −4G | PROTEIN −4G

ASPARAGUS IN LEMON AND PARMESAN

INGREDIENTS

- 1 bunch asparagus, about 250g//9oz
- 15ml of olive oil
- Salt to taste
- ½ lemon, squeezed
- 45g//1.5oz grated parmesan cheese to sprinkle

METHOD

1. Trim and discard the woody ends of the asparagus. Wash and pat dry.
2. Preheat the air fryer to 200C//400F.
3. In a bowl, toss the asparagus in the olive oil so it's coated all over.
4. In the air fryer, cook the asparagus at 200C//400F for 2–5 minutes. Pause the cooking to shake the asparagus at intervals.
5. Serve immediately with a squeeze of fresh lemon and sprinkle with parmesan.

Nutritional Information per Serving:

SERVES −4 | CALORIES −103KCAL | FAT −7G | CARBOHYDRATES −5G | PROTEIN −7G

ALOO GOBI

INGREDIENTS

- 1 medium cauliflower cut into florets (about 570g//1.25lb of florets)
- 1 potato, peeled and cubed
- 1 onion, thinly sliced
- 85g//3oz chopped tomato
- 30ml of olive oil
- 1/2 teaspoon of garlic powder
- 1/2 teaspoon of ground cumin
- 1/2 teaspoon of ground turmeric
- 1 teaspoon of ground coriander
- 1/2 teaspoon of red chilli powder
- Salt to taste
- Optional: 1 teaspoon of lime juice
- Optional: fresh chopped coriander

METHOD

1. Preheat the air fryer to 190C//380F.
2. Put all the ingredients together in a large bowl and mix well.
3. Spread an even layer of the aloo gobi mixture in the air fryer and cook at 190C//380F for about 12–15 minutes.
4. Transfer to a serving bowl, sprinkle with lime juice and top with chopped coriander.

Nutritional Information per Serving:

SERVES −4 | CALORIES −267KCAL | FAT −8G | CARBOHYDRATES −11G | PROTEIN −3G

INDIAN BATATA VADA

INGREDIENTS

For the Filling:

- 300g//10.5oz boiled potatoes
- 1 small piece of ginger, grated
- 1 green chilli, finely chopped
- 1/8 teaspoon ground turmeric
- 1/4 teaspoon red chilli powder
- 1/4 teaspoon salt

For the Batter:

- 60g//2oz chickpea flour, for the batter
- 12g//0.4oz semolina
- 125ml water
- Pinch of baking soda
- 1/4 teaspoon ground turmeric
- 1/4 teaspoon red chilli powder
- Pinch of salt
- Spray cooking oil

METHOD

1. Mash the boiled potatoes in a bowl with the ginger, chilli, red chilli powder, turmeric, and salt.
2. Use a large spoon to scoop out the potato mixture and create small balls. Set them to one side.
3. To create the batter, whisk the water and chickpea flour together.
4. Add the baking soda, salt, ground turmeric, red chilli powder and semolina and mix well.
5. Pre heat the air fryer to 200C/400F, then once hot, reduce the heat to 180C//360F.
6. Dip the potato balls in the batter mix then cook the first batch in the air fryer for 6–7 minutes.
7. Pause the air fryer, spritz the potato balls with cooking oil, and cook for a further 6–7 minutes at the same temperature.
8. Serve hot with ketchup.

Nutritional Information per Serving:

SERVES –4 | CALORIES –208KCAL | FAT –2.5G | CARBOHYDRATES –38.6G | PROTEIN –9.1G

BEETS WITH ORANGE GREMOLATA AND GOATS CHEESE

INGREDIENTS

- 3 medium fresh golden beets
- 3 medium fresh beets
- 30ml lime juice
- 30ml orange juice
- 1/2 teaspoon sea salt
- 15g//0.5oz fresh parsley, finely chopped
- 15g//0.5oz fresh sage, finely chopped
- 1 garlic clove, finely chopped
- 1 teaspoon grated orange zest
- 115g//4oz crumbled goat cheese
- 15g//0.5oz sunflower kernels

METHOD

1. Trim the tops of the beets and scrub them thoroughly.
2. Wrap the beets tightly in a double layer of foil.
3. Preheat air fryer to 200C//400F.
4. Put the wrapped beets in a single layer on a tray in the air fryer.
5. Cook at 200C/400F for about 45–55 minutes, or until tender.
6. Open the foil carefully to let the steam escape. Take care not to burn yourself on the steam.
7. When the beets are cool enough to touch, peel them, cut in half and slice.
8. Place the sliced beets in a serving bowl with the lime juice, orange juice and salt, and toss together. Make sure the beets are thoroughly coated in the juices.
9. In a small bowl, combine the parsley, sage, garlic and orange zest and sprinkle generously over the beets.
10. Serve warm or chilled, topped with goat cheese and sunflower kernels.

Nutritional Information per Serving:

SERVES –4 | CALORIES –49KCAL | FAT –1G | CARBOHYDRATES –9G | PROTEIN –2G

OKRA WITH SMOKED PAPRIKA

INGREDIENTS

- 450g//1lb fresh okra pods
- 15ml of olive oil
- 15ml of lemon juice
- 1/2 teaspoon smoked paprika
- 1/4 teaspoon salt
- 1/8 teaspoon garlic powder
- 1/8 teaspoon pepper

METHOD

1. Preheat air fryer to 190C//375F.
2. Add ALL the ingredients to a bowl and toss together.
3. Place the seasoned okra on a greased tray in air fryer. Cook at 190C//375F for 15–20, stirring occasionally, until light brown and tender.

Nutritional Information per Serving:

SERVES –4 | CALORIES –57KCAL | FAT –4G | CARBOHYDRATES –6G | PROTEIN –2G

STARTERS, SIDES AND SNACKS – FISH DISHES

CRISPY CRAB CAKES

INGREDIENTS

- 400g//14oz lump crabmeat
- 60g//2oz of mayonnaise
- 45g//1.5oz of breadcrumbs (alternatively, use ordinary bread toasted and finely crushed)
- 30g//1oz plain flour
- 1 egg
- 1 medium green onion, sliced
- 1/2 red bell pepper, seeded and diced
- 15ml of Worcestershire sauce
- 15g//0.5oz of cajun
- Juice from ½ a lemon

METHOD

1. Place ALL the ingredients together in a large bowl and mix well.
2. Preheat the air fryer to 180C//360F.
3. Shape the mixture into small balls and flatten into burger shapes.
4. Put the crab cakes in the air fryer and cook at 180C//360F for 10–12 minutes until crisp.
5. Serve hot with sweet chilli sauce.

Nutritional Information per Serving:

SERVES –4 | CALORIES –275KCAL | PROTEIN –25G | CARBOHYDRATES –13G | FAT –2G

PRAWN COCKTAIL

INGREDIENTS

For the Cocktail Sauce:

- 115g//4oz ketchup
- 2 teaspoons of Worcestershire sauce
- 1 teaspoon of prepared horseradish
- 1 teaspoon of fresh lemon juice
- 1/4 teaspoon of celery salt
- 1/4 teaspoon of garlic powder
- Salt and pepper to taste
- Fresh lemon slices
- 1 small cucumber, sliced

For the Prawns:

- 450g//1lb raw prepared prawns
- Spray cooking oil
- Salt and pepper to taste

METHOD

1. Stir the ketchup, Worcestershire sauce, horseradish, fresh lemon juice, celery salt, garlic powder, salt, and black pepper together in a bowl until well combined. Set to one side.
2. Rinse the prawns and pat them dry with kitchen roll.
3. Preheat the air fryer to 200C//400F.
4. Spray the prawns lightly with cooking oil, add salt and pepper to taste, then place in the air fryer in a single layer.
5. Cook at 200C//400F for 8–12 minutes, or until cooked through.
6. Allow to cool completely. Put in the fridge until ready to serve.
7. Serve in small bowls on a bed of fresh lettuce with the prawn cocktail. Garnish with fresh lemon and cucumber slices.

Nutritional Information per Serving:

SERVES –6 | CALORIES –106KCAL | PROTEIN –16G | CARBOHYDRATES –6G | FAT –2G

TUNA FISH CAKES

INGREDIENTS

- 425g//15oz can of tuna, drained (or 450g//1lb fresh tuna, diced)
- 3 eggs
- Zest of 1 lemon
- 1 tablespoon of freshly squeezed lemon juice
- 60g//2oz of breadcrumbs
- 45g//1.5oz of parmesan cheese, grated
- 1 stalk of celery, finely chopped
- 45g//1.5oz of spring onions, thinly sliced
- 1/2 teaspoon of garlic powder
- 1/2 teaspoon of dried mixed herbs
- Salt and pepper to taste

METHOD

1. Mix the eggs, lemon zest, lemon juice, breadcrumbs, parmesan cheese, celery, onion, garlic powder, dried herbs, salt, and pepper together in one bowl until combined.
2. Fold the tuna into the mixture, but do not overmix.
3. Preheat the air fryer to 185C//360F.
4. Line the air fryer with baking paper and spray lightly with cooking oil.
5. Use a tablespoon to scoop out the tuna mixture and create burger shapes. The mixture should make about 10 fishcakes.
6. If the fishcakes are too soft to handle, then chill in the fridge for about an hour before cooking to firm them up.
7. Spray the fishcakes with oil, then cook for 10 minutes at 185C//360F. Make sure that you pause the cooking halfway, turn the fishcakes over, spray again with oil, and cook for the remainder of the time.
8. Serve with your favourite sauce or with fresh lemon slices.

Nutritional Information per Serving:

SERVES – MAKES ABOUT 10 FISHCAKES | CALORIES – 101KCAL | PROTEIN – 13G | CARBOHYDRATES – 5G | FAT – 3G

COCONUT PRAWN

● ●

INGREDIENTS

- 30g//1oz of cornflour
- 1 teaspoon of salt
- 2 egg whites
- 130g//4.5oz coconut flakes
- 230g//8oz of large raw prawns

For the Yoghurt Sauce:

- 150g//5oz of Greek style vanilla yoghurt
- 4g//0.15oz of coconut flakes
- 45g//1.5oz of marmalade
- 30g//1oz of crushed pineapple

METHOD

1. Mix the corn flour and salt in a bowl together.
2. Put the egg whites in a second, separate bowl.
3. Add the coconut to a third bowl.
4. Preheat the air fryer to 170C//330F.
5. Taking one prawn at a time, dip each one into the corn flour, then into the egg whites, then into the coconut. At each stage make sure the prawn is thoroughly covered.
6. Spray the air fryer with cooking oil and lay the prawns in a single layer without overcrowding it. Cook in batches if necessary.
7. Cook at 170C//330C for 10–15 minutes.
8. While the prawns are cooking, combine all the ingredients for the yoghurt sauce and mix thoroughly until combined. Add a little pineapple juice to the sauce to thin it if required.
9. Serve the prawns on a bed of lettuce with the yoghurt sauce.

Nutritional Information per Serving:

SERVES – 4 | CALORIES – 191KCAL | PROTEIN – 13G | CARBOHYDRATES – 18G | FAT – 6G

DIPPING FISH STICKS

INGREDIENTS

For the Lemon Caper Sauce:

- 70g//2.5oz of natural Greek yoghurt
- 155g//5.5oz mayonnaise
- 15g//0.5oz tablespoon of capers, drained
- 15g//0.5oz of fresh chives, finely chopped
- 1 teaspoon of fresh lemon juice
- Salt and pepper to taste

For the Fish Sticks:

- Cooking oil spray
- 450g//1lb skinless cod fillets, about 1-inch thick, rinsed, and dried
- 3 egg whites
- 15g//0.5oz Dijon mustard
- ½ of a freshly squeezed lemon
- 1/8 teaspoon paprika
- Salt and pepper to taste

For the Crumbs:

- 150g//5oz of breadcrumbs
- 1 1/2 teaspoons Old Bay seasoning
- (Cajun seasoning makes a good alternative)
- 2 teaspoons dried parsley flakes
- 1/2 teaspoon paprika

METHOD

1. Mix all the ingredients for the lemon caper sauce together in one bowl. Combine thoroughly to a smooth sauce. Set to one side.
2. Prepare the fish dipping sticks by cutting into slices approximately 2-inches long and 1-inch wide. Set to one side.
3. In a second bowl, mix up the egg whites, Dijon mustard, lemon juice, paprika, salt and pepper.
4. In a third bowl, combine the breadcrumbs with the seasonings.
5. Preheat the air fryer to 190C//370F.
6. Make sure the fish is dry, then dip each stick into the egg mixture and then into the breadcrumbs. Make sure the fish sticks are coated thoroughly in the mixture at each stage.
7. Cook in batches to prevent overcrowding.
8. Line the air fryer and lightly spray with cooking oil. Place the crumbed fish sticks into the air fryer and spritz again with the cooking oil.
9. Cook for about 7–8 minutes at 190C//370F, turning the fish sticks over about halfway through the cooking.

Nutritional Information per Serving:

SERVES –2 TO 4 (ONE SERVING IS 5 FISH STICKS) | CALORIES –229KCAL | PROTEIN –31G | CARBOHYDRATES –15G | FAT –4G

GARLIC PRAWN STARTER

INGREDIENTS

- 450g//1lb of raw prawns, ready to cook
- Cooking oil spray
- 1/4 teaspoon garlic powder
- Salt and pepper to taste
- Fresh lemon wedges
- Optional: chopped parsley and/or chilli flakes to garnish

METHOD

1. Preheat the air fryer to 200C//400F.
2. Add the oil, garlic powder, salt, and pepper into one bowl and mix. Add the prawns and toss in the seasoned oil until thoroughly coated.
3. Put the prawns into the air fryer and cook at 200C//440F for 10–14 minutes. Pause cooking and shakes a couple of times throughout.
4. Serve the garlic prawns on a bed of lettuce with a squeeze of fresh lemon, and a sprinkle of parsley and chilli flakes.

Nutritional Information per Serving:

SERVES –2–3 | CALORIES –166KCAL | PROTEIN –25.9G | CARBOHYDRATES –1.9G | FAT –5.4G

WHITE FISH TACOS

INGREDIENTS

- 1 teaspoon of chilli powder
- 1 teaspoon of oregano
- ½ teaspoon of garlic powder
- ½ teaspoon of onion powder
- ½ teaspoon of paprika
- Salt and pepper to taste
- ½ teaspoon of cayenne powder, optional
- 700g//1.5lb of fresh white fish, rinsed and dried
- Olive oil cooking spray
- 6–8 soft tortillas (flour or corn)

METHOD

1. Mix all the seasonings together in a bowl.
2. Preheat the air fryer to 200C//400F.
3. Pat the fish dry with kitchen roll, then spritz lightly with the cooking oil.
4. Dip or rub the seasonings into the fish, coating it entirely in the spices.
5. Spray the air fryer basket with cooking oil and put a single layer of the seasoned fish in. Spritz the top of the fish with the olive oil.
6. Air fry the fish at 200C//400F for 8 to 10 minutes.
7. Cut the fish up and serve in a bowl ready to create your tacos.

Nutritional Information per Serving:

SERVES –6 TO 8 | CALORIES –392KCAL | PROTEIN –75.8G | CARBOHYDRATES –11.7G | FAT –4.6G

STARTERS, SNACKS AND SIDES – MEAT DISHES

CHEESY PEPPERONI CRISPS

INGREDIENTS

- 12 slices sandwich style pepperoni
- 115g//4oz shredded mozzarella cheese
- 60g//2oz parmesan cheese plus extra for sprinkling
- 5g//0.2oz seasoned breadcrumbs
- Olive oil cooking spray

METHOD

1. Use baking paper to line the air fryer, spray with olive oil cooking spray and sprinkle the parmesan cheese to lightly cover the paper.
2. Place the pepperoni in a single layer over the top of the pepperoni.
3. Mix the breadcrumbs, the remaining parmesan, and the mozzarella. Sprinkle on top of the pepperoni.
4. Spritz over the top of the cheesy pepperoni with olive oil and cook for 7 minutes at 200C//400F. The pepperoni crisps should be crispy and golden brown in colour.
5. NB: Don't turn over during cooking as with some other foods.
6. Transfer the cheesy pepperoni crisps to a bowl using tongs and serve. They taste great with a pizza sauce.

Nutritional Information per Serving:

SERVES −2 | CALORIES −94KCAL | PROTEIN −7G | CARBOHYDRATES −2G | FAT −6G

BACON AND BROCCOLLI QUICHE CUPS

INGREDIENTS

- 4 bacon strips, chopped
- 15g//0.5oz of broccolli, broken into small florets
- 15g//0.5oz of chopped onion
- 1 garlic clove, finely chopped
- 3 eggs
- 15g//0.50oz of dried parsley flakes
- Salt and pepper to taste
- 115g//4oz shredded cheddar cheese
- 30g//1oz of chopped tomato

METHOD

1. Fry the chopped bacon in a pan until crispy. Transfer to paper towels to soak up the liquid and keep what is in the frying pan to use again.
2. Using the same pan and the liquid from the bacon, add the broccoli and onion to and cook for 2–3 minutes until tender. Add the garlic and cook for a further minute.
3. Whisk the eggs, parsley, salt, and pepper in a separate bowl until thoroughly combined. Add the cheese, tomato, bacon, and broccoli mixture, and stir.
4. Preheat the air fryer to 200C//400F.
5. Pour the quiche mixture evenly between 2 greased 10–oz. ramekins, and place in the air fryer.
6. Cook at 200C//400F for 20–25 minutes or until a knife inserted in the centre comes out clean.
7. Serve hot or cold.

Nutritional information per Serving:

SERVES −2 | CALORIES −301KCAL | PROTEIN −19G | CARBOHYDRATE −5G | FAT −23G

BACON AND TURKEY BURGER BITES

INGREDIENTS

- 900g//2lbs minced turkey
- 120g//4oz centre cut raw bacon, minced
- 30g//1oz yellow mustard
- 1/2 teaspoon of onion powder
- Salt to taste
- Pepper to taste
- 1 head of butter lettuce
- 30 cherry tomatoes
- 2–3 jalapeño sliced in 30 thin slices, optional
- 30 dill pickle chips or slices
- Ketchup, mayo and/or yellow mustard, optional for dipping

METHOD

1. In a bowl, use your hands to mix the beef, bacon, mustard, salt, onion powder and pepper.
2. Use a tablespoon to scoop out the mixture to create 30 burger bites about the size of a golf ball.
3. Preheat the air fryer to 200C//400F.
4. Arrange the burger bites in a single layer in the air fryer. Cook in batches if they will not all fit.
5. Cook at 200C//400F for about 8 to 10 minutes turning about halfway through cooking. Cook for longer if you prefer the meat well-done.
6. Skewer the burger bites with salad vegetables and pickles and serve with a selection of dipping sauces.

Nutritional Information per Serving:

SERVES –15 (2 BURGERS PER SERVING) | CALORIES – 125KCAL | PROTEIN – 13.5G | CARBOHYDRATES – 2G | FAT – 6.5G

TURKEY BREAKFAST BURGERS

INGREDIENTS

- 450g//1 lb turkey mince
- 1 teaspoon of light brown sugar
- 15g//0.50z of sage, freshly chopped
- Salt to taste
- 3/4 teaspoon of smoked paprika
- 1/2 teaspoon of crushed red pepper flakes
- 1/2 teaspoon of crushed fennel seeds
- 1/2 teaspoon of garlic powder
- Olive oil cooking spray

METHOD

1. Combine all the ingredients in a bowl and mix thoroughly.
2. Form into burger shapes about ¼ of an inch thick.
3. Preheat the air fryer to 200C//400F.
4. Spray the air fryer with cooking oil and arrange the burgers in the air fryer in a single layer with space between each one. You may need to cook in batches rather than overfill the air fryer.
5. Cook for 5–8 minutes at 200C//400F until crispy and golden, turning halfway through.

Nutritional Information per Serving:

SERVES –4 | CALORIES – 188KCAL | PROTEIN – 23G | CARBOHYDRATES – 4G | FAT – 9G

FRITTATA WITH SAUSAGE

INGREDIENTS

- 8 eggs
- 240ml mascarpone
- 200g//7oz of grated cheddar
- 6 sausages cut into quarters
- 1 large, sweet potato
- 1 medium courgette
- 15ml of olive oil
- 2 spring onions, thinly sliced
- 1 teaspoon of dried parsley
- Salt and pepper to taste
- Optional: sliced cherry tomatoes
- Optional: a sprinkle of basil

METHOD

1. Preheat the air fryer to 180C//360F.
2. Peel and dice the sweet potato into cubes. Cut the courgette into medium slices, then quarter each slice.
3. Put the sweet potato cubes and courgette slices into a bowl and add the olive oil, salt, pepper, and parsley. Use your hands to mix the ingredients thoroughly.
4. Put the mixture into the air fryer and cook at 180C//360F for about 5 minutes.
5. Give the air fryer a shake, then add the sausages on top.
6. Cook for a further 12 minutes at 180C//360F.
7. Load the mixture evenly into a silicon flan dish, along with the sliced spring onion. Top with grated cheese and set to one side.
8. In a jug, beat the eggs, and slowly add in the mascarpone and combine. Add the seasoning and parsley.
9. Pour the egg mixture evenly over the top of the dish containing the sweet potato and courgette. Decorate with cherry tomato halves as well as a sprinkle of basil.
10. Put the dish in the air fryer and cook for 17 minutes at 180C//360F, followed by another 5 minutes at 170C//340F. Check with a cocktail stick in the centre and if it comes out clean then the frittata is cooked.
11. Cut into slices and chill before serving.

Nutritional Information per Serving:

SERVES –4 TO 6 | CALORIES –414KCAL | PROTEIN –24G | CARBOHYDRATES –11G | FAT –30G

MINI QUICHE SNACK USING LEFTOVER MEAT
• •

INGREDIENTS

- 6 cherry tomatoes
- ¼ green pepper
- 425g//15oz leftover meat
- 4 eggs
- 2 garlic cloves, finely chopped
- 2 teaspoons of basil
- Salt and pepper to taste
- 40ml of milk

METHOD

1. Dice the tomatoes, green pepper, and meat for the filling. Share the filling evening between 6 small silicone bowls.
2. Preheat the air fryer to 180C//360F.
3. Beat the egg and seasonings together and pour over the top of the fillings in the silicone bowls.
4. Put the silicone moulds into the air fryer and cook at 180C//360F for 12 minutes.
5. Serve hot or cold.

Nutritional Information per Serving:

SERVES –6 | CALORIES –49KCAL | PROTEIN –5G | CARBOHYDRATES –1G | FAT –3G

LEFTOVER BEEF HASH
• •

INGREDIENTS

- 255g//9oz of leftover beef
- 3 small, sweet potatoes
- 2 peppers (different colours)
- 15ml of olive oil
- 1 teaspoon of paprika
- 1 teaspoon of dried coriander
- Salt and pepper to taste

METHOD

1. Peel and dice the sweet potatoes. Remove the seeds and stem from the pepper and dice.
2. Preheat the air fryer to 180C//360F.
3. In a bowl, combine the diced sweet potato, pepper, oil, and seasonings. Mix well with your hands.
4. Place in the air fryer and cook at 180C//360F for about 12 minutes.
5. Meanwhile, cut the beef into chunks.
6. When the 12 minutes cooking time is complete, add the beef, give the air fryer a shake, then cook for a final 3 minutes at the same temperature.
7. Serve.

Nutritional information per Serving

SERVES −2 TO 4 | CALORIES −338KCAL | PROTEIN −7G | CARBOHYDRATES −76G | FAT −2G

BREAKFAST SAUSAGE AND POTATO HASH

INGREDIENTS

- 6 medium potatoes
- 1 white onion
- 6 sausages
- 15ml of olive oil
- 15g//0.5oz of dried basil
- Salt and pepper to taste

METHOD

1. Preheat the air fryer to 160C//320F.
2. Peel the potatoes and onions, dice into pieces and put in a bowl together.
3. Add the basil, salt, pepper, and olive oil and use your hands to mix thoroughly.
4. Cut the sausages into quarters.
5. Add the potato mixture to the air fryer and put the sausage pieces on top.
6. Cook at 160C//320F for about 15 minutes.
7. Give the air fryer a shake, then cook for a further 3 minutes at the same temperature.
8. Serve.

Nutritional Information per Serving:

SERVES −4 TO 6 | CALORIES −859KCAL | PROTEIN −39G | CARBOHYDRATES −5G | FAT −75G

CHEESE AND HAM STROMBOLI

INGREDIENTS

- Pizza dough for one standard pizza
- 30g//1oz of pizza sauce
- 400g//14oz of grated cheese
- 300g//10.6oz leftover ham
- 1 egg, beaten
- Optional: a sprinkle of mixed dried herbs
- Optional: 45g//1.5oz of black olives, chopped

METHOD

1. Make (or purchase) your pizza dough.
2. Roll the pizza dough into a rectangular shape.
3. Layer the dough with pizza sauce, grated cheese, olives, and shredded ham. Sprinkle with the dried herbs if you choose to.
4. Preheat the air fryer to 160C//320F.
5. Lift one side of the rectangle and begin rolling inwards so that the filling is on the inside of the stromboli.
6. Cut small slits into the top of the stromboli and brush the dough with egg wash.
7. Cook in the air fryer for 12–15 minutes at 160C//320F.
8. Slice and serve.

Nutritional Information per Serving:

SERVES –4 | CALORIES –560KCAL | PROTEIN –54G | CARBOHYDRATES –5G | FAT –35G

CHEESE, BACON, AND POTATO HASH

INGREDIENTS

- 1kg//2.2lb of white potatoes
- 1 medium onion
- 30g//1oz of bacon bits
- 60g//2oz grated cheddar cheese
- 15ml of olive oil
- 1 teaspoon of dill
- 1 teaspoon of parsley
- 1 teaspoon of garlic powder
- 1 teaspoon of chives, chopped
- Salt and pepper to taste

METHOD

1. Preheat the air fryer to 200C//400F.
2. Peel, slice and rinse your potatoes, and allow to drain.
3. Hold the bacon and cheese in 2 separate bowls until ready to use.
4. Put the potatoes into the air fryer with the rest of the ingredients. Keep the cheese and bacon separate.
5. Turn the air fryer temperature down and cook for 15 minutes at 160C//320F.
6. Once the potato mix is cooked, add the bacon, and cook for a further 5 minutes at the same temperature.
7. After 5 minutes, transfer the bacon and potato mixture to a layer of silver foil and return to the air fryer.
8. Top the potatoes with grated cheddar cheese, increase the temperature to 200C//400F, and cook for another 5 minutes. Serve.

Nutritional Information per Serving:

SERVES –6 TO 8 | CALORIES –317KCAL | PROTEIN –11G | CARBOHYDRATES –49G | FAT –10G

CLASSIC PIGS IN BLANKETS

INGREDIENTS

- 725g//1.6lb pack of bacon
- 500g//1.1lb pack of small sausages (about 30 cocktail sausages)

METHOD

1. Remove the packaging from your bacon and sausages.
2. Preheat the air fryer to 180C//360F.
3. Wrap the bacon firmly around the sausages and secure with a cocktail stick.
4. Put the sausages and bacon in the air fryer and cook for about 8 minutes at 180C//360F.
5. Serve.

Nutritional Information per Serving:

SERVES −6 | CALORIES −835KCAL | PROTEIN −31.6G | CARBOHYDRATES −1.4G | FAT −77.6G

STUFFED PEPPERS

INGREDIENTS

- 6 bell peppers (mix your colours)
- 450g//1lb minced beef
- 15-30ml of taco seasoning
- 200g//7oz cooked rice
- 3 spring onions, thinly sliced
- 85g//3oz of black beans
- 170g//6oz frozen corn
- Optional: 230g//8oz of grated cheese, plus additional for topping

METHOD

1. In a saucepan, brown the minced beef and add the taco seasoning.
2. Stir in the remaining ingredients and mix thoroughly.
3. Cut the tops off the peppers, remove the stalks and the seeds. Wash and pat dry.
4. Cut the peppers in half from top to bottom, and stuff them with the minced beef mixture.
5. Cook in the air fryer for 10 minutes at 180C//350F.
6. Sprinkle the remaining cheese on top of the peppers and cook for a further 5 minutes.
7. Serve with tortilla chips, salsa, and sour cream.

Nutritional Information per Serving:

SERVES −6 | CALORIES −367KCAL | PROTEIN −21G | CARBOHYDRATES −25G | FAT −20G

SWEET POTATO TOPPED WITH CHICKEN AND VEGETABLES

INGREDIENTS

- 2 sweet potatoes, skin on
- 230g//8oz chicken cut into bite size pieces
- 1 bell pepper cut into bite size pieces
- 1 small red onion, finely chopped
- 85g//3oz frozen corn
- 85g//3oz of black beans
- 7.5ml oil of choice
- ½ teaspoon of cumin
- ½ teaspoon of brown sugar
- ½ teaspoon of paprika
- ¼ teaspoon of chilli powder
- Salt and pepper to taste

METHOD

1. Wash and scrub the sweet potatoes thoroughly and pierce with a fork a few times.
2. Preheat the air fryer to 190C//380F.
3. Rub oil all over the sweet potatoes. Place in the air fryer, sprinkle with salt and cook for about 20 minutes at 190C//380F.
4. Meanwhile, combine the chicken, corn, bell pepper, red onion and black beans with the oil and seasonings.
5. Open the air fryer and add the chicken and vegetables mixture. Cook for a further 10 minutes, then give the vegetable a stir in the air fryer basket. Adjust cooking time as required to ensure the potatoes are cooked through.
6. Once finished cooking, remove, and cut open the sweet potatoes. Top with the chicken and vegetables and enjoy.
7. Add your own toppings as appropriate.

Nutritional Information per Serving:

SERVES –2 | CALORIES –473KCAL | PROTEIN –20G | CARBOHYDRATES –72G | FAT –13G

BREAKFAST SHIRRED EGGS

INGREDIENTS

- 2 teaspoons unsalted butter, at room temperature
- 2 thin slices of ham, about 56g//2oz in total weight
- 4 eggs
- 30ml of double cream
- Salt and pepper to taste
- 45g//1.5oz finely grated parmesan cheese
- ⅛ teaspoon of smoked paprika
- 2 teaspoons fresh chives, chopped finely
- Optional: toasted bread, for serving

METHOD

1. Butter a flan tin and line with the ham so that the bottom and sides are covered.
2. In a separate bowl, whisk one of the eggs with the cream, and salt and pepper to taste.
3. Pour the egg mixture into the flan tin, then break the 3 remaining eggs over the top. Season with salt and pepper and sprinkle with the parmesan cheese.
4. Put into the air fryer and cook for 12 minutes at 160C//320F.
5. Remove the flan tin from the air fryer and with the help of a spatula, transfer the shirred eggs to a plate.
6. Garnish with the paprika and chives and serve warm.
7. Optional: Place the eggs on the toasted bread for a heartier meal if preferred.

Nutritional Information per Serving:

SERVES –2 | CALORIES – 319KCAL | PROTEIN – 22.3G | CARBOHYDRATES – 2.9G | FAT – 24.6G

BREAKFAST EGG POPPERS

INGREDIENTS

- 7 eggs
- 15ml of double cream
- 20g//0.7oz cheddar cheese shredded
- 4 slices cooked bacon, chopped
- 15ml of milk
- 2 spring onions, thinly sliced
- ¼ teaspoon mustard powder
- Salt and pepper to taste

METHOD

1. Preheat air fryer to 175C//340°F.
2. In a bowl, whisk the eggs, cream, mustard powder, salt and pepper until pale yellow and fluffy.
3. Divide the bacon, cheese, and spring onions between the individual small bowls (or muffin tins). Pour over the egg mixture, sharing evenly between each one.
4. Cook at 175C//340F for about 7 minutes, pause to stir, then cook for a further 7 minutes. The eggs are ready when they are just about set.
5. Rest for 5 minutes before serving.

Nutritional Information per Serving:

SERVES –4 | CALORIES – 134KCAL | PROTEIN – 8G | CARBOHYDRATES – 1G | FAT –11G

SCOTCH EGGS

• •

INGREDIENTS

For the Turkey Sausage:

- 450g//1lb minced turkey
- 1 teaspoon of sage

- 1/8 teaspoon of marjoram
- 1/4 teaspoon of red pepper flakes

- Salt and pepper to taste

For the Scotch Eggs:

- 6 hard–boiled eggs
- 100g//3.5oz of breadcrumbs

- 2 large eggs, beaten
- Salt and pepper to taste

- Optional: fresh chopped parsley as a garnish

METHOD

1. Combine the herbs and spices together in a large bowl.
2. Add the turkey mince and use your hands to mix thoroughly with the spices.
3. Divide the turkey mixture into 6 even balls and flatter into a thin burger shape.
4. Place a hardboiled egg into the middle of each burger shape and wrap the turkey around the eggs, sealing it on all sides.
5. Set the turkey wrapped eggs to one side.
6. Preheat the air fryer to 200C//400F.
7. In a separate bowl, break the two eggs and whisk. Put the breadcrumbs on a separate plate nearby.
8. Spray the air fryer with cooking oil. Dip each turkey wrapped egg in the beaten egg, then in the breadcrumbs. Place on a heatproof tray and when they are all dipped, transfer to the air fryer.
9. Cook for 12 minutes at 200C//400F, turning halfway through.
10. Serve hot or cold with a dipping sauce.

Nutritional information per Serving:

SERVES –6 | CALORIES –202KCAL | FAT –7G | CARBOHYDRATES –7G | PROTEIN –26G

CARAMELISED CRISPY BACON TWISTS WITH DIPPY EGGS

• •

INGREDIENTS

- 1 pack of bacon strips, any kind
- 1 teaspoon of brown sugar
- Salt and pepper to taste

- 4 soft boiled eggs
- Spray cooking oil

METHOD

1. Preheat the air fryer to 200C//400F. Spray the air fryer lightly with cooking oil.
2. Twist each bacon strip tightly and place in the air fryer.
3. Sprinkle over the top with brown sugar.
4. Cook at 200C//400F for about 4–5 minutes.
5. Turn all the bacon strips over, then cook for a further 5–7 minutes at the same temperature.
6. While the bacon is cooking, prepare your soft–boiled dippy eggs.
7. Serve and enjoy!

Nutritional information per Serving:

SERVES –6 | CALORIES –9KCAL | FAT –1G | CARBOHYDRATES –0G | PROTEIN –1G

PROTEIN BOXES FOR LUNCHBOXES
● ●

INGREDIENTS

- 2 x boneless skinless chicken breasts
- 60ml of olive oil
- Salt and pepper to taste
- ¼ teaspoon of dried oregano or basil
- ¼ teaspoon of onion powder
- ¼ teaspoon of smoked paprika
- 60ml of lemon juice
- 4 eggs
- 150g//5oz of raw almonds
- 150g//5oz of grapes
- 3 mozzarella cheese sticks, each cut into 4 pieces (other cheeses can be used)
- 3 cheddar cheese sticks, each cut into 4 pieces (other cheeses can be used

METHOD

1. Whisk to combine the olive oil, lemon juice, salt, pepper, herbs, onion powder, and paprika.
2. Toss the chicken breasts in the bowl with the marinade and coat completely. Place in the fridge to marinate for at least 30 minutes.
3. Preheat the air fryer to 200C//400F and spray with oil.
4. Place the chicken in the air fryer and cook for 15–20 minutes or until cooked. Turn halfway through cooking to ensure it's cooked through.
5. Set aside to cool before slicing into 1/2 inch slices.
6. Adjust the temperature of the air fryer to 130C//260F and place the 4 eggs into the air fryer. Cook for 17 minutes at the new temperature.
7. Cool the eggs and peel.
8. Divide the sliced chicken, the almonds and grapes, and the cheese sticks pieces between four partitioned sandwich boxes. Put an egg in each sandwich box.
9. Sprinkle with salt and pepper if desired, place lids on the containers and save until ready to eat. The protein boxes can be stored in the fridge for up to 3 days.

Nutritional information per Serving:

SERVES –4 | CALORIES –603KCAL | FAT –44G | CARBOHYDRATES –15G | PROTEIN –40G

BREAKFAST CASSEROLE

INGREDIENTS

- 4 eggs
- 30ml of double cream
- 450g//1lb of Italian sausage, already cooked
- 130g//4.5oz of tomatoes and green chillies, diced
- 60g//2oz of shredded cheddar cheese
- 2 teaspoons Italian seasoning

METHOD

1. Put the cooked Italian sausage, diced tomatoes, chillies, and Italian seasoning in a bowl together and mix thoroughly.
2. Stir in the shredded cheese.
3. Gradually whisk the eggs and cream into the sausage mixture.
4. Preheat the air fryer to 170C//340F.
5. Pour the mixture evenly between 4 ramekins and top with shredded cheese.
6. Place the ramekins in the air fryer and cook for 5 to 8 minutes at 170C//340F.
7. When the eggs are set the food is cooked.
8. Serve and enjoy.

Nutritional information per Serving:

SERVES –4 | CALORIES –560KCAL | FAT –18G | CARBOHYDRATES –9G | PROTEIN –32G

STARTERS, SIDES AND SNACKS – BREADS AND CAKES

EASY LOW–FAT HOT CROSS FRUIT BUNS

INGREDIENTS

- 150g//5oz of plain flour
- 2 teaspoons of baking powder
- 30g//1oz of white sugar
- 3/4 teaspoon of cinnamon

For the Icing:

- 30g//1oz of icing sugar
- 1 teaspoon milk or water

- Pinch of salt
- 280g//10oz of fat–free Greek yoghurt
- 30g//1oz of raisins

- 1 egg, beaten

METHOD

1. Place baking paper on a baking sheet or line the air fryer. Spray with cooking oil to prevent it sticking.
2. Put the flour, baking powder, sugar, cinnamon, and salt in a bowl together and mix well.
3. Add the yoghurt and raisins to the dry mixture and fold in with a fork until combined.
4. Knead the dough on a lightly floured surface until it is slightly sticky but comes away cleanly.
5. Preheat the air fryer to 165C//325F.
6. Divide the dough into 8 equal balls and transfer directly to the air fryer, or onto the baking sheet if you're using one.
7. Cook in batches at 165C//325F for 11–12 minutes, or until a lovely golden brown.
8. Transfer to a wire rack to cool for at least 30 minutes before icing.
9. For the icing: in a small bowl, whisk the icing sugar with the milk (or water) until smooth, but not too runny.
10. Use an icing bag, or drizzle with a spoon to create an icing cross over the surface of the buns.

Nutritional Information per Serving:

SERVES –8 (2 BUNS IS 1 SERVING) | CALORIES –230KCAL | PROTEIN –10.5G | CARBOHYDRATES –46G | FAT –0.5G

SO–EASY LOW–FAT BAGELS

INGREDIENTS

- 150g/5oz of plain flour
- 2 teaspoons baking powder
- Pinch of salt

- 280g//10oz of fat–free Greek yoghurt
- 1 egg, beaten

- Optional toppings: try bagel seasoning, sesame seeds, poppy seeds, dried garlic flakes, dried onion flakes etc.

METHOD

1. Combine the flour, baking powder and salt in a bowl and mix well. Stir in the yoghurt with a fork until well combined.
2. Knead the dough on a light floured surface until it is still tacky but comes away clean.
3. Divide into 4 equal balls, then roll each one into a fat sausage shape. Bring the ends together to form a bagel shape.
4. Preheat the air fryer to 130C//280F.
5. Brush with egg wash and sprinkle your choice of seasoning over the top.
6. Place in batches in the air fryer and cook for 15 to 16 minutes at 130C//280F until golden brown.
7. Leave to cool for 15 minutes before serving.

Nutritional Information per Serving:

SERVES –4 (1 BAGEL IS 1 SERVING) | CALORIES –152KCAL | PROTEIN –10G | CARBOHYDRATES –26.5G | FAT –0.3G

GARLIC BUTTER NAAN

INGREDIENTS

- 1 x 7g//0.2oz sachet of active dry yeast
- 60ml of water
- 2 teaspoons of sugar
- 540g//19oz of plain flour

- 175ml of milk
- 200g//7oz of Greek yoghurt
- 40ml of olive oil
- 6 garlic cloves, finely chopped
- 1 teaspoon of baking powder

For the Garlic Butter:

- 6 garlic cloves, finely chopped
- 70g//2.5oz butter
- A sprig of chopped fresh parsley

METHOD

1. Stir the yeast, sugar, and warm water together in a jug and leave to stand for 10 minutes.
2. Use a stand mixer with dough hook for the next stage if you have one or mix by hand.
3. Combine the flour, milk, yoghurt, garlic, oil, baking powder, salt with the yeast mixture to create a soft dough.
4. On a floured service, knead the dough for about 5 minutes.
5. Put the dough in an oiled bowl and cover. Set aside in a warm place for an hour.
6. When the dough has doubled in size, remove from the bowl, cut 10 equal pieces, and roll them into a ball.
7. Preheat your air fryer to 185C//370F and spray with cooking oil.
8. Flatten each ball out to a size that will fit in your air fryer, place inside and cook one at a time at 185C//370F for about 6 minutes. Turn over and cook for 3 more minutes.
9. In the meantime, make your garlic butter. Melt the butter with the garlic and parsley.
10. Brush the naan immediately with the garlic butter as it comes out of the air fryer.
11. Serve as a side to a curry dish.

Nutritional Information per Serving:

SERVES −10 | CALORIES −316KCAL | PROTEIN −8G | CARBOHYDRATES −43G | FAT −13G

SHARING BREAD ROLLS

INGREDIENTS

- 1 x 7g//0.2oz packet of dried yeast
- 280ml milk
- 2 teaspoons of sugar
- 450g//1lb of plain flour
- 70g//2.5oz of butter
- 15ml of olive oil
- 15ml of coconut oil
- Salt and pepper to taste
- Optional: egg wash to brush over the top of the dough

METHOD

1. Stir the yeast, sugar, and milk together in a jug and leave to stand for 10 minutes.
2. Use a stand mixer with dough hook for the next stage if you have one or mix by hand.
3. Combine the flour, butter, olive and coconut oils and salt and pepper with the yeast mixture to create a soft dough.
4. On a floured service, knead the dough for about 5 minutes.
5. Put the dough in an oiled bowl and cover. Set aside in a warm place for an hour.
6. When the dough has doubled in size, remove from the bowl.
7. Create several medium bread rolls and put them in the air fryer in a single layer with sides touching.
8. Brush the tops with the egg wash if you want to at this point.
9. Air fry at 180C//360F for about 15 minutes.
10. Remove from air fryer and allow to cool on a wire rack.

Nutritional Information per Serving:

SERVES −9 | CALORIES −652KCAL | PROTEIN −15G | CARBOHYDRATES −90G | FAT −26G

OATMEAL COOKIES

INGREDIENTS

- 150g//5oz of self–raising flour
- 150g//5oz of rolled oats
- 70g//2.5oz of butter, cold, cut into cubes
- 70g//2.5oz of caster sugar
- 2 teaspoons of golden syrup
- 2 teaspoons of vanilla essence
- 15 ml whole milk
- Optional: squirty cream

METHOD

1. Mix the flour and the sugar in a bowl, then add the cubes of refrigerated butter.
2. Rub the butter and flour together in your fingertips to combine. The finished mixture should look like coarse breadcrumbs.
3. Stir in the oats, golden syrup, and vanilla.
4. Add a little milk at a time and stir with your hands to create a large ball of dough.
5. Roll the dough out onto a floured surface and cut out cookies with cookie cutters.
6. Preheat your air fryer to 180C//360F.
7. Line your air fryer and spritz a little cooking oil, then place your cookies inside in a single layer so they are not touching.
8. Cook for 8 minutes at 180C//360F.
9. Turn the temperature down a little to 160C//320F and cook for a further 3 minutes.
10. Leave on a wire rack to cool, then serve.

Nutritional Information per Serving:

SERVES –SERVING BASED ON 2–3 STANDARD COOKIES | CALORIES –339KCAL | PROTEIN –6G |

CARBOHYDRATES –50G | FAT – 12G

CHOCOLATE CHIP COOKIES

INGREDIENTS

- 115g//4oz unsalted butter, melted
- 100g//3.5oz of brown sugar
- 60g//2oz white sugar
- 1 egg
- 1 teaspoon of vanilla extract
- 240g//8.5oz of plain flour
- 1 teaspoon of baking soda
- ¼ teaspoon of salt
- 170g//6oz of semi–sweet chocolate chips

METHOD

1. In a bowl, beat both sugars with the melted butter until light and fluffy, then gradually stir in the egg and vanilla before beating the mixture for a final 30 seconds.
2. Add all the remaining ingredients and stir until combined. Put in the fridge to chill for about 30 minutes.
3. Line the air fryer with baking paper, then preheat to 160C//325F.
4. Use a tablespoon to scoop out dough balls and place them into the air fryer on the baking paper. (You may need to cook in batches.)
5. Cook at 160C//325F for about 5–7 minutes until cooked through.
6. Allow to cool on a wire rack before serving.

Nutritional Information per Serving:

SERVES –1 COOKIE (MAKES 18 COOKIES) | CALORIES –179KCAL | PROTEIN –2G | CARBOHYDRATES –22G | FAT –9G

BLUEBERRY MUFFINS

INGREDIENTS

- 170g//6oz of rolled oats
- 3 medium bananas
- 2 eggs
- 240ml of Greek yoghurt
- 30g//1oz of honey
- ½ teaspoon of vanilla essence
- 1 teaspoon of baking powder
- 50g//1.7oz blueberries

METHOD

1. Peel and chop your bananas.
2. Keep the blueberries to one side but place all the other ingredients into the blender.
3. Blend until the batter is smooth and creamy with no lumps.
4. Preheat the air fryer to 180C//360F.
5. Distribute the muffin batter evenly between your silicone muffin cases.
6. Add about 8 blueberries to each muffin case. Push 4 into the batter mix and let 4 settle just on top.
7. Cook for 12 minutes at 180C//360F and allow to cool before serving.

Nutritional Information per Serving:

SERVES –1 MUFFING (MAKES 6 TO 8 MUFFINS.) | CALORIES –203KCAL | PROTEIN –9G | CARBOHYDRATES –36G | FAT – 4G

GARLIC BREAD

INGREDIENTS

- 500g//1.1lb of ready–made pizza dough
- 15ml of olive oil
- 1 teaspoon of dried parsley
- 2 teaspoons of garlic puree
- Salt and pepper to taste

METHOD

1. If you have a bread maker, then cook up a batch of pizza dough.
2. Mix the other ingredients in a small bowl.
3. On a floured surface, roll out the pizza dough into 2 round pizza shapes (make sure that they will fit in your air fryer!).
4. Spread the oil and garlic mixture evenly over your pizza bread.
5. Gently prick holes all over the pizza bread with a fork, then brush the garlic and oil mixture evenly all over the upper surface.
6. Place in the air fryer and cook at 160C//320F for about 10 minutes.

Nutritional Information per Serving:

SERVES –4 | CALORIES –384KCAL | PROTEIN –7G | CARBOHYDRATES –60G | FAT – 1G

PIZZA DOUGH BALLS

INGREDIENTS

- Any leftover pizza dough, at room temperature, or make a new batch
- 1 teaspoon of mustard
- 1 teaspoon of garlic puree
- 100g//3.5oz of grated mozzarella
- 60g//2oz of soft cheese
- 15ml of olive oil
- 2 teaspoons of dried rosemary
- Salt and pepper to taste
- Optional: Harissa sauce

METHOD

1. Bring your pizza dough up to room temperature and knead briefly on a floured surface.
2. Set the dough and olive oil to one side for later and mix all the other ingredients in a bowl until you have a paste.
3. Take the dough and divide it evening into 8 balls, which you will then flatten out like a pancake. Put a 1/3 teaspoon of the paste in the middle, then bring the edges of the dough shape up around the paste and seal at the top. The paste should now be occupying a little compartment in the centre of the dough ball. Squash them very gently into a dough ball.
4. Brush the dough balls with oil and place them in the air fryer.
5. Cook for 10 minutes at 180C//320F for 10 minutes.
6. Turn the temperature of the air fryer down a little to 160C//320F and cook for a further 5 minutes. Serve with your favourite dipping sauce.

Nutritional Information per Serving:

SERVES –2 | CALORIES –153KCAL | PROTEIN –6G | CARBOHYDRATES –2G | FAT – 14G

PUMPKIN BREAD
••

INGREDIENTS

- 2 eggs
- 60g//2oz of banana flour
- 130g//4.5oz of fresh pumpkin puree
- 60g//2oz of rolled oats
- 70g//2.5oz of Greek yoghurt
- 2 teaspoons of vanilla essence
- 85g//3oz of honey
- Pinch of nutmeg

METHOD

1. Put the oats to one side and place all the other ingredients into a mixing bowl. Combine until smooth and creamy. Use a hand mixer if appropriate.
2. Use a fork to gently fold in the oats.
3. Preheat your air fryer to 180C//360F.
4. Pour your mixture into a greased and/or lined baking tin. Make sure it fits your air fryer first.
5. Cook for 15 minutes at 180C//360F.
6. Remove from the fryer and allow to cool before serving.

Nutritional Information per Serving:

SERVES –4 | CALORIES –229KCAL | PROTEIN –8G | CARBOHYDRATES –29G | FAT – 8G

BANANA BREAD
•••

INGREDIENTS

- 230g//8oz of self–raising flour
- 1/4 teaspoon of bicarbonate of soda
- 70g//2.5oz of butter
- 170g//6oz of caster sugar
- 2 eggs
- 450g//1lb of peeled bananas (weight without skins)
- Optional: 100g//3.50z of chopped walnuts

METHOD

1. Preheat the air fryer to 180C//350F.
2. Grease a tin that will fit the air fryer.
3. Mix the bicarbonate of soda with the flour in a bowl.
4. In a second bowl, cream the butter and sugar until it is pale and fluffy in texture. Stir in the eggs gradually with a little of the flour at a time.
5. Fold in the remaining flour and optional walnuts.
6. Mash the peeled bananas and stir them into the final mixture.
7. Scoop the banana bread mixture into the prepared tin and cook for 10 minutes at 180C//350F. Reduce the temperature a little to 170C//335F and cook for a further 15 minutes.
8. Allow to cool on a wire rack, then serve.

Nutritional Information per Serving:

SERVES −6 | CALORIES −530KCAL | PROTEIN −10.7G | CARBOHYDRATES −77.5G | FAT − 22.1G

AFRICAN CHIN CHIN

INGREDIENTS

- 440g//15.5oz of plain flour
- ½ teaspoon baking powder
- ½ teaspoon salt
- 130g//4.5oz of sugar
- 1 ½ teaspoons grated nutmeg
- 1 teaspoon of grated lime zest
- 70g//2.5oz butter
- 1 egg, beaten
- 180ml milk

METHOD

1. Mix the flour, baking powder, salt, sugar, nutmeg, and lime zest together in a large bowl.
2. Add the butter and rub between your fingers until you have a mixture resembling coarse breadcrumbs.
3. Add the egg and milk and mix thoroughly until you have a sticky dough ball.
4. Knead the dough on a floured surface for about 5 minutes, adding a little more flour as required until the dough is smooth, elastic and no longer sticky. (Use your stand mixer with the dough hook if that is preferable.)
5. Divide the dough into two equal pieces and roll each section out to about ⅛ inches thick.
6. Preheat the air fryer to 150C//300F.
7. Create dough shapes as preferred. Use the internet for inspiration! Some prefer dough balls, squares, chip shapes, or even use dough cutters!
8. Spray the air fryer with cooking oil and add the Chin Chin in a single layer. You may need to cook in batches depending on the size of your air fryer.
9. Cook for 15−18 minutes at 150C//300F. Give the basket a shake and cook for a further 2 minutes if needed.
10. Serve hot or cold.

Nutritional Information per Serving:

SERVES −4 | CALORIES − 421KCAL | PROTEIN − 9G | CARBOHYDRATES − 58G | FAT − 17G

TAPIOCA CAKE

INGREDIENTS

- 450g//1lb grated tapioca
- 85g//3oz sugar
- 250ml coconut milk
- Pinch of salt
- 1 egg, beaten
- 15g//0.5oz unsalted butter, at room temperature
- 1/4 teaspoon ground turmeric
- 30g//1oz desiccated coconut

METHOD

1. Mix the tapioca and sugar in a large bowl until combined.
2. Add the coconut milk, salt, beaten egg, and turmeric powder and mix well.
3. Stir in the softened butter, then the desiccated coconut. Make sure the mixture is thoroughly combined.
4. Preheat the air fryer to 160C//320F.
5. Pour the mixture into a lined baking pan, place in the air fryer and cook for 15 minutes at 160//320F.
6. Turn the heat up to 180C//360F. Continue cooking for a further 10–15 minutes until golden brown.
7. Transfer to a wire cooling rack and allow to cool. Cut and serve.

Nutritional Information per Serving:

SERVES –6 TO 8 | CALORIES –494KCAL | PROTEIN –2.4G | CARBOHYDRATES –89.5G | FAT –15.2 G

BREAKFAST BRAN MUFFINS
• •

INGREDIENTS

- 70g//2.5oz of All Bran or Fiber One cereal (or similar)
- 220ml of buttermilk
- 85g//3oz unsweetened applesauce
- 1 egg
- 150g//5oz brown sugar
- 1 teaspoon of pure vanilla extract
- 150g//5oz of plain flour
- 1 teaspoon of baking powder
- 1 teaspoon of baking soda
- 1 teaspoon of salt

METHOD

1. Combine the cereal and buttermilk in a bowl and leave to stand for about 20 minutes.
2. In a separate bowl, mix the applesauce, egg, vanilla together.
3. In a third bowl, combine the brown sugar, flour, baking powder, baking soda, and salt.
4. Finally, put the 3 mixtures into one bowl and mix until well combined.
5. Preheat the air fryer to 160C//320F. Spray the muffin tins lightly with cooking oil.
6. Pour the muffin batter into the tins until each one is about 2/3 full.
7. Put the muffins in the air fryer and cook at 160C//320F for 12–15 minutes.
8. Allow to cool on a wire rack for a few minutes, serve and enjoy.

Nutritional Information per Serving

SERVES –6 | CALORIES –122KCAL | FAT –1G | CARBOHYDRATES –27G | PROTEIN –3G

BREAKFAST APPLE MUFFINS
• •

INGREDIENTS

For the Muffin Mix:

- 60g//2oz of plain flour
- 1 teaspoon of baking powder
- 1 teaspoon of ground cinnamon
- Pinch of salt
- 45g//1.5oz of brown sugar
- 30g//1oz melted butter
- 1 egg yolk
- 30ml of double cream
- 1 teaspoon of vanilla extract
- 60g//2oz of chopped apples
- Spray cooking oil

For the Crumb Topping:

- 30g//1oz of plain flour
- 60g//2oz of brown sugar
- 1 teaspoon ground cinnamon
- 45g//1.5oz of butter

METHOD

1. Mix the flour, baking powder, ground cinnamon, sugar, and salt together in a bowl.
2. Add the egg, melted butter, vanilla extract, and double cream. Mix well until combined.
3. Fold in the chopped apples.
4. Spray the ramekins or muffin tins with spray cooking oil and distribute the muffin mix evenly between them.
5. For the topping, use your fingers to rub together the flour, brown sugar, cinnamon, and white sugar until it resembles coarse breadcrumbs.
6. Preheat the air fryer to 160C//320F.
7. Sprinkle the topping mix over the muffins.
8. Put the muffin tins/ramekins into the air fryer and cook for 12–14 minutes at 160C//320F.
9. Allow to cool for a few minutes before eating.

Nutritional Information per Serving

SERVES −2 | CALORIES −704KCAL | FAT −40G | CARBOHYDRATES −82G | PROTEIN −7G

CORNBREAD MUFFINS

● ●

INGREDIENTS

- 120g//4oz plain flour
- 160g//5.5oz of yellow cornmeal
- 1 teaspoon salt
- 15g//0.5oz of baking soda
- 300ml of buttermilk
- 60g//2oz corn kernels
- 2 large eggs
- 60g//2oz granulated sugar
- 80ml of vegetable oil

METHOD

1. Combine the flour, yellow cornmeal, salt, baking powder, baking soda, and sugar together in a bowl.
2. Add the buttermilk, eggs, corn kernels, and vegetable oil and mix well.
3. Preheat the air fryer to 170C//330F.
4. Spray the muffin tins lightly with cooking oil, then evenly fill each one to about 2/3 full of the muffin mixture.
5. Cook for about 12 minutes at 170C//330F.
6. Allow to cool on a wire rack for a few minutes before serving.

Nutritional Information per Serving:

SERVES −6 | CALORIES −352KCAL | FAT −4G | CARBOHYDRATES −49.3G | PROTEIN −8G

SAVOURY CHEESE AND BACON MUFFINS

● ●

INGREDIENTS

- 300g//10.5oz of plain flour
- 85g//3oz of shredded cheddar cheese
- 2 teaspoons of baking powder
- 1 teaspoon of dried basil
- Pinch of salt
- 15ml of olive oil
- 1 egg
- 80ml of milk
- 60g//2oz cooked, chopped bacon

METHOD

1. Mix the flour, cheddar cheese, baking powder, dried basil, salt together.
2. Add the olive oil, egg, crumbled bacon, and milk and mix to combine.
3. Preheat the air fryer to 180C//350F.
4. Spray the muffin tins lightly with cooking oil.
5. Pour the muffin mixture evenly among the muffin tins to about 2/3 full.
6. Place the muffins into the air fryer and cook for about 15 minutes at 180C//350F.
7. Check the muffins with a toothpick pushed into the centre of the muffin. If it comes out clean, then they are done. Cook for a further 5 minutes if necessary and check again.
8. Allow to cool on a wire rack for a few minutes before serving.

Nutritional Information per Serving:

SERVES −24 MUFFINS | CALORIES −486KCAL | FAT −20G | CARBOHYDRATES −49.3G | PROTEIN −29.5G

BREAKFAST HONEY MUFFINS

INGREDIENTS

- 600g//21oz of plain flour
- 100g//3.5oz sugar
- 30g//1oz of baking powder
- Pinch of salt
- 80ml milk
- 60g//2oz of melted butter
- 85g//3oz of honey
- 1 egg

METHOD

1. Mix the flour, sugar, baking powder, and salt together in a bowl, then add the milk, melted butter, honey and egg.
2. Then mix in the milk, melted butter, honey, and egg.
3. Mix well to make a batter.
4. Preheat the air fryer to 160C//320F.
5. Spray the muffin tins lightly with cooking oil, then distribute the mixture evenly between them to about 2/3 full.
6. Place in the air fryer and cook for 12 minutes at 160C//320F.
7. If they are not quite done, cook for a further 3–4 minutes and check again.
8. Allow to cool on a wire rack for a few minutes, then serve with butter.

Nutritional Information per Serving:

SERVES −24 | CALORIES −139KCAL | FAT −2.4G | CARBOHYDRATES −26.6G | PROTEIN −2.9G

EXCLUSIVE BONUS

40 Weight Loss Recipes

&

14 Days Meal Plan

Scan the QR-Code and receive
the FREE download:

MAINS – AIRFRYER COOKBOOK

MAINS – VEGETARIAN DISHES

EVERYONE'S FAVOURITE CHIPS

Air fried chips are one of the first foods people cook after purchasing their first air fryer!

INGREDIENTS

- 2–3 medium to large potatoes, peeled and chipped into even pieces about 1–1.5cms thick
- 15-30ml of olive oil
- Seasonings

METHOD

1. After chipping your potatoes, rinse in cold, clean water and dry thoroughly.
2. Put the olive oil into the air fryer and preheat to 180C//350F.
3. Add the dried chips taking care not to overfill the air fryer basket and shake so that the chips are coated in the olive oil.
4. Cook for 20–30 minutes at 180C//350F, shaking the basket every 5–10 minutes so the chips do not clump together.
5. Cook to your preference. If you prefer your chips well–browned, then leave them in the air fryer for a little longer; cook for less time if you prefer them golden.
6. Serve immediately with your favourite vegetable, fish, or meat accompaniments. Season to taste.

Nutritional Information per Serving:

SERVES –4 | CALORIES –191KCAL | CARBOHYDRATE –25.1G | PROTEIN –2.7G | FAT –9.6G

MEDITERRANEAN STYLE STIR FRY VEGETABLES

INGREDIENTS

- 1 aubergine
- 1 courgette (mix your colours: try ½ a green courgette, ½ a yellow courgette)
- 250g//9oz button mushrooms
- Peppers, 1 green, 1 red
- 2 garlic cloves, peeled and chopped
- 100ml of white wine
- 15ml of vegetable oil
- Salt and pepper

METHOD

1. Cut the aubergine into semi–circular slices and cover with salt for 30 minutes (this absorbs any excess moisture).
2. Cut the courgette into thin circles.
3. Chop the mushrooms in half.
4. Slice the peppers into thin strips and remove the seeds.
5. Peel and chop the garlic.
6. Preheat the air fryer to 180C//360F.
7. Rinse the excess salt off the aubergine and put it in the bottom of the air fryer pan with the chopped garlic.
8. Add the rest of the vegetables and pour the wine and the oil over the top.
9. Cook for 20–30 minutes at 180C//360F.
10. Serve immediately with boiled white or brown rice.

EASY VEGETABLE FRITTERS

INGREDIENTS

- 2 medium potatoes
- 255g//9oz of frozen mixed vegetables, thawed and drained
- 130g//4.5oz of frozen peas, thawed and drained
- 1 coarsely chopped onion
- 15g//0.5oz of ground flaxseed, optional
- 30g//1oz of fresh coriander, finely chopped
- 60g//2oz of plain flour
- 1/2 teaspoon sea salt
- Olive oil cooking spray

METHOD

1. Peel the potatoes and grate them into a large bowl.
2. Stir the thawed vegetables, chopped onion (and optional ground flax seed) into the potato mixture.
3. Add the whisked egg and coriander and stir in, followed by the flour and salt. Mix thoroughly.
4. Preheat the air fryer to 180C//356°F.
5. Divide the mixture into equal parts to make 12 fritters and spray lightly with the cooking oil.
6. Place the fritters carefully into the air fryer taking care not to overfill it and cook at 180C//356°F for about 15 minutes, turning halfway. Depending on the size of your air fryer, you may need to cook the fritters in batches.

ROASTED CAULIFLOWER TACOS

INGREDIENTS

- 1kg//2.2lbs of cauliflower florets
- 30ml of olive oil
- 1/2 teaspoon of tajin
- 1/2 teaspoon smoked paprika
- Salt to taste
- 6 street tortillas (6–inch corn tortillas)
- Pickled red onions (recipe below)
- 90ml of Peruvian green sauce (Aji Verde) for topping
- Optional: sour cream
- Optional: fresh chopped coriander to garnish

For the Pickled Red Onions:

- 1 red onion, peeled and sliced into rounds
- 120ml of apple cider vinegar
- 70ml of water
- 15g//0.5oz of sugar
- Salt to taste
- 2 bay leaves

METHOD

1. Preheat the air fryer to 200C//400F and spray with cooking oil.
2. Toss the cauliflower, olive oil, tajin, smoked paprika and salt in a bowl together and combine so that the cauliflower is coated in the seasoning.
3. Add the cauliflower florets to the air fryer and cook for 12–15 minutes at 200C//400F until browned and tender. Give the cauliflower a shake halfway through cooking.
4. Create your taco: Fill your tortilla wrap with the cauliflower and red onion pickle topped with Peruvian green sauce, sour cream and chopped coriander.

For the Pickled Red Onions:

1. Bring the vinegar, water, sugar, and salt gently to the boil in a saucepan on the hob and simmer until the sugar dissolves.
2. Put the onions in a safe, heatproof bowl and pour the vinegar over the top so they are completely covered.
3. Allow to cool, cover, then store overnight in the fridge.

Nutritional Information per Serving
Serves – 3

CALORIES –284KCAL | CARBOHYDRATES –22.5G | PROTEIN –8.5G | FAT –21.5G

MACARONI CHEESE

INGREDIENTS

- 150g//5oz elbow macaroni pasta
- 240ml of water
- 120g//4oz of double cream
- 230g//8oz shredded cheddar cheese (keep ¼ back in a separate bowl)
- 1 teaspoon of mustard powder
- Salt and pepper to taste
- 1/4 teaspoon of garlic powder
- Optional: chopped ham, bacon crumbs or corn kernels

METHOD

1. Preheat the air fryer to 185C//360F.
2. Put all the ingredients into a large saucepan and mix thoroughly. Remember to set aside ¼ of the cheese in a separate bowl.
3. Put the mixture in the air fryer and cook for 8–10 minutes at 185C//360F.
4. Open the air fryer and stir in the remaining ¼ of cheddar cheese.
5. Close the air fryer and continue cooking for a further 10 minutes at 185C//360F.
6. Once cook, allow to cool. The mixture will thicken slightly.
7. Serve topped with ham or bacon bits. Alternatively, garnish with corn kernels, and a little ground pepper.

Nutritional Information per Serving:

SERVES –4 | CALORIES –530KCAL | PROTEIN –22G | CARBOHYDRATES –41G | FAT –31G

SWEET POTATO CASSEROLE WITH PECAN TOPPING

INGREDIENTS

- 3 medium sweet potatoes, peel, washed and cubed
- 120ml of coconut milk
- 60g//2oz of brown sugar
- 1 teaspoon of ground cinnamon

For the Pecan Topping:

- 150g//5oz of chopped pecan nuts
- 60g//2oz brown sugar
- 60g//2oz of butter
- 60g//2oz of plain flour
- 1 teaspoon of ground cinnamon

METHOD

1. Boil the sweet potato cubes in a saucepan of hot water for about 10 minutes until soft, then drain, transfer to a bowl and mash.
2. Add the brown sugar, coconut milk and cinnamon to the mashed potato and stir to combine.
3. Transfer the mixture to a prepared casserole dish and set to one side.
4. Preheat the air fryer to 170C//340F.
5. To make the pecan topping, mix the flour, sugar, chopped pecan nuts and cinnamon in a bowl. Add the melted butter and stir until crumbly.
6. Sprinkle the pecan mixture over the top of the sweet potato casserole.
7. Place the filled casserole dish in the air fryer and cook for about 16 minutes at 170C//340F. Serve and enjoy.

Nutritional Information per Serving:

SERVES –4 | CALORIES –572KCAL | PROTEIN –5G | CARBOHYDRATES –65G | FAT –35G

ROASTED PARMESAN BRUSSEL SPROUTS WITH BUTTERNUT SQUASH

INGREDIENTS

- About 450g//1lb brussels sprouts
- 280g//10oz of diced butternut squash
- 45ml of olive oil
- 1 teaspoon of garlic powder
- Salt and pepper to taste
- 30g//1oz breadcrumbs
- 45g//1.5oz of parmesan cheese

METHOD

1. Clean the sprouts and cut in half. Peel the butternut squash and dice.
2. In a bowl, mix the olive oil, salt, pepper and garlic powder. Add the sprouts and butternut and toss to coat with the seasoned oil.
3. Preheat the air fryer to 195C//390C.
4. Prepare the breadcrumb by mixing with the parmesan cheese in a bowl.
5. Transfer the sprouts and squash to the air fryer and cook for 10 minutes at 195C//390F.
6. Open the air fryer, sprinkle the cheesy breadcrumb mixture over the vegetables, and cook for a further 5 minutes.
7. Serve warm.

Nutritional Information per Serving:

SERVES –4 | CALORIES –252KCAL | PROTEIN –10G | CARBOHYDRATES –24G | FAT –15G

FRIED BROWN RICE

INGREDIENTS

- 1 large carrot, peeled and chopped into small pieces
- 2 spring onions, thinly sliced
- 1–inch piece of ginger, grated/finely chopped
- 15ml of vegetable oil
- Salt and pepper to taste
- 370g//13oz of long–grain brown rice
- 1 garlic clove, finely chopped
- 2 ½ teaspoons of soy sauce
- 2 teaspoons of toasted sesame oil
- 1 egg, beaten
- 70g//2.5oz frozen peas, thawed

METHOD

1. Preheat the air fryer to 200C//400F.
2. Put the carrot, spring onion, ginger, vegetable oil, and salt into a non–stick pan and place in the air fryer. Cook for about 5 minutes at 200C//400F, stirring halfway through.
3. Add the brown rice, garlic, soy sauce, sesame oil, salt and pepper to the air fryer and mix.
4. Cook for a further 5 minutes at 200C//400F.
5. Open the air fryer and pour the egg onto the rice on one side, and the peas over the other side.
6. Cook again for about 4 minutes at 200C//400F until the vegetables are tender and the egg is just set.
7. Serve hot, topped with thinly sliced spring onion.

Nutritional Information per Serving:

SERVES –2 | CALORIES –440KCAL | PROTEIN –12G | CARBOHYDRATES –62G | FAT –16G

HOMEMADE PIZZA

Note – put your pizza together inside your air fryer.

INGREDIENTS

- 2 x 230g//8oz packets of ready–made pizza dough or make your own
- 15ml of olive oil
- 60g//2oz of crushed tomatoes
- 1 garlic clove, finely chopped
- 1/2 teaspoon of oregano
- Salt and pepper to taste.
- 230g//8oz mozzarella ball, cut into slices about ¼"
- Basil leaves, for garnish

METHOD

1. From your pizza dough, create 2 x 8" pizza rounds (or matched to the size of your air fryer if smaller). Brush one side of each with olive oil.
2. Put one pizza, oil side up, into the air fryer ready to top.
3. In a separate bowl, combine the crushed tomatoes, garlic, oregano and salt and pepper to taste.
4. Spread half of the tomato mixture in an even layer over the pizza base in the air fryer. Leave a bare 1/2–inch crust around the edge.
5. Add half of the sliced mozzarella to the top of the pizza.
6. Cook for 10–12 minutes at 200C//400F until the cheese is melted and the crust is golden.
7. Lift carefully from the air fryer and garnish with fresh basil leaves.
8. Repeat the process with the second pizza, cut into slices and serve.

Nutritional Information per Serving:

SERVES 2 | CALORIES –772KCAL | PROTEIN –35G | CARBOHYDRATES –61.7G | FAT –40.3G

JAPANESE TERIYAKI VEGETABLES

INGREDIENTS

- 1 small broccoli
- 4 mushrooms
- 1 pepper, any colour
- 1 medium courgette
- 15ml of olive oil
- 2 teaspoons of Chinese 5 spice
- Salt and pepper to taste
- 45ml of teriyaki sauce

METHOD

1. Chop the vegetable and toss them in a bowl with the Chinese 5-spice, salt, and pepper.
2. Preheat the air fryer to 180C//360F.
3. Pour the olive oil into the bowl of chopped vegetables and mix well.
4. Transfer the seasoned vegetables to the air fryer and cook for 14 minutes at 180C//360F.
5. Move the vegetables from the air fryer to the bowl and stir in the teriyaki sauce.
6. Place the ingredients on a foil layer and return to the air fryer.
7. Cook for a further 5 minutes at 180C//360F.
8. Serve with cooked rice.

Nutritional Information per Serving:

SERVES −4 | CALORIES −240KCAL | PROTEIN −14G | CARBOHYDRATES −34G | FAT −9G

BEAN BURGER

INGREDIENTS

- 170g//6oz of frozen sweetcorn
- 170g//6oz of drained chickpeas
- 115/g//4oz of cooked green lentils
- 6g//0.2oz of pumpkin seeds
- ¼ of a red onion, thinly sliced
- 100g//3.5oz of cheddar cheese
- 3 cloves of garlic, finely chopped
- 10g//0.3oz of chopped coriander
- 45ml of peri peri sauce
- Salt and pepper to taste
- Breadcrumbs

For the Garnish:

- 4 burger buns
- Shredded lettuce
- Sliced tomato
- 30g//1oz of ketchup
- 18g//0.6oz of peri peri sauce
- 60g//2oz of mayonnaise
- Freshly squeezed juice of ¼ lemon

METHOD

1. Put all the burger ingredients (excluding the garnish) into a bowl and mix thoroughly. Use a stand or hand mixer if you have one.
2. Add the breadcrumbs and combine thoroughly.
3. Preheat air fryer to 180C//360F.
4. Form burger shapes and dip in breadcrumbs. Completely cover the bean burger.
5. Put the burgers into the air fryer and cook for 12 minutes at 180C//360F.
6. Meanwhile, in a small dish, mix the mayonnaise with the lemon juice. In a separate dish, mix the ketchup with the peri peri sauce.
7. Assemble your burger as follows:
8. Lemon mayonnaise on the bottom section of the bun.
9. Add a layer of lettuce, then sliced tomato.
10. Place your burger on the tomato.
11. Spread a layer of the ketchup–peri peri marinade on the top part of the burger bun and place on top.
12. Enjoy!

Nutritional Information per Serving:

SERVES –4 | CALORIES –921KCAL | PROTEIN –42G | CARBOHYDRATES –120G | FAT –32G

ONE–POT VEGETARIAN FRIED RICE

INGREDIENTS

- 45g//1.5oz of butter, melted
- 3 onions, peeled and chopped
- 6 cloves of garlic, finely chopped
- 3 eggs, beaten
- 540g//19oz of uncooked basmati rice
- 180ml of soy sauce
- 1litre of vegetable broth or stock
- 355g//12.5oz of mixed frozen vegetables

METHOD

1. Preheat the air fryer to 175C//350F and lightly spritz with cooking oil spray.
2. Put the melted butter, garlic, and onion into a non–stick pan and place in the air fryer. Cook for about 5 minutes at 175C//350F, stirring halfway through.
3. Then add the beaten egg and cook for another minute to scramble it.
4. Add the basmati rice, soy sauce, stock, salt, and pepper to the air fryer and stir in thoroughly. Cook for a further 10 minutes at 175C//350F.
5. Pause the air fryer to add the frozen vegetables and cook for a final 5-6 minutes or until the vegetables are cooked through and the stock has been absorbed.
6. Serve and enjoy!

Nutritional Information per Serving:

SERVES –12 | CALORIES –254KCAL | PROTEIN –7.3G | CARBOHYDRATES –45.6G | FAT –4.4G

CLASSIC EGG FRIED RICE

INGREDIENTS

- 200g//7oz of leftover rice
- 60g//2oz of frozen peas
- 100g//3.5oz of frozen stir fry mix
- 15ml of olive oil
- 60ml of soy sauce
- 15ml of Worcester sauce
- 30g//1oz of Chinese 5-Spice
- Olive oil cooking spray
- Scrambled eggs
- 2 eggs
- 1 teaspoon of butter
- Salt and pepper

METHOD

1. Crack your eggs into a ramekin and stir in butter, milk and salt and pepper. Place in the air fryer and cook for 8 minutes at 18C0/360F.
2. When the air fryer beeps add the eggs and all other ingredients into a bowl and mix well with a fork.
3. Spray a baking pan that is suitable for the air fryer with olive oil spray and then load in your rice mixture.
4. Coo for 10 minutes at 180C//360F, stir and then cook for a further 5 minutes at the same temperature.
5. Check that its piping hot before serving.

Nutritional Information per Serving:

SERVES -4 | CALORIES -419KCAL | PROTEIN -17G | CARBOHYDRATES -53G | FAT -16G

COURGETTE PASTA BAKE

INGREDIENTS

- 230g//8oz of pasta
- 450g//1lb of courgettes, chopped
- 30g//1oz onion, chopped
- 2 teaspoons of dried parsley
- 1 teaspoon of dried oregano
- Salt and pepper to taste
- 4 eggs, beaten
- 60ml of vegetable oil
- 120g//4oz of plain flour
- 1 teaspoon of baking powder
- ¼ teaspoon of salt
- 15g//0.5oz of butter, melted
- 45g//1.5oz parmesan cheese

METHOD

1. Put the pasta into a large saucepan of boiling water and cook for 8–10 minutes. Once cooked, drain and set aside.
2. Put the vegetables, herbs, and spices together in a bowl and mix thoroughly.
3. Mix in the eggs and vegetable oil.
4. In a separate bowl, combine the flour, baking powder and salt, and add to the vegetable mixture.
5. Finally, add the cheese and the melted butter. Mix it all together thoroughly.
6. Preheat the air fryer to 160C//320F.
7. Transfer the mixture to a heat proof casserole dish and place in the air fryer.
8. Cook for 15 minutes at 160C//320F.
9. After the 15 minutes, look at your casserole. Does it look cooked? Mine was cooked and I removed. If you need more time, add some. Otherwise, remove and let cool, slightly.

Nutritional Information per Serving:

SERVES -4 | CALORIES -659KCAL | PROTEIN -20G | CARBOHYDRATES -59G | FAT -39.1G

HALLOUMI FAJITAS

INGREDIENTS

- 230g//8oz halloumi
- 3 peppers of different colours
- 1 small red onion
- 1 teaspoon of olive oil
- 15g//0.5oz of fajita seasoning mix
- Salt and pepper to taste

METHOD

1. Slice halloumi lengthways and set aside.
2. Slice the onions and pepper into thin strips and season with salt and pepper.
3. Preheat the air fryer to 180C//360F.
4. Toss the peppers, onion, olive oil, and fajitas seasoning in a bowl and mix well.
5. Add the halloumi, taking care not to break it up.
6. Place in the air fryer and cook for 8 minutes at 180C//360F.
7. Serve in a bowl ready to load into wraps.

Nutritional Information per Serving:

SERVES –4 | CALORIES –894KCAL | PROTEIN –55G | CARBOHYDRATES –36G | FAT –61G

GREEK SALAD WITH FRIED HALLOUMI

INGREDIENTS

- 230g//8oz of halloumi
- Sliced cucumber
- Cherry tomatoes, cut in half (use different coloured tomatoes if you have them)
- 150g//5oz of mixed olives
- ½ medium red onion
- 200g//7oz salad rocket leaves
- 2 teaspoons of dried oregano
- Olive oil cooking spray
- 4 teaspoons of olive oil for drizzling

METHOD

1. Preheat the air fryer to 180C//360F.
2. Cut the halloumi into cubes and sprinkle with oregano.
3. Cook the halloumi in the air fryer for 6 minutes at 180C//360F.
4. Meanwhile, toss rocket leaves, cherry tomatoes, mixed olives, and red onion into a salad bowl. Drizzle a little olive oil over the top.
5. Add the cooked halloumi.
6. Serve warm.

Nutritional Information per Serving:

SERVES –4 | CALORIES –575KCAL | PROTEIN –29G | CARBOHYDRATES –11G | FAT –48G

VEGGIE BURGERS

INGREDIENTS

- 500g//1.1lb of sweet potato
- 800g//1.8lb of cauliflower
- 200g//7oz of carrots
- 170g//6oz of chickpeas, drained
- 240g//8.5oz of breadcrumbs
- 100g//3.5oz of grated mozzarella
- 15g//0.5oz of dried mixed herbs
- 15g//0.5oz of basil
- Salt and pepper to taste

METHOD

1. Peel and chop the vegetables into small pieces. Steam until tender.
2. Drain and dry any moisture from the vegetables so that they are dry.
3. Add the chickpeas to the vegetables and mash together so they are well combined.
4. Mix in the breadcrumbs and seasonings. Shape into burgers.
5. Pre heat the air fryer to 180C//360F.
6. Roll in the mozzarella so the burgers are completely covered in grated cheese.
7. Line the air fryer and spritz with a little cooking oil spray as the cheese will melt, then put the burgers in.
8. Cook at 180C//360F for 10 minutes. Turn the temperature to 200C//360F and cook for another until crusty on the outside.
9. Serve in burger buns with a side of salad.

Nutrition Nutritional Information per Serving:

SERVES –4 | CALORIES –373KCAL | PROTEIN –16G | CARBOHYDRATES –60G | FAT –8G

LENTIL BURGERS
• •

INGREDIENTS

- 170g//6oz of cooked green lentils
- 1 large, sweet potato
- 6 medium carrots
- 1 small red onion, peel and finely chopped
- 60g//2oz of flour
- 1 teaspoon of garlic puree
- 1 teaspoon of basil
- 1 teaspoon of oregano
- 1 teaspoon of thyme
- 1 teaspoon of paprika
- 1 teaspoon of harissa
- Salt and pepper to taste

METHOD

1. Peel and chop the sweet potato and carrots and steam until tender.
2. Place the potato, carrot, onion, and lentils in a bowl together. Add the seasonings.
3. Mash thoroughly to combine.
4. Preheat the air fryer 200C//400F.
5. Make into burgers and roll in oats until thoroughly covered.
6. Place the burgers in the air fryer and cook 12 minutes at 200C/400F. Turn the burgers, and cook for another 5 minutes.

Nutritional Information per Serving:

SERVES –4 | CALORIES –77KCAL | PROTEIN –2G | CARBOHYDRATES –16G | FAT –1G

FAMILY FAVOURITE BUBBLE AND SQUEAK
• •

INGREDIENTS

- 500g//1.1lb of cooked, mashed potato
- 200g//7oz of leftover cooked cabbage (or sprouts)
- 100g//3.5oz of leftover meat
- 30g//1oz of grated cheddar cheese
- 2 teaspoons of thyme
- Salt and pepper to taste

METHOD

1. Preheat the air fryer to 180C//360F.
2. Put all the ingredients in a bowl and mix to combine.
3. Load the mixture into the air fryer and at and cook for 8 minutes at 180C//360F.
4. Turn the temperature to 200C//400F and cook for a further 4–5 minutes.
5. Serve hot with tomato ketchup and fried eggs for a hearty breakfast or evening meal.

Nutritional Information per Serving:

SERVES −4 | CALORIES −1067KCAL | PROTEIN −40G | CARBOHYDRATES −209G | FAT −10G

EASY AND HEALTHY CHICKPEA CURRY

INGREDIENTS

- 425g//15oz can of chickpeas, drained and dried
- 70g//2.5oz of your favourite curry sauce
- 15g//0.5oz of garam masala
- 2 teaspoons of curry powder
- 1 teaspoon of ground cumin
- Olive oil cooking spray
- Optional: Naan Bread optional

METHOD

1. Preheat the air fryer to 200C//400F.
2. Add the chickpeas (make sure they are dry), spritz with olive oil cooking spray, and season with the garam masala, curry powder and ground cumin.
3. Cook for 12–15 minutes at 200C//400F, giving them a shake at intervals.
4. Transfer to a suitable heat safe container and pour in your curry sauce. Mix thoroughly.
5. Turn the temperature down to 180C//360F and cook for another 5 minutes.
6. Serve hot with cooked rice and naan bread.

*Nutritional Information per Serving:

SERVES −4 | CALORIES −128KCAL | PROTEIN −3G | CARBOHYDRATES −11G | FAT −7G

*Nutritional information may vary depending on choice of curry sauce.

POTATO GNOCCHI

INGREDIENTS

- 500g//1.1lb of cooked, mashed potato
- 1 egg
- 45g//1.5oz of plain flour
- 100g//3.5oz of grated cheese
- 1 teaspoon of oregano
- 15g//0.5oz of basil
- 1 teaspoon of thyme
- Salt and pepper
- Extra 20g//0.7oz of flour

METHOD

1. In a bowl, put the mashed potato, egg, cheese, flour and seasoning. Mix until well combined.
2. Preheat the air fryer to 200C//400F.
3. Divide the gnocchi mix into 8 equal pieces and roll each one into a thin sausage shape.
4. Cut each sausage shape into 1cm gnocchi pieces.
5. Place the gnocchi into the air fryer in a single layer without touching. You may need to cook in batches.
6. Cook for 6 minutes at 200C//400F.
7. Serve hot.

Nutritional Information per Serving:

SERVES –4 | CALORIES –608KCAL | PROTEIN –23G | CARBOHYDRATES –110G | FAT –10G

VEGETARIAN COURGETTE BALLS

INGREDIENTS

- 170g//6oz of rolled oats
- 150g//5oz of courgette
- 45g//1.5oz of feta cheese
- 1 egg, beaten
- 1 teaspoon of lemon rind
- 6 basil leaves, sliced thinly
- 1 teaspoon of dill
- 1 teaspoon of oregano
- Salt and pepper to taste

METHOD

1. Grate the courgette and squeeze out any excess water.
2. Mix the egg and courgette together in a bowl. Add the cheese and seasonings but set aside the oats.
3. Put the oats in a blender and blend until they look like fine breadcrumbs. Add them to the bowl a little at a time, as the mixture will thicken quickly.
4. Preheat your air fryer to 200C//400F. Line with foil or baking paper.
5. Create your meatball shapes out of the mixture and place in the air fryer in a single layer with plenty of space between each one.
6. Cook for 10 minutes at 200C//400F.
7. Serve hot with spaghetti.

Nutritional Information per Serving:

SERVES –4 | CALORIES –203KCAL | PROTEIN –9G | CARBOHYDRATES –29G | FAT –6G

MOZZARELLA RICE BALLS

INGREDIENTS

- 625g//1.3lb of leftover risotto
- 100g//3.5oz of breadcrumbs
- Salt and pepper to taste
- 1/4 teaspoon of garlic powder
- Olive oil cooking spray
- Mozzarella, room temperature
- Serve with arrabbiata sauce and a parsley garnish

METHOD

1. Set aside the breadcrumbs in one bowl, and the mozzarella in another.
2. With your hands, roll 2 tablespoons of risotto into a golf ball size and flatten it. Put a teaspoon of mozzarella in the centre, then roll back up into a golf ball with the mozzarella in the centre.
3. Roll the rice ball in the breadcrumbs ensuring a good coverage. Place in the fridge for about an hour to firm up.
4. When you're ready to start cooking, reheat the air fryer to 190C//380F.
5. Line the air fryer with foil or baking paper and add the coated rice balls in a single layer with space between each one. Spritz with cooking oil.
6. Cook at 190C//380F for about 6–8 minutes, turning halfway through. The risotto balls should turn a golden brown.
7. Serve with parsley and Arrabbiata sauce.

Nutritional Information per Serving:

SERVES –4 | CALORIES –153KCAL | PROTEIN –2G | CARBOHYDRATES –31G | FAT –2G

BUTTERNUT SQUASH GNOCCHI

INGREDIENTS

For the Gnocchi:

- 500g//1.1lb of cooked, mashed butternut squash
- 1 egg yolk
- 45g//1.5oz of semolina
- 45g//1.5oz of pasta flour
- Pinch of sugar
- Pinch of salt
- Pinch of nutmeg
- Spray cooking oil

For the Cheese Sauce:

- 50ml of milk
- 75ml of cream
- 200g//7oz of camembert cheese
- A splash of white wine
- Fresh chopped thyme to taste

METHOD

1. Put the mashed squash and egg yolk into a bowl and add salt, sugar and nutmeg to taste. Add the flour and work to a smooth, thick dough. Add a little more flour if it feels too wet.
2. Divide the gnocchi mix into 8 equal pieces and roll each one into a thin sausage shape. Cut each sausage shape into 1cm gnocchi pieces. Set to one side while you make your cheese sauce.
3. Put all your cheese sauce ingredients in a saucepan and bring gradually to a simmer, stirring constantly to remove any lumps.
4. Simmer until the ingredients have blended and the sauce has thickened, stirring constantly to remove any lumps.
5. Place the gnocchi into the air fryer in a single layer without touching. You may need to cook in batches.
6. Cook for 6 minutes at 200C//400F.
7. Open the air fryer and remove the gnocchi. Transfer the cheese sauce to a heatproof pan and add the cooked gnocchi.
8. Place in the air fryer and cook for a further 3–4 minutes until piping hot.
9. Serve and enjoy!

Nutritional Information per Serving:

SERVES –4 | CALORIES –330KCAL | CARBOHYDRATE –34.6G | PROTEIN –14.7G | FAT –14.8G

ONE-POT BROCCOLI AND CHEESE CASSEROLE

INGREDIENTS

- 450g//1lb of fresh broccoli florets, steamed until tender
- 230g//8oz of cream cheese, room temperature
- 65ml of sour cream
- 85g//3oz of shredded cheddar
- Salt and pepper to taste
- 60g//2oz of crushed (Ritz) crackers
- 45g//1.5oz of butter, melted

METHOD

1. In a large bowl, add the cream cheese, sour cream, and cheddar to cooked broccoli and mix.
2. Preheat the air fryer to 180C//350F.
3. Lightly spray a heat safe casserole dish with cooking spray and transfer the broccoli mixture into it. Cover with foil.
4. Cook in the air fryer for 10 minutes at 180C//350F.
5. In a separate bowl, mix the crushed crackers and butter together.
6. Once cooked, remove the foil from the casserole dish and sprinkle the crushed crackers over the top of the broccoli mix.
7. Put the casserole dish back into the air fryer without the foil and cook for a further 5 minutes at 180C//350F.
8. Serve immediately and enjoy.

Nutritional Information per Serving:

SERVES –6 | CALORIES –332KCAL | PROTEIN –9G | CARBOHYDRATES –14G | FAT –27G

GARLIC MUSHROOM RISOTTO

INGREDIENTS

- 300g//11oz of arborio or risotto rice
- 1 onion, peeled and finely chopped
- 3 garlic cloves, finely chopped
- 85g//3oz frozen peas
- 15ml of Worcestershire sauce
- 300g//10.5oz sliced mushrooms
- 1.4litres of vegetable stock
- 30ml of white wine vinegar
- Lemon juice squeezed from half a lemon
- 1 handful of fresh parsley, chopped
- 85g//3oz of pecorino cheese
- Olive oil cooking spray

METHOD

1. Preheat the air fryer to 200C//400F and spray with a little cooking oil.
2. Add the chopped onions, garlic and 200g of the mushrooms. Splash in the Worcestershire sauce. Spritz again with cooking oil.
3. Cook for 5 minutes at 200C//400F.
4. Add the rice and cook again for a further 3 minutes at the same temperature.
5. Pour in the vegetable stock, white wine vinegar and the remaining mushrooms and cook for 45 minutes at 200C//400F.
6. Finally, stir in the peas, lemon juice, pecorino cheese and chopped parsley. Season with black pepper and cook for another 3 minutes.
7. Serve with a sprig of parsley.

Nutritional Information per Serving:

SERVES –6 | CALORIES –323KCAL | PROTEIN –12G | CARBOHYDRATES –48.9G | FAT –10.5G

ONE–POT CREAMED CORN CASSEROLE

INGREDIENTS

- 120g//4oz of melted butter
- 30g//1oz of plain flour
- 70g//2.5oz of sugar
- 2 eggs, beaten
- ½ teaspoon of garlic salt
- 120ml of milk
- 1 can of sweetcorn, drained
- 1 can of creamed corn

METHOD

1. Whisk the flour and melted butter. Add in the milk, beaten eggs and sugar and whisk some more.
2. Add the garlic salt, and both cans of corn. Combine thoroughly.
3. Preheat the air fryer to 160C//320F.
4. Pour the mixture into a heat safe bowl and place in the air fryer. Cook at 160C//320F for 40–45 minutes.
5. Once cooked, allow to cool for 10 minutes before serving.

Nutritional Information per Serving:

SERVES –6 | CALORIES –365KCAL | PROTEIN –7G | CARBOHYDRATES –46G | FAT –19G

ONE–POT ISRAELI SHAKSHUKA

INGREDIENTS

- 3 eggs
- 100g//3.5oz chopped green peppers
- 15g//0.5oz chopped onion
- 100g//3.5oz chopped tomatoes
- 30g//1oz of fresh chopped coriander
- 250g//9oz of tomato puree
- 125ml of water
- 30ml of olive oil
- 1 teaspoon of paprika
- 1/2 teaspoon of cumin seeds
- 1/2 teaspoon of ground nutmeg
- Salt and pepper to taste

METHOD

1. Set the eggs to one side until needed.
2. Preheat the air fryer to 175C//345F.
3. Add all the ingredients to a heat safe bowl that fits your air fryer and combine all the ingredients. Mix thoroughly.
4. Cook for 15 minutes at 175C//345F. Stir halfway.
5. Open the air fryer and make 3 little wells for the eggs in the sauce. Crack one egg into each little well. Cook for another 5 minutes at 175C//345F.
6. Serve hot sprinkled with coriander.

Nutritional Information per Serving:

SERVES –3 | CALORIES –195KCAL | PROTEIN –7.7G | CARBOHYDRATES –12G | FAT –14.3G

SWEET POTATO SOUFFLE

INGREDIENTS

- 1 sweet potato, peeled, baked, and mashed
- 30g//1oz of melted butter
- 1 egg, yolk and egg white separated
- 60ml whole milk
- Salt and pepper to taste
- Breadcrumbs
- Pecans, for garnish

METHOD

1. In a mixing bowl, mash the potato, half the melted butter, egg yolk, milk and salt together. Set to one side.
2. In a separate bowl, whisk the egg white until it forms stiff peaks.
3. Fold the whisked egg white gently into the potato mix.
4. Preheat the air fryer to 165C//330F.
5. Grease 4 small ramekins with olive oil spray and fill each with the sweet potato mixture to ¾ full.
6. Put the ramekins in the air fryer and bake at 165C//330F for 15 minutes. You may need to work in batches depending on the size of your air fryer.
7. Transfer the ramekins to a wire cooling rack, and sprinkle with chopped pecans and breadcrumbs.
8. Cool for 10 minutes before serving.

Nutritional Information per Serving:

SERVES –4 | CALORIES –156KCAL | PROTEIN –3.8G | CARBOHYDRATES –12.1G | FAT –10.6G

ROAST SQUASH SOUP
• •

INGREDIENTS

- 1.13kg//2.5lb of peeled and diced butternut squash
- 2 medium carrots, peeled and cut into 1–inch pieces
- 1 large onion, peeled and cut into 1/2–inch–thick wedges
- 4 garlic cloves, finely chopped
- 2 garlic cloves, whole
- 1 red fresno chilli, cut in half, no seeds
- 4 sprigs of fresh thyme
- 60ml of olive oil (shared into 2 portions of 30ml each)
- Salt and pepper to taste
- 30g//1oz of pumpkin seeds
- 1/4 teaspoon of smoked paprika
- Sour cream and crusty bread, for serving
- 800ml of water or vegetable stock

METHOD

1. Preheat the air fryer to 200C//400F.
2. Set aside the chopped garlic and 30ml of olive oil for later.
3. Meanwhile, toss the chopped squash, carrots, onion, whole garlic cloves, chilli pepper, thyme, 30ml of the oil, salt, and pepper to taste in a bowl together and mix.
4. Place in the air fryer and cook at 200C//400F for about 30 minutes, until the vegetables are tender, but firm.
5. While the air fryer is cooking, put the chopped garlic and the remaining 30ml of oil in a saucepan on a medium heat. Stir until the garlic lightly browns on the edges, about 2 minutes.
6. Add the pumpkin seeds, the paprika and a pinch of salt, and cook for a further minute.
7. Put everything into a blender, add 200ml of water and blend.
8. Gradually add an additional 600ml of water until it reaches your desired consistency.
9. Refrigerate and reheat when needed. Serve topped with cream and spiced pumpkin seeds.

Nutritional Information per Serving:

SERVES –4 | CALORIES –280KCAL | PROTEIN –5G | CARBOHYDRATES –36G | FAT –15.5G

MAINS – TOFU

Note: blocks of tofu need to be drained and dried before using. Once you have patted the surface dry with kitchen roll, it is usually best to stand the tofu on a plate between sheets of kitchen roll, usually with a second plate on top to weigh it down. This will squeeze the liquid out onto the plate while the kitchen roll soaks up the rest. Change the kitchen roll and drain the liquid from the plate every now and again until no more water comes out.

TOFU IN SWEET HONEY GARLIC SAUCE

INGREDIENTS

- 400g//14oz of extra firm tofu cut into 1" cubes, dried with kitchen towel

For the Honey Garlic Sauce:

- 175ml of chicken or vegetable stock
- 7g//0.25oz of honey

- 15g//0.5oz of cornflour
- 1 teaspoon of garlic powder
- ½ teaspoon of paprika

- 30ml of soy sauce
- 2 garlic cloves, finely chopped
- ½ teaspoon of ground ginger

- ½ teaspoon of onion powder
- ½ teaspoon of salt
- Cooking spray

- 7g//0.25oz of cornflour
- 15ml of water

METHOD

1. Toss the cubes of tofu into a large bowl with the cornflour, garlic powder, paprika, onion powder, and salt. The tofu should be completely coated.
2. Preheat the air fryer to 190C//360F and spray with cooking oil (or line the air fryer with foil or baking paper).
3. Put the tofu in an even layer in the air fryer and spray oil over the top.
4. Cook for 18 minutes at 190C//360F giving the tofu a shake after the first 10 minutes cooking time.
5. Make sure the tofu is returned to a single layer in the air fryer and cook for another 8 minutes at 190C//360F.
6. While waiting, make the sauce by mixing the chicken broth, honey, soy sauce, garlic, and ginger in a saucepan over medium heat.
7. Bring gently to the boil, reduce the heat and simmer for about 5 minutes until the sauce reduces and the flavours combine.
8. Whisk the water and cornflour together in a small bowl then pour into the saucepan. Simmer for a further 5 minutes or until the sauce thickens.
9. When the tofu is cooked, toss into a bowl with about 100ml of the honey garlic sauce.
10. Serve the tofu with a drizzle of extra sauce.

Nutritional Information per Serving:

SERVES –4 | CALORIES –107KCAL | PROTEIN –9.5G | CARBOHYDRATES –9.5G | FAT –4.5G

CRISPY SEASONED TOFU

INGREDIENTS

- 450g//16oz of extra firm tofu cut into 1" cubes and dried
- 1 teaspoon of garlic powder
- ½ teaspoon of onion powder
- 1 teaspoon of paprika
- ½ teaspoon of sea salt
- 2 teaspoons of cornflour
- 7.5ml of light soy sauce
- ½ teaspoon of sesame oil
- ¼ teaspoon of ground black pepper

METHOD

1. Preheat the air fryer to 200C//400F and spray with oil.
2. Toss the tofu cubes in a bowl with the soy sauce.
3. Gradually add the seasoning ingredients and the oil and coat the tofu thoroughly in the mixture.
4. Place the tofu in an even single layer and cook for 10 minutes at 200C/400F. Give the tofu a shake halfway through cooking.
5. Serve and enjoy!

Nutritional Information per Serving:

SERVES –4 | CALORIES –110KCAL | PROTEIN –11G | CARBOHYDRATES –5G | FAT –6G

HONEY SOY TOFU

INGREDIENTS

- 450g//16oz of extra firm tofu cut into 1" cubes, dried with kitchen towel
- 45g//1.5oz of potato starch
- ½ teaspoon of ground ginger

- 2 teaspoons of onion powder
- 1 teaspoon of paprika
- Salt and pepper to taste
- 2 teaspoons of garlic powder
- Cooking spray

For the Ginger Honey Sauce:

- 60ml of soy sauce
- 50g//1.8oz of brown sugar
- 20ml of lime juice
- ¼ teaspoon of toasted sesame oil

- 2" piece of fresh ginger, finely grated
- 70g//2.5oz of honey
- 70g//2.5oz of sambal (or other hot chilli paste will do)

- 2 garlic cloves, finely chopped
- 2 teaspoons rice wine
- 60ml of water, plus extra as needed
- 2 teaspoons of cornflour

For Serving:

- 1 teaspoon spring onions, finely sliced
- ½ teaspoon of sesame seeds
- 1 fresh lime, cut into wedges

METHOD

1. In a bowl, mix the potato starch, ground ginger, onion powder, paprika, black pepper, garlic powder, and salt. Toss in the tofu cubes and coat well on all sides.
2. Preheat the air fryer to 200C//400F and spray with cooking oil.
3. Shake off the excess from the seasoned tofu and working in batches (if necessary) place in the air fryer in a single layer. Cook at 200C//400F for 12 minutes until crispy. Give the tofu a shake halfway through cooking.
4. While the tofu is cooking, in a saucepan on the hob, combine the soy sauce, brown sugar, lime juice, sesame oil, ginger, honey, sambal, garlic, and rice wine. Bring to a gentle simmer for about 6–7 minutes until the sauce starts to thicken.
5. In a separate small bowl, whisk together the water and cornflour and add to the sauce, stirring and cooking for another 2–3 minutes.
6. When the tofu is cooked, transfer to a bowl and pour over enough sauce to coat it thoroughly. Any remaining sauce can be saved for dipping.
7. Serve sprinkled with sesame seeds and chopped spring onions over steamed rice with mixed vegetables. Add a squeeze of lime.

Nutritional information per Serving:
SERVES –24 PIECES | CALORIES –48KCAL | FAT –1G | CARBOHYDRATE –8G | PROTEIN –2G

MISO TOFU

• •

INGREDIENTS

- 450g//16oz of extra firm tofu cut into ½" cubes, dried with kitchen towel
- 30g//1oz of miso paste
- Optional: 1 teaspoon of sriracha hot sauce
- 15g//0.5oz of brown sugar
- 2 teaspoons of sesame oil
- 2 teaspoon of soy sauce
- 1 spring onion, sliced thinly
- 15g//0.5oz of sesame seeds

METHOD

1. Prepare the tofu sauce by mixing the miso, sriracha, brown sugar, sesame oil, and soy sauce together in a bowl until blended.
2. Preheat the air fryer to 200C//400F and spray with cooking oil and/or line with foil or greaseproof paper.
3. Gently put a small crisscross cut in the surface of the tofu cubes without cutting through.
4. Place the tofu cubes into the air fryer and brush a thick layer of sauce onto the tofu, lightly dabbing the crisscross surface so the sauce can get into the crevices.
5. Cook for 10–12 minutes at 200C//400F, brushing a layer of the sauce on the tofu every 3–4 minutes until the sauce is caramelized.
6. Serve sprinkled with green onion and sesame seeds.

Nutritional Information per Serving:
SERVES –4 | CALORIES –147KCAL | PROTEIN –11G | CARBOHYDRATES –9G | FAT –8G

PEKING TOFU BALLS

INGREDIENTS
For the Meatballs:

- 450g//16oz of extra firm tofu cut into ½" cubes, dried with kitchen towel
- 3 dried shitake mushrooms, soaked until softened and cut into small pieces
- 60g//2oz of steamed carrots
- 60g//2oz bamboo shoots, thinly sliced (fresh or canned)
- 60g//2oz of breadcrumbs
- 30g//1oz of cornflour
- 20ml of soy sauce
- 1 teaspoon of garlic powder
- Salt and pepper to taste

For the Sauce:

- 15ml of olive oil
- 4 garlic cloves, finely chopped
- 30ml of soy sauce
- 30g//1oz of tomato ketchup
- 15g//0.5oz of sugar

METHOD
1. Put all the ingredients for the tofu balls into a food processor and mix until well combined.
2. Preheat air fryer to 190C//380F and line with greased paper.
3. Form the mixture into small balls and place in the air fryer. Spray some cooking oil over the top.
4. Cook for 10 minutes at 190C//360F, shaking them once during cooking.
5. Meanwhile, in a frying pan on the hob, sauté the garlic in the olive oil for 2–3 minutes, then stir in the soy sauce, tomato ketchup, and sugar. Cook until the sauce thickens.
6. When cooked, roll the meatballs thoroughly in the sauce and serve garnished with sliced spring onions and sprinkled with sesame seeds.

Nutritional Information per Serving:

SERVES –4 | CALORIES –251KCAL | PROTEIN –13.8G | CARBOHYDRATES –32.4G | FAT –9.4G

TOFU WITH MANGO SALSA

INGREDIENTS

- 450g//1lb of extra firm tofu dried and cut into even cubes
- 15ml of olive oil
- 15ml of soy sauce
- Optional: Thai peanut sauce
- Optional: chopped peanuts

For the Mango Salsa:

- 2 large ripe mangos, peeled, stoned and diced
- 1/2 medium red bell pepper, deseeded, washed and chopped
- 4 spring onions, thinly sliced
- 30g//1oz of chopped fresh coriander
- 30ml of lime juice
- Salt and pepper to taste
- 150g//5oz of shredded purple or green cabbage

METHOD

1. Preheat the air fryer to 180C//350F.
2. Spread the tofu cubes evenly across a piece of greaseproof paper and drizzle with olive oil and soy sauce.
3. Lift the greaseproof paper and tofu into the air fryer together and cook at 180C//350F for about 18 minutes.
4. Prepare the mango salsa by combining all the ingredients into a bowl and mixing thoroughly together. Season with salt and pepper to taste.
5. Serve the tofu over rice, accompanied by the mango salsa.
6. Top with peanut sauce and chopped peanuts.

Nutritional Information per Serving:

SERVES –4 | CALORIES –230KCAL | PROTEIN –11.6G | CARBOHYDRATES –31.8G | FAT –9G

TOFU COCONUT CURRY

INGREDIENTS

- 450g//16oz of extra firm tofu dried and cut into 1" cubes
- 30g//1oz of cornflour
- 30ml of soy sauce

For the Vegetable Curry:

- 15ml of olive oil
- 450g//16oz of green beans chopped
- 1 red bell pepper, chopped
- 1 garlic clove, chopped

- 1 inch of fresh ginger, grated
- 1 small onion, diced
- 1 teaspoon of turmeric powder
- 1 teaspoon of curry powder

- 1 x 340g//12 oz can of coconut cream
- 120ml of water
- 1/4 teaspoon of black pepper
- Juice of 1 lime

METHOD

1. Sit the tofu cubes in a bowl with the soy sauce. Mix the cornflour with a little water then blend into the bowl with the soy sauce and tofu so that each piece is coated.
2. Preheat the air fryer to 195C//380F and spray with oil.
3. Add the tofu in an even layer and cook for 15 minutes at 195C//380F, giving the tofu a shake halfway through cooking.
4. While waiting for the tofu, saute the olive oil, green beans, red bell pepper, white onion, garlic, and ginger in a large pan for 5 minutes on medium heat. Toss occasionally.
5. When the vegetables are softened, increase the temperature in the pan to high and add the coconut cream, turmeric powder, curry powder, black pepper, and water. Bring to a gentle bowl, then bring to a simmer.
6. Add the cooked tofu to the pan of vegetable curry and mix well. Simmer for further 10 minutes.
7. Serve over cooked rice, and sprinkle with chopped coriander and lime juice.

Nutritional Information per Serving:

SERVES –4 | CALORIES –590KCAL | PROTEIN –21G | CARBOHYDRATES –73.2G | FAT –27.6G

GARLIC AND GINGER TOFU

INGREDIENTS

- 450g//1lb of extra firm tofu dried and cut into 1/2" cubes
- 1 inch piece of fresh ginger, grated
- 2 garlic cloves, finely chopped
- 15ml of sesame seed oil
- 120ml of soy sauce
- 30ml of rice vinegar
- 2 teaspoons of maple syrup
- ½ teaspoon of cornflour

METHOD

1. Preheat the air fryer to 195C//380F.
2. Place the cubes of tofu in an even layer in the air fryer and spray with cooking oil.
3. Cook at 195C//380F for 20 minutes. Give the tofu a shake about halfway through cooking.
4. When it's crisp, remove from the air fryer and set to one side.
5. In a bowl whisk the ginger, garlic, sesame seed oil, soy sauce, rice vinegar, maple syrup and cornflour until well combined.
6. Transfer the sauce to a saucepan on low heat and simmer for a few minutes until the sauce thickens.
7. Add the cooked tofu in and simmer for a further 2–3 minutes.
8. Serve with rice and top with sesame seeds.

Nutritional Information per Serving:

SERVES –3 | CALORIES –337KCAL | PROTEIN –29.2G | CARBOHYDRATES –16.5G | FAT –19.2G

MAINS – QUORN DISHES

FRIED RICE WITH QUORN FILLETS (VEGAN OPTION AVAILABLE)

INGREDIENTS

- 2 Quorn fillets, defrosted and sliced (Vegan fillets available)
- 320g//11oz cold cooked rice
- 75ml of soy sauce
- 230g//8oz of mixed frozen vegetables
- Optional: 100g//3.5oz of firm tofu, crumbled
- 1 teaspoon of sesame oil
- 1 teaspoon of vegetable oil
- 2 spring onions, chopped for garnish
- Salt to taste

METHOD

1. Combine the cold rice with the frozen vegetables, tofu (if using) and sliced Quorn fillets.
2. Preheat the air fryer to 180C//350F and line with baking paper.
3. Add the soy sauce and oil to the rice and mix well to combine.
4. Put the rice mixture into the air fryer and cook for 15 minutes at 180C//350F. Stir a couple of times during cooking to prevent the food clumping.
5. Serve hot, sprinkled with chopped spring onions.

Nutritional Information per Serving:

SERVES –2 | CALORIES –584KCAL | PROTEIN –26.1G | CARBOHYDRATES –80.7G | FAT –16.8G

QUORN FILLETS WITH CRISPY DORITO CRUMB

INGREDIENTS

- 4 vegetarian Quorn fillets
- 150ml buttermilk (alternative 130ml of milk +1 tablespoon apple cider vinegar)
- 90g//3oz of tangy cheese tortilla chips
- 1 egg, beaten
- 30g//1oz of plain flour
- Salt and pepper to taste
- Salsa to serve

METHOD

1. Put the Quorn fillets into a bowl and cover with buttermilk. Cover the bowl and place in the fridge to marinate for at least 4 hours.
2. When ready to cook, preheat the air fryer to 180C//350F and line with greaseproof paper.
3. In a separate bowl, crush the tortilla chips to crumbs (this can be done in a food processor if you have one) and set aside.
4. Place the beaten egg in a second shallow bowl.
5. In a final bowl, blend the flour, salt, and pepper.
6. Drain the Quorn and discard the buttermilk. Press the Quorn on the flour and roll to coat. Next, dip in the egg, shake off the excess, then press the fillet firmly into the tortilla chips.
7. Put the coated Quorn fillets into the air fryer and cook for 10 minutes at 180C//350F.
8. Serve with salsa and Mexican style rice.

Nutritional Information per Serving:

SERVES –4 | CALORIES –712KCAL | PROTEIN –17.9G | CARBOHYDRATES –34.6G | FAT –17.1G

QUORN KATSU CURRY

INGREDIENTS

- 1 pack of Quorn Crunchy Fillet Burger, still frozen
- 230g//8oz of uncooked white rice

For the Slaw:

- 150g//5oz of shredded cabbage
- 30ml of rice wine vinegar
- 1 teaspoon of salt

For the Katsu Sauce:

- 115g//4oz of ketchup
- 30ml of soy sauce
- 15g//0.5oz of brown sugar
- 15ml of mirin
- 1½ teaspoons of Worcestershire sauce
- ½ teaspoon of dried ginger
- ½ teaspoon of garlic powder

METHOD

1. Cook the rice according to package Method and set aside.
2. Preheat the air fryer to 200C//400F and spray with cooking oil.
3. Put the still-frozen contents of the packet of Quorn Crunchy Fillet Burger in the air fryer and cook for 6 minutes 200C/400F. Turn the fillet burgers and cook for another 6 minutes.
4. Meanwhile, in a large mixing bowl, toss the shredded cabbage with vinegar and salt and let sit until ready to serve.
5. In a separate bowl, whisk together all of the ingredients for the Katsu sauce.
6. Once cooked, slice the burgers into 1" thick strips.
7. Serve the sliced burgers with rice, Katsu sauce and slaw. Garnish with chopped spring onions and a lemon wedge.

Nutritional Information per Serving:

SERVES –2 | CALORIES –610KCAL | PROTEIN –19.9G | CARBOHYDRATES –123G | FAT –3.4G

MAINS – FISH DISHES

GARLIC BUTTER SALMON WITH GREEN BEANS

INGREDIENTS

- 5 garlic cloves, finely chopped
- 15g//0.5oz of parmesan cheese, grated
- Juice of 1 lemon
- 1 teaspoon of Italian herb seasoning (shop bought or make your own)
- 60g//2oz of melted butter
- Pinch of coarse sea salt
- 300g//10.5oz of fresh green beans
- 4 salmon fillets, approximately 170g//6oz each
- Olive oil cooking spray
- Ground black pepper
- Optional: torn fresh parsley

METHOD

1. Mix the garlic, parmesan, lemon juice, Italian seasoning, and melted butter together in a bowl, and season with salt.
2. Cut four sheets of baking paper big enough to place a piece of salmon with extra around to fold over.
3. Divide the green beans evenly between the 4 sheets of baking paper and spray lightly with the cooking oil.
4. Place the salmon fillets on top of the green beans and brush with the garlic butter sauce. Season with freshly ground pepper.
5. Preheat the air fryer to 180C//350F.
6. Fold the sheets in half across each piece of salmon and roll the remaining sides up to create four neat little parcels. Place each parcel carefully in the air fryer.
7. Cook at 180C//350F for about 8–10 minutes or until cooked through.
8. Once cooked, remove from the parcel, garnish with parsley and a little more parmesan.
9. Serve immediately.

Nutritional Information per Serving:

SERVES –4 | CALORIES –150KCAL | PROTEIN –32G | CARBOHYDRATES –0G | FAT –2G

SUGARED GARLIC SALMON

INGREDIENTS

- 450g//1lb salmon (or 4 pieces)
- Salt and pepper to taste
- 30g//1oz of brown sugar
- 1 teaspoon of chilli powder
- 1/2 teaspoon of paprika
- 1 teaspoon of Italian seasoning
- 1 teaspoon of garlic powder

METHOD

1. Lightly salt and pepper the salmon.
2. In a separate bowl, mix the remaining ingredients together.
3. Rub the seasoning all over the salmon.
4. Preheat the air fryer to 200C//400F.
5. Place the salmon skin side down and cook for 10 minutes at 200C//400F.
6. Serve hot or cold.
   Delicious with baby new potatoes and seasonal vegetables, or a crisp mixed leaf salad.

Nutritional Information per Serving:

SERVES –4 | CALORIES –190KCAL | PROTEIN –23G | CARBOHYDRATES –7G | FAT –7G

GLAZED CHILLEAN SEA BASS

INGREDIENTS

- 2 x 170g//6oz Chilean sea bass fillets
- 15g//0.5oz of unsalted butter
- 85g//3oz of white miso paste
- 15ml of rice wine vinegar
- 85g//3oz of maple syrup or honey
- 30ml of mirin
- 1/2 teaspoon of ginger paste
- Salt and pepper to taste

METHOD

1. First, turn on the air fryer and preheat 195C//375F and spray with cooking oil.
2. Brush oil all over the fish fillets and sprinkle with fresh cracked pepper.
3. Put the fish in the air fryer skin side down and cook at 195C//375F for 12–15 minutes until the top begins to turn golden brown.
4. Meanwhile, melt the butter in a pan over a medium heat on the hob. Stir in the miso paste, rice wine vinegar, maple syrup, mirin, and ginger paste, bring to a boil and remove immediately from the heat.
5. Remove the fish from the air fryer when it is cooked and using a pastry brush or the back of a spoon, spread the sauce all over the fish.
6. Return to the air fryer for another 2 minutes at 195C//375F until the glaze is caramelised and top with chopped spring onions and sesame seeds.

Nutritional Information per Serving:

SERVES –2 | CALORIES –524KCAL | PROTEIN –23G | CARBOHYDRATES –23G | FAT –29G

SWEET AND SPICY SALMON

INGREDIENTS

- 450g//1lb of wild salmon fillets (four pieces)
- Salt and pepper to taste
- 60ml of sweet red chilli sauce
- 1 teaspoon of Sriracha sauce
- 1" piece of fresh ginger, grated
- Thinly sliced spring onions, for garnish

METHOD

1. Preheat the air fryer to 200C//400F. Spray with olive oil.
2. Put the salmon into the air fryer and season with salt.
3. Combine the red chilli sauce, sriracha and ginger in a bowl together and brush over the salmon.
4. Cook at 200C//400F for 8 to 10 minutes.
5. Serve with a garnish of thinly sliced spring onions.

Nutritional Information per Serving:

SERVES −4 | CALORIES −202KCAL | PROTEIN −22.5G | CARBOHYDRATES −6.5G | FAT −7G

CAJUN PRAWNS

INGREDIENTS

- 15g//0.5oz of cajun or creole seasoning
- 450g//1lb of extra jumbo prawns, ready to eat
- 170g//6oz of cooked, turkey or chicken Andouille sausage
- 230g//8oz courgette (cut into ½ moon slices, 1/2−inch thick)
- 230g//8oz of squash (cut into ½ moon slices, 1/4−inch thick)
- 1 large red bell pepper, seeded and cut into thin 1−inch pieces
- Salt to taste
- 30ml of olive oil

METHOD

1. Toss the prawns and the Cajun seasoning in a large bowl and coat thoroughly.
2. Next, add the sausage, courgette, squash, bell peppers, and salt. Add the olive oil and toss to coat the meat and vegetables.
3. Preheat the air fryer to 200C//400F and spray with cooking oil.
4. Put the prawns and vegetables into the air fryer and cook for 8 minutes, shaking at intervals. Cook in batches if necessary due to a small air fryer.
5. Once all the batches are cooked, return the first one to the air fryer and cook an extra 1 minute to reheat if necessary.
6. Serve.

Nutritional Information per Serving:

SERVES −4 | CALORIES −284KCAL | PROTEIN −31G | CARBOHYDRATES −8G | FAT −14G

WHITE FISH SEASONED WITH GARLIC AND LEMON

INGREDIENTS

- 340g//12oz of white fish (2 fillets approximately 6oz each)
- 1/2 teaspoon of garlic powder
- 1/2 teaspoon of lemon pepper seasoning
- Optional: 1/2 teaspoon onion powder
- Salt and pepper to taste
- Fresh chopped parsley
- Lemon wedges

METHOD

1. Preheat the air fryer to 185C//360F and spritz with cooking oil.
2. Wash the fish fillets and pat them dry.
3. Spray the fillets and season them with garlic powder, lemon pepper, onion powder, salt, and pepper. Repeat for the other side.
4. Line the air fryer with greased paper and put the fish on top of the paper in the air fryer. Add a few lemon wedges near the fish.
5. Cook for 6–12 minutes at 185C//360F, or until cooked thoroughly.
6. Top with chopped parsley and lemon wedges.

Nutritional Information per Serving:

SERVES –4 | CALORIES –169KCAL | PROTEIN –34G | CARBOHYDRATES –1G | FAT –3G

FAVOURITE FISH AND CHIP DINNER

INGREDIENTS

For the Chips:

- 2 large russet potatoes, scrubbed, peel and cut into ¼ inch chips
- 30ml of olive oil
- ½ teaspoon of salt

For the Fish:

- 680g//1.5lb of white fish (cod fillets preferably)
- 160g//5.5oz of dry pancake mix
- 120ml of buttermilk
- 1 egg
- 100g//3.5oz of breadcrumbs
- Salt and pepper to taste
- ½ teaspoon paprika

METHOD

1. Put the chips in a bowl of cold water to soak for about 30 minutes. Remove, drain and pat dry.
2. In a clean bowl, toss the chips with the oil and salt.
3. Preheat the air fryer to 200C//400F and spritz with cooking oil.
4. Put the potatoes into the air fryer and cook for 8–10 minutes at 200C//400F. Shake, then cook for a further 10 minutes or until they are crisp and golden brown.
5. Remove from the air fryer, place on a plate and keep warm.
6. Meanwhile, prepare the fish while the chips are cooking. Rinse with clean cold water and pat dry.
7. In a clean bowl, whisk together the egg and buttermilk. In a second bowl, combine the breadcrumbs and seasonings. In a third bowl, have the pancake mixture ready.
8. Dip the fish into the egg and buttermilk, then straight into the pancake mixture.
9. Immediately dip the same piece of fish into the egg mixture again, and then into the breadcrumbs. Repeat with the other fish.
10. Once dipped in all coatings, place the fish in the air fryer, spray liberally with cooking oil, then cook for 12 minutes at 200C//400F.
11. Briefly return the chips and cook 1–2 minutes just to heat through.
12. Serve!

Nutritional Information per Serving:

SERVES –4 | CALORIES –451KCAL | PROTEIN –40G | CARBOHYDRATES –41G | FAT –14G

SPICED COD
• •

INGREDIENTS

- 60ml of Italian salad dressing
- 1/2 teaspoon of sugar
- Salt and pepper to taste
- 1/8 teaspoon of garlic powder
- 1/8 teaspoon of curry powder
- 1/8 teaspoon of paprika
- 2 cod fillets (170g//6oz each)
- 15g//0.5oz of butter

METHOD

1. In a bowl, combine the Italian salad dressing with all the seasonings. Toss in the cod fillets, coating them thoroughly with the seasonings. Allow to rest for 15 minutes before cooking.
2. Preheat the air fryer to 185C//370F and spray with cooking oil.
3. Put the fillets in a single layer into the air fryer and cook at 185C//370F for about 8–10 minutes, until the fish begins to flake easily with a fork.
4. Serve topped with butter.

Nutritional Information per Serving:

SERVES –2 | CALORIES –168KCAL | PROTEIN –27G | CARBOHYDRATES –2 G | FAT –5G

SUSHI BOWL

INGREDIENTS

- 250g//9oz of cooked jasmine rice or sushi rice
- 230g//8oz of salmon
- 150g//5oz of cucumber, diced
- 1 large avocado, peeled and diced
- 70g//2.5oz of water chestnuts, drained
- 60g//2oz of carrots, peeled and diced thinly
- 30g//1oz of snow peas or sugar snap peas
- 60g//2oz of radishes, sliced
- 1 spring onion, thinly sliced
- 30g//1oz of butter beans or fava beans
- 30ml of sriracha Sauce
- 30g//1oz of Japanese mayo
- 30ml of soy sauce
- Salt and pepper to taste

METHOD

1. Begin by cooking your rice and preparing all your vegetables.
2. Preheat the air fryer to 200C//400F and lightly spray with cooking oil.
3. Season the salmon with salt and black pepper.
4. Put the salmon in the air fryer and cook for 3–5 minutes at 200C//400F.
5. Layer a clean dish with the rice, vegetables, and salmon.
6. Serve drizzled with the sauces.

Nutritional Information per Serving:

SERVES –4 | CALORIES –503KCAL | PROTEIN –20G | CARBOHYDRATES –71.9G | FAT –15.2G

HOMEMADE FISH FINGERS

INGREDIENTS

- 2 large cod fillets
- 2 eggs, beaten
- 460g//16oz of breadcrumbs
- 460g//16oz of plain flour
- 30ml of lemon juice
- 30g//1oz of parsley
- 2 teaspoons of dill
- Extra – 2 teaspoons of dried parsley
- 2 teaspoons of dried basil
- Salt and pepper to taste

METHOD

1. Pat your cod fillets dry.
2. Take 3 clean bowls. In the first bowl, whisk the egg with the lemon juice. In the second bowl blend the flour with the tablespoon of dried parsley. In the third bowl mix the breadcrumbs with the remainder of the seasonings. Keep the 3 bowls in the following order – flour, egg, breadcrumbs – and close to each other.
3. Preheat your air fryer to 180C//360F. Spray the air fryer wit cooking oil.
4. Season the cod fillets with salt and pepper and cut lengthways and then in half. You should have 8 pieces.
5. Place the fish fingers into the flour, then straight into the egg, and finally into the breadcrumbs, pressing so that they are well coated with each.
6. Put into the air fryer and cook for 10 minutes at 180C//360F until they are nice and crispy.
7. Serve with chips or new potatoes.

Nutritional Information per Serving:

SERVES –4 | CALORIES –1733KCAL | PROTEIN –196G | CARBOHYDRATES –182G | FAT –18G

FISHY NUGGETS

INGREDIENTS

- 2 large cod fillets cut into 1" chunks
- 2 eggs, beaten
- 460g//16oz of breadcrumbs
- 460g//16oz of plain flour
- 30ml of lemon juice
- 30g//1oz of parsley
- 2 teaspoons of dill
- Extra – 2 teaspoons of dried parsley
- 2 teaspoons of dried basil
- Salt and pepper to taste

METHOD

1. Pat your cod fillets dry.
2. Take 3 clean bowls. In the first bowl, whisk the egg with the lemon juice. In the second bowl blend the flour with the tablespoon of dried parsley. In the third bowl mix the breadcrumbs with the remainder of the seasonings. Keep the 3 bowls in the following order – flour, egg, breadcrumbs – and close to each other.
3. Preheat your air fryer to 180C//360F. Spray the air fryer wit cooking oil.
4. Season the cod fillets with salt and pepper and cut lengthways and then in half. You should have 8 pieces.
5. Place the fish nuggets into the flour, then straight into the egg, and finally into the breadcrumbs, pressing so that they are well coated with each.
6. Put into the air fryer and cook for 8 minutes at 180C//360F until they are nice and crispy.
7. Serve with chips or new potatoes.

Nutritional Information per Serving:

SERVES –4 | CALORIES –1733KCAL | PROTEIN –196G | CARBOHYDRATES –182G | FAT –18G

THAI FISHCAKES

INGREDIENTS

For the Fish:

- 1 salmon fillet, rinsed and patted dry
- 1 cod fillet, rinsed and patted dry
- 1 pollock fillet, rinsed and patted dry
- 2 teaspoons of dill
- Salt and pepper to taste

For the Potatoes:

- 300g//10.5oz of baby potatoes
- 2 teaspoons of olive oil
- Salt and pepper to taste
- 15g//0.5oz of butter

For the Coating:

- 2 eggs, beaten
- 460g//16oz of breadcrumbs
- 460g//16oz of plain flour
- 30ml of lemon juice
- 30g//1oz of parsley
- 2 teaspoons of dill
- Extra – 2 teaspoons of dried parsley
- 2 teaspoons of dried basil
- Salt and pepper to taste

For the Fishcakes:

- 2 teaspoons of coriander
- 2 teaspoons of Thai 7 Spice
- 2 teaspoons of sweet paprika
- 5g//0.2oz of fresh parsley, shredded
- Salt and pepper to taste
- 15g//0.5oz of butter

METHOD

1. Preheat the air fryer to 180C//360F. Spray with cooking oil.
2. Place the fish on a chopping board and season well with the salt, pepper and dill.
3. Put the fish into the air fryer and cook at 180C//360F for about 8 minutes.
4. Remove the fish from the air fryer and use a fork to flake the fish and set aside in a bowl.
5. Combine the potatoes, olive oil, salt and pepper in a bowl and mix well with your hands to ensure a good covering of oil.
6. Load the potato mixture into the air fryer and cook at 180C//360F for 17 minutes. Remove from the air fryer to a bowl and mash with the butter.
7. Add the cooked fish and the fishcake seasoning to the potato mix and mash everything together thoroughly.
8. When cooled, form into little fishcake shapes.
9. Next, take 3 clean bowls. In the first bowl, whisk the egg with the lemon juice. In the second bowl blend the flour with the tablespoon of dried parsley. In the third bowl mix the breadcrumbs with the remainder of the seasonings. Keep the 3 bowls in the following order – flour, egg, breadcrumbs – and close to each other.
10. Place the fish cakes firstly into the flour, then into the egg, and finally press into the breadcrumbs and ensure a good coating of the mixture at each stage.
11. Place into the air fryer in a single layer. Cook in batches if you need to due to the size of your air fryer. Cook at 180C//360F for about 10 minutes until the fishcakes are golden and crispy.
12. Enjoy served with a sweet chilli dipping sauce.

Nutritional Information per Serving:

SERVES –4 | CALORIES –868KCAL | PROTEIN –68G | CARBOHYDRATES –105G | FAT –17G

KING PRAWN AND MANGO CURRY

INGREDIENTS

- 1 large onion, roughly chopped
- 1 red pepper, roughly chopped
- Spray cooking oil
- 45g//1.5oz of mild curry paste (preferably korma)
- 1 mango, peeled, stone removed and diced (or 200g//7oz of fresh mango chunks)
- 1 x 400g//14oz tin tomatoes
- 1 x 400g//14oz tin coconut milk
- 300g//10.5oz cooked and peeled king prawns
- Handful of flaked almonds
- Fresh coriander leaves, chopped

METHOD

1. Preheat the air fryer to 220C//425F and spritz lightly with oil.
2. Put the onion and red pepper in the air fryer and spray liberally with cooking oil. Cook at 220C//425F for 8 minutes.
3. Next, stir in the curry paste and cook for another 2 minutes at the same temperature.
4. Stir in the mango, chopped tomatoes and coconut milk, and cook for another 10 minutes.
5. Add the prawns and cook for another 5 minutes until heated thoroughly.
6. Serve with rice, sprinkled with flaked almonds and fresh chopped coriander.

Nutritional Information per Serving:

SERVES –4 | CALORIES –444KCAL | PROTEIN –19.3G | CARBOHYDRATES –33.9G | FAT –28.2G

TANDOORI SALMON

INGREDIENTS

- 360g//13oz of salmon cut into approximately 12 x 30g//1oz cubes
- 1/2 cucumber, diced
- 1 small teaspoon of fresh green chilli, finely chopped
- 1/2 red onion, finely chopped
- 1 small tomato
- 10g//0.3oz tandoori spice powder
- 3 small pots of natural yoghurt
- 10g//0.3oz ground cumin
- 30 leaves of fresh mint

METHOD

1. In a bowl, coat the salmon cubes with the tandoori spice powder. Cover the bowl and refrigerate for at least an hour.
2. In a separate bowl, blend ¼ of the yoghurt with the chilli, mint, cumin, salt and pepper. Leave to steep in the fridge until ready to use.
3. Prepare your vegetables so they are ready to use.
4. Preheat the air fryer to 200C//400F and spritz with cooking oil.
5. Cook the salmon at 200C//400F for 5 to 6 minutes. If you prefer your salmon well-done, then check, season with salt and pepper to taste and cook for a further 4–5 minutes.
6. Remove the spiced yoghurt from the fridge and mix with the remaining yoghurt, tomato, cucumber and chopped onion.
7. Serve the salmon immediately topped with the sauce. Serve extra sauce on the side in individual glasses.
8. Garnish with mint leaves.

Nutritional Information per Serving:

SERVES –4 | CALORIES –208KCAL | PROTEIN –22.5G | CARBOHYDRATES –11.4G | FAT –8.7G

SMOKED SALMON RISOTTO WITH ASPARGUS

INGREDIENTS

- 310g//11oz of pearl barley
- 85g//3oz of onion, finely chopped
- 125ml of white wine
- 500ml chicken stock
- 1 garlic clove, peeled and finely chopped
- Cooking oil spray
- 500g//1.1lb blanched asparagus tips
- 115g//4oz frozen peas
- 85g//3oz grated parmesan
- 10g//0.3oz of grated lemon zest
- 10g//0.3oz of finely chopped fresh dill
- 130g//4.5oz of smoked salmon cut into thin slices
- Salt and pepper to taste

METHOD

1. Preheat the air fryer to 200C//400F. Spritz with cooking oil spray.
2. Add the barley, onion, garlic, salt and pepper to the air fryer and spray again with cooking oil. Cook at 200C//400F for 8 minutes.
3. Meanwhile, in a saucepan over a low heat, gently stir the wine, broth and water until it steams but does not boil.
4. Pour half of the liquid into the air fryer with the vegetables and cook at 200C//400F for about 20 minutes.
5. Add the remaining liquid to the air fryer and cook for a further 25 minutes. The liquid should be nearly absorbed and the barley, tender, but firm.
6. Finally, add the asparagus, peas, parmesan cheese, lemon zest and dill. Cook for a further 2 minutes so that all the ingredients are hot and well mixed.
7. Plate and serve with the smoked salmon.

Nutritional Information per Serving:

SERVES −4 | CALORIES −555KCAL | PROTEIN −25.7G | CARBOHYDRATES −75.3G | FAT −16.9G

SALMON IN SESAME SEEDS

INGREDIENTS

- 500g//1.1lb of salmon in cubes
- 20ml of soya sauce
- 20ml of lemon juice
- 15g//0.5oz of honey
- 15g//0.5oz of sesame
- 1 teaspoon of paprika
- Salt and pepper to taste

METHOD

1. Preheat the air fryer to 200C//400F and spray with cooking oil.
2. Toss the salmon in a large bowl with all the ingredients, ensuring it's fully coated.
3. Put all the contents of the bowl together into the air fryer.
4. Cook for 10–12 minutes at 200C//400F.
5. Serve hot.

Nutritional Information per Serving:

SERVES −4 | CALORIES −202KCAL | PROTEIN −25.3G | CARBOHYDRATES −4.7G | FAT −9.5G

TROUT IN GARLIC, LEMON, AND PARSLEY MARINADE

INGREDIENTS

- 700g//1.5lb of fresh trout, filleted (about 1 large whole trout)
- 100g//3.5oz of butter, melted
- 30ml of freshly squeezed lemon juice
- 2 garlic cloves, finely chopped
- Enough plain flour to coat the trout
- Salt and pepper to taste
- Lemon slices for garnish
- 10g//0.4oz of fresh chopped parsley

METHOD

1. Wash and dry the trout and cut into 6 pieces.
2. In a bowl, blend the melted butter, lemon juice and garlic. Toss in the fish slices so they are well coated in the sauce. Cover the bowl, place in the fridge, and leave to marinate for two hours.
3. Place the flour in a shallow bowl ready to coat your trout pieces.
4. Preheat your air fryer to 200C//400F and spray with cooking oil.
5. Taking one slice at a time, coat each piece of trout in flour, sprinkle with salt and pepper and place in the air fryer. Spray again with cooking oil.
6. Cook at 200C//400F for 11 minutes.
7. Serve garnished with chopped parsley and lemon slices just before serving.

Nutritional Information per Serving:

SERVES –6 | CALORIES –420KCAL | PROTEIN –33.5G | CARBOHYDRATES –16.7G | FAT –23.6G

PRAWN LETTUCE WRAPS

INGREDIENTS

- 30ml of fresh lemon juice
- 30g//1oz of pepper paste (Korean Gochujang, Sriracha, Thai Chilli Paste can all be used)
- 50ml of olive oil
- 10g//0.4oz of honey
- 1 garlic clove, finely chopped
- 1cm piece of fresh ginger, grated
- 700g//1.5lb of cooked large prawns
- 1 head of iceberg lettuce, leaves separated, washed and drained
- 2 cucumbers, sliced
- 1 bunch of small radishes, sliced
- Mint and basil, for serving

METHOD

1. Preheat the air fryer to 200C//400F and line with greased foil. Spritz with cooking oil spray.
2. Whisk together the lemon juice, pepper paste, oil and honey, then stir in the garlic and ginger.
3. Toss the prawns into the mixture to coat thoroughly.
4. Place the coated prawns in the air fryer in a single layer and cook at 200C//400F for about 10 minutes.
5. Serve the prawns immediately in lettuce and topped with cucumbers, radishes, mint and basil.

Nutritional Information per Serving:

SERVES –6 | CALORIES –230KCAL | PROTEIN –36G | CARBOHYDRATES –13G | FAT –4.5G

HONEY AND LIME PRAWNS

INGREDIENTS

- 450g//1lb large prawns, ready to use
- 20ml of olive oil
- 20ml of freshly squeezed lime juice (can be replaced with lemon if necessary)
- 20g//0.7oz honey
- 2 garlic cloves, finely chopped
- Salt and pepper to taste
- Lime wedges
- Coriander

METHOD

1. Whisk the olive oil, lime juice, honey, garlic and salt together in a large bowl. Toss in the prawns and leave to marinate in the fridge for about 20–30 minutes.
2. Heat the air fryer to 200C//400F, spritz with cooking oil spray and line with greased foil.
3. Place the marinated prawn into the air fryer.
4. Cook at 200C/400F for 2 minutes, give the prawns a good stir or shake, and cook for another 2–3 minutes at the same temperature.
5. Serve with lime wedges and coriander.

Nutritional Information per Serving:

SERVES –4 | CALORIES –187KCAL | PROTEIN –23G | CARBOHYDRATES –7G | FAT –7G

TUNA STEAKS

INGREDIENTS

- 2 garlic cloves, finely chopped
- 1" piece of fresh ginger, grated
- 15g//0.5oz of brown sugar
- 15ml of olive oil
- 60ml of soy sauce
- 2 tuna steaks

METHOD

1. Whisk all the ingredients except the tuna steaks in a bowl together until thoroughly combined.
2. Toss the tuna into the bowl of marinade and coat thoroughly. Cover and leave at room temperature to marinate for 10 to 15 minutes.
3. Preheat your air fryer to 185C//360F and spray with oil.
4. Remove the tuna from the marinade, and place in the air fryer. Discard any remaining marinade. Place the tuna steaks in the air fryer for 5 minutes, flipping at 3 minutes.
5. Cook for 3 minutes at 185C//360F, turn over, and cook at the same temperature for a further 2 minutes. (Note: if you prefer your tuna steaks well done, then cook for a further 3–5 minutes.)

Nutritional Information per Serving:

SERVES –4 | CALORIES –313KCAL | PROTEIN –41G | CARBOHYDRATES –8G | FAT –12G

MASALA FRIED FISH

INGREDIENTS

- 500g//1.1lb of pearl spot fish, washed, gutted and prepped

For the Marinade:

- 30ml of vegetable oil
- 1 teaspoon of apple cider vinegar
- 2 teaspoons of ginger garlic paste
- 2 teaspoons of chopped curry leaves
- 1.5 teaspoons of red chilli powder
- 1 teaspoon of turmeric powder
- Salt and pepper to taste

For the Topping:

- 1.5 teaspoons of coconut oil
- 10g//0.4oz of onion, chopped
- About 10–12 curry leaves
- 7 garlic cloves, skin on, crushed
- Salt to taste
- 1/2 teaspoon of red chilli flakes

METHOD

1. Mix all the marinade ingredients thoroughly in a bowl together to create a thick paste.
2. Take your prepared fish and cut a few small shallow gashes into the flesh.
3. Coat the fish thoroughly with the marinade on both sides, making sure it is evenly coated and applied especially to the cuts.
4. Cover and marinate the fish in the refrigerator for at least 15–20 minutes.
5. Preheat the air fryer to 200C//400F and spray with cooking oil.
6. Place the marinated fish in the air fryer and cook for about 15 minutes at 200C//400F. (If your fish is bigger than 500g, it may need a few minutes longer).
7. Meanwhile, heat the coconut oil gently in a pan on the hob. Add the onion, curry leaves and garlic with a pinch of salt. Fry for about 5–6 minutes.
8. Add the red chilli flakes and remove from the heat.
9. Serve the fish hot sprinkled with the topping mixture.

Nutritional Information per Serving:

SERVES –4 | CALORIES –181KCAL | PROTEIN –20.6G | CARBOHYDRATES –3G | FAT –8.9G

COD WITH LEMON AND DILL
• •

INGREDIENTS

- 4 cod loins, washed and patted dry with kitchen roll
- 60g//2oz of melted butter
- 6 garlic cloves, finely chopped
- Freshly squeezed juice of 1 lemon
- 30g//1oz of fresh dill, chopped
- Salt and pepper to taste

METHOD

1. Combine the melted butter with the garlic, lemon juice, dill and salt in a large bowl.
2. Toss in the cod loins one at a time making sure they are thoroughly coated in the marinade. Make sure to press the garlic into the flesh so it doesn't fall off.
3. Preheat the air fryer to 185C//370F and lightly spray with cooking oil.
4. Place the cod loins in one layer in the air fryer so that there is space between each one.
5. Cook for 10 minutes at 185C//370F, then remove carefully from the fryer.
6. Serve hot garnished with lemon and butter.

Nutritional Information per Serving:

SERVES –4 | CALORIES –302KCAL | PROTEIN –42G | CARBOHYDRATES –3G | FAT –13G

CRUMB TOPPED SOLE
• •

INGREDIENTS

- 45g//1.5oz of mayonnaise
- 45g//1.5oz of parmesan cheese, grated
- 2 teaspoons mustard seed
- Salt and pepper to taste
- 680g//1.5lb of sole fillets (approximately 4 fillets, 6 ounces each)
- 115g//4oz of soft breadcrumbs
- 1 spring onion, finely chopped
- 1/2 teaspoon ground mustard
- 15g//0.5oz of melted butter
- Cooking spray

METHOD

1. Blend the mayonnaise, 25g of parmesan cheese (save the rest for the breadcrumb mix later), mustard seed, salt, and pepper, to a well–mixed paste.
2. Preheat the air fryer to 190C//370F and spray with cooking oil.
3. Spread the mayonnaise mixture over the sole fillets, taking care to ensure an even coating all over.
4. Place the fish in a single layer in the air fryer – you may need to cook in batches – and spray lightly with a little more cooking oil.
5. Cook for about 5 minutes at 190C//375F until the fish flakes easily with a fork.
6. While the fish is cooking, combine the breadcrumbs with the onion, mustard powder, remaining parmesan cheese and the butter.
7. Spoon the breadcrumb mix over the sole fillets and pat gently. Spray with cooking oil.
8. Cook at 190C//375F for another 2–3 minutes until golden brown.
9. Serve sprinkled with chopped spring onions.

Nutritional Information per Serving:

SERVES –4 | CALORIES –233KCAL | PROTEIN –24G | CARBOHYDRATES –8G | FAT –11G

MAINS – HAM AND PORK DISHES

SPICED PORK FILLETS

INGREDIENTS

- 900g//2lb of pork tenderloin steak
- 30ml of olive oil
- 3 garlic cloves, finely chopped
- 30g//1oz of brown sugar
- 2 teaspoons of chilli powder
- 2 teaspoons of ground cumin
- 2 teaspoons of onion powder
- 1 teaspoon of thyme
- Salt and pepper to taste

METHOD

1. Remove the tenderloin from any packaging and pat dry with kitchen roll.
2. Slip the point of a knife under the silver skin of the pork and gently cut and pull to remove it.
3. Put all the dry ingredients in a bowl and mix thoroughly.
4. Pour in the olive oil, add the garlic and mix again until combined.
5. Rub the seasoning mixture all over the pork.
6. Preheat the air fryer to 200C//400F.
7. Put the seasoned pork tenderloin into the air fryer. Cook for 16–17 minutes at 200C//400F.
8. Remove the pork from the air fryer and allow to rest for a few minutes before serving.

Nutritional Information per Serving:

SERVES –8 | CALORIES –248KCAL | PROTEIN –32G | CARBOHYDRATES –6G | FAT –10G (PORK TENDERLOIN IS ONE OF THE LEA-NEST CUTS OF PORK)

GLAZED HAM

INGREDIENTS

- 1kg//2.2lb cooked, boneless ham joint with netting removed
- 115g//4oz brown sugar
- 85g//3oz honey
- Juice of 1 orange (alternatively, 60ml orange juice)
- 30g//1oz of mustard (or 30ml of apple cider vinegar)
- 1/4 teaspoon of cinnamon
- 1/4 teaspoon of cloves
- Ground pepper to taste

METHOD

1. The ham should be at room temperature before cooking, so remove it from the fridge 2 hours before preparing.
2. For the glaze, put the brown sugar, honey, orange juice, mustard (or apple cider vinegar), cinnamon, cloves, and black pepper into a small saucepan.
3. Warm gently on low heat and stir until the ingredients are blended and the sugar has dissolved. Turn off the heat and leave to one side.
4. Preheat the air fryer to 180C//350F.
5. Use a sharp knife to crisscross the ham with ½ inch cuts.
6. Lay the ham on a piece of foil large enough to fold over the top of the meat joint.
7. Brush the glaze all over the ham and fold the foil tightly over the top.
8. Cook the ham at 180C//350F for 25 minutes.
9. Open the air fryer and the foil and brush the ham with a little more glaze (don't use all the glaze now as you will need some for serving).
10. Reseal the foil tightly and cook for a further 25 minutes at 180C//350F.
11. When it's cooked, open the foil and arrange it into a shallow basket to hold the ham and the meat juices contained.
12. Brush the ham with a little more glaze, increase the heat a few degrees in the air fryer and cooked for 5 minutes more. The glaze should be nicely caramelised.
13. Rest the ham for 5 minutes before serving.
14. Serve any remaining meat juices and glaze in a gravy boat with the ham.

Nutritional Information per Serving:

SERVES –4 TO 6 | CALORIES –348KCAL | PROTEIN –25G | CARBOHYDRATES –19G | FAT –25G

CRISPY BREADED PORK CHOPS

INGREDIENTS

- Olive oil spray
- 6 boneless pork chops, patted dry with kitchen roll
- Salt and pepper to taste
- 1 egg, beaten
- 100g//3.50oz of breadcrumbs
- 35g//1.2oz of crushed cornflakes crumbs
- 15g//0.50oz of grated parmesan cheese
- 1 1/4 teaspoon of sweet paprika
- 1/2 teaspoon of garlic powder
- 1/2 teaspoon of onion powder
- 1/4 teaspoon of chilli powder

METHOD

1. In a bowl, combine the breadcrumbs, crushed cornflakes, parmesan cheese, and all the seasonings. Set to one side.
2. In a separate bowl place the beaten egg and set to one side.
3. Preheat the air fryer to 200C//400F. Spray lightly with cooking oil.
4. Season the pork chops all over with salt.
5. Take each pork chop in turn and place it first in the beaten egg, then into the crumb mixture, pressing lightly so that the crumbs will stick.
6. Put in the air fryer in a single layer, spritz the top of the chops with cooking oil, and cook for about 12 minutes at 200C//400F.
7. Serve.

Nutritional Information per Serving:

SERVES –6 | CALORIES –378KCAL | PROTEIN –33G | CARBOHYDRATES –8 G | FAT –13G

BARBECUE PORK BELLY BITES

INGREDIENTS

- 450g//1lb pork belly, rinsed and patted dry, diced into ¾ inch pieces
- 1 teaspoon of Worcester sauce
- 1/2 teaspoon of garlic powder
- Salt and pepper to taste
- Optional: 60ml of BBQ sauce

METHOD

1. Preheat the air fryer to 200C//400F.
2. Put the diced pork into a bowl and season with the Worcester sauce, garlic powder, salt and pepper. Cover the bowl and marinate for about 30–60 minutes.
3. Spread the pork in an even layer in the air fryer and cook for 10–18 minutes at 200C//400F. Turn the pork about halfway through cooking.
4. Check the pork and if you prefer it well done, add another 2–5 minutes of cooking time.
5. Serve seasoned with additional salt and pepper to taste, and drizzle with BBQ sauce.

Nutritional Information per Serving:

SERVES –4 | CALORIES –590KCAL | PROTEIN –11G | CARBOHYDRATES –1G | FAT –60G

PARMESAN PORK CHOPS

INGREDIENTS

- 500g//18oz of pork chops (as 3 x 170g//6 oz individual chops), rinsed and patted dry
- Salt and pepper to taste
- Garlic powder to taste
- Smoked paprika to taste
- 50g//1.7oz of breadcrumbs
- 60g//2oz of parmesan cheese, grated
- 30g//1oz of chopped parsley, plus additional for garnish
- 1 egg, beaten
- Cooking spray
- 60g//2oz of mozzarella cheese, grated
- 240ml of marinara sauce, warm

METHOD

1. Combine the breadcrumbs, parmesan cheese and chopped parsley in a bowl and set to one side.
2. In a second bowl place the beaten egg.
3. On a clean surface, season the pork shops with salt, pepper, garlic powder, and smoked paprika to your taste.
4. Preheat the air fryer to 190C//380F and spray with cooking oil.
5. Dip each pork chop in egg then press gently into the seasoned breadcrumbs, coating them completely. Lightly spray both sides of coated pork chops with cooking spray immediately before cooking.
6. Put the pork chops in the air fryer and cook at 190C//380F for 8–12 minutes. Turn the pork chops over about halfway through.
7. Finally top with mozzarella cheese and cook for an extra 2 minutes until the cheese is melted.
8. Serve warm with marinara sauce.

Nutritional Information per Serving:

SERVES –3 | CALORIES –495KCAL | PROTEIN –53G | CARBOHYDRATES –18G | FAT –22G

CARIBBEAN BONE–FREE PORK CHOPS

INGREDIENTS

- 2 bone–free pork chops about 170g//6oz each
- 30ml of olive oil
- 1 teaspoon of light brown sugar
- 40g//1.4oz of jerk seasoning (use less if you prefer a less spicy meal)
- Salt to taste

METHOD

1. Combine the brown sugar, jerk seasoning, and salt until blended. Set to one side.
2. Lightly spray both sides of the pork shops then coat all over with the seasoning rub, cover, and leave to marinate for 30 minutes.
3. Preheat the air fryer to 190C//375F and lightly spray with oil.
4. Put the seasoned pork chops into the air fryer and cook at 190C//375F for 5–6 minutes. Turn the pork chops and cook for another 5–6 at the same temperature.
5. When cooked, transfer to a place and allow to rest for 5 minutes.
6. Serve with a tossed salad, rice, or pasta.

Nutritional Information per Serving:

SERVES –2 | CALORIES –350KCAL | PROTEIN –4G | CARBOHYDRATES –4 G | FAT –14G

SWEET AND SOUR PORK

INGREDIENTS

For the Sauce:

- 115g//4oz of unsweetened crushed pineapple, undrained
- 120ml of cider vinegar
- 50g//1.7oz of white sugar
- 45g//1.5oz of packed dark brown sugar
- 60g//2oz ketchup
- 15ml of soy sauce
- 1–1/2 teaspoons of Dijon mustard
- 1/2 teaspoon of garlic powder

For the Pork:

- 1 pork tenderloin (approximately 340g//0.75lb cut in half)
- Salt and pepper to taste
- Cooking spray
- Optional: spring onions, thinly sliced

METHOD

1. Combine all the sauce ingredients in a saucepan, and over a low heat gently bring to the boil. Simmer for about 6–8 minutes until the sauce thickens, stirring occasionally.
2. Preheat air fryer to 180C//350F and spray with cooking oil.
3. Season the pork with salt and pepper and place on greased paper in the air fryer. Spray with cooking oil.
4. Cook at 180C//350F for about 7–8 minutes.
5. Turn the pork and pour about 30ml of sauce over the it.
6. Cook for a further 10–12 minutes at 180C//350F.
7. Once the pork is removed from the air fryer, let it stand for about 5 minutes before serving.
8. Serve with the remaining sauce, topped with spring onions.

Nutritional Information per Serving:

SERVES –4 | CALORIES –502KCAL | PROTEIN –35G | CARBOHYDRATES –72G | FAT –7G

ONE–POT – SAUSAGE, ONIONS, PEPPERS AND POTATOES (1)

INGREDIENTS

- 340g//12oz smoked sausage sliced into ½ inch pieces
- 200g//½lb baby potatoes cut into quarter
- 170g//6oz of sliced mushrooms
- 1 medium bell pepper, sliced
- 1 onion diced
- 2 teaspoons of smoke paprika
- 1 teaspoon of garlic powder
- 1 teaspoon of onion powder
- Salt and pepper to taste
- ½ teaspoon of cumin
- ½ teaspoon of coriander
- ½ teaspoon of turmeric

METHOD

1. Toss the smoked sausage, onions, peppers, potatoes, and mushrooms in a large bowl with the olive oil. Stir to ensure a good coating of oil.
2. Preheat the air fryer to 180C//350F and spray liberally with olive oil cooking spray.
3. Put all the ingredients into the air fryer together and cook at 180C//350F for about 18–22 minutes until the potatoes are cooked. Serve.

Nutritional Information per Serving:

SERVES –6 | CALORIES –280KCAL | PROTEIN –9G | CARBOHYDRATES –15 G | FAT –21G

QUICK ONE–POT ITALIAN SAUSAGE AND PEPPER DINNER (2)

INGREDIENTS

- 8 Italian sausages, still frozen (or any thick butcher's sausages)
- 3 bell peppers (green, yellow, red), stalk and seed removed, sliced lengthwise
- 1 small onion, thinly sliced
- ½ teaspoon of olive oil
- ½ teaspoon of oregano
- ½ teaspoon of garlic powder
- ½ teaspoon of pork seasoning
- Salt and pepper to taste

METHOD

1. Preheat the air fryer to 180C//360F and spray with cooking oil.
2. Put the still–frozen Italian sausages into the air fryer and cook for 10 minutes at 180C//350F.
3. In a bowl, combine the olive oil with the seasonings and toss in the peppers and onions. Mix well with your hands.
4. Now separate the sausages in the air fryer and add the pepper and onion mixture. Give the air fryer a good stir and cook for another 10 minutes at 180C//360F.
5. Serve.

Nutritional Information per Serving:

SERVES –4 | CALORIES –1640KCAL | PROTEIN –67G | CARBOHYDRATES –21G | FAT –142G

PORK AND APPLE BURGERS AND CHIPS

INGREDIENTS

- 60g//2oz of minced pork meat
- 2 medium apples, peeled, cored and grated
- 100g//3.5oz of cheese, grated
- 1 teaspoon of garlic puree
- 15g//0.5oz of thyme
- 15g//0.5oz of mixed herbs

For the Chips:

- 10ml of olive oil
- 1 extra teaspoon of thyme (for seasoning the chips)
- Salt and pepper to taste

METHOD

1. In a large bowl, combine the pork mince, grated apple, all seasonings (save the extra teaspoon of thyme), and grated cheese.
2. Using your hands, mix thoroughly then create your four pork and apple burger shapes. Indent the top of each one with your thumb. Set to one side.
3. Preheat the air fryer to 180C//350F and spritz with cooking oil.
4. Now toss your chipped potatoes into a large bowl with the olive oil, salt, pepper and the extra teaspoon of thyme. Use your hands to mix well.
5. Load the chips into the air fryer and cook at 180C//350F for 5 minutes.
6. When the 10 minutes is up, add the burgers in with the chips and cook for a further 10 minutes at 180C//350F.
7. Finally, turn the burgers over, shake the chips up, then cook for a further 8 minutes.
8. Add the burgers to burger buns and serve with the chips.

Nutritional Information per Serving:

SERVES –4 | CALORIES –517KCAL | PROTEIN –32G | CARBOHYDRATES –15 G | FAT –37G

ONE–POT HARVEST CASSEROLE

INGREDIENTS

- 100g//3.50z of fresh sprouts, cleaned and chopped into quarters
- 1 sweet potato, peeled and chopped into cubes
- ½ medium white onion, peeled and sliced
- 2 red apples, peeled, cored, and diced into cubes
- 2 green apples, peeled, cored, and diced into cubes
- 4 sausages, sliced into medium chunks
- 3 slices of thick bacon, crumbled
- 15ml of olive oil
- 60g//2oz of dried thyme
- Salt and pepper to taste

METHOD

1. Preheat the air fryer to 180C//360F and spray with cooking oil.
2. Load the apple, onion, sprouts and sweet potato pieces into a bowl with the olive oil, thyme, salt, and pepper. Use your hands to mix so that everything is coated with the oil.
3. Put all the seasoned vegetables into the air fryer and cook at 180C//360F for 8 minutes.
4. When the 8 minutes is complete, add the sausage and bacon on top of the vegetables and cook at the same temperature for a further 10 minutes.
5. Turn the temperature up to 200C//400F, give the air fryer a stir and cook another 2 minutes at 200C//400F.
6. Serve.

Nutritional Information per Serving:

SERVES –4 | CALORIES –1123KCAL | PROTEIN –37G | CARBOHYDRATES –81G | FAT –74G

TRADITIONAL HAM, EGG AND CHIPS

INGREDIENTS

- 2 ham steaks, still frozen
- 15ml of olive oil
- 2 large white potatoes, peeled, washed, dried and chipped
- Salt and pepper to taste
- Optional: fried egg
- Optional: tinned pineapple

METHOD

1. Preheat the air fryer to 180C//360F and spray with cooking oil.
2. Toss the chips into a bowl with the olive oil and season with salt and pepper. Make sure the chips are fully coated.
3. Put the chips into the air fryer and cook at 180C//360F for 10 minutes.
4. Open the air fryer, put the still frozen ham steaks on top and cook for another 10 minutes at 180C//360F.
5. Now is a good time to fry your eggs and drain the can of pineapple.
6. Serve the ham steaks topped with pineapple rings, with chips and fried egg.

Nutritional Information per Serving:

SERVES –2 | CALORIES –469KCAL | PROTEIN –48G | CARBOHYDRATES –30G | FAT –17G

THAI MINCED PORK (OR TURKEY)

INGREDIENTS

- 450g//1lb of pork (or turkey) mince
- 230g//8oz of green beans cut into 1-inch lengths
- 15g//0.5oz of garlic, finely chopped

- 15ml of oyster sauce
- 15ml of sesame oil
- 15ml of soy sauce
- 30ml of fish sauce
- 1 teaspoon of cornflour
- Salt and pepper to taste

- Optional: 15ml of sriracha hot sauce
- Optional: Thai basil to garnish

For the Poached Eggs:

- 4 eggs
- 60ml of water

METHOD

1. In a large bowl, use your clean hands to mix the minced meat with the sesame oil, oyster sauce, soy sauce, fish sauce and sriracha hot sauce (optional) thoroughly.

   Set aside to marinate for 30 minutes.

   Preheat the air fryer to 190C//380F.
2. Grease a 4–cup muffin tray, or 4 individual muffin cups (depending on the size of your air fryer). Put a little water into each muffin cup, then crack an egg into it.
3. Put the eggs into the air fryer and cook at 190C//380F for 7–8 minutes for an egg with runny yolk, or 9–10 minutes for a firm egg yolk.
4. Remove the eggs from the air fryer when cooked.
5. Next, put the chopped garlic, green beans and olive oil into air fryer and mix. Cook at 180C//360F for 5 minutes, stirring once halfway through cooking.
6. Add the marinated mincemeat and cook for 12minutes, stirring every 3–4 minutes until meat is cooked.
7. Serve the meat and egg over rice, sprinkled with a Thai basil garnish.

Nutritional Information per Serving (based on minced turkey):

SERVES –4 | CALORIES –277KCAL | PROTEIN –30.5 G | CARBOHYDRATES –8.2G | FAT –14.2G

5 SPICE PORK

INGREDIENTS

- 230g//8oz of pork shoulder, cut into thick slices
- 30ml of soy sauce
- 10ml of rice wine
- 1 teaspoon of cornflour
- 2 garlic cloves, finely chopped
- 1 teaspoon of sesame oil
- 1/2 teaspoon of sugar
- 1/2 teaspoon of Chinese five spices powder
- 60g//2oz of plain flour
- Salt to taste

- White pepper powder to taste
- Optional: chilli pepper, thinly sliced
- Optional: chopped coriander

METHOD

1. Toss the pork slices in a bowl with all the main ingredients except the plain flour. Ensure the pork slices are well coated, then cover the bowl and marinate the meat for at least 1 hour.
2. Preheat the air fryer to 195C//380F and spray with cooking oil.
3. Put the plain flour in a shallow dish and dip the pork in it, shaking off any excess. Put the pork slices to one side for about 5–10 minutes until you don't see dry flour.
4. Put the pork slices into the air fryer and spritz with cooking oil. Cook at 195//380F for 12–14 minutes, turning once during cooking. The pork slices should look nice and crisp when cooked.
5. Serve topped with the chopped chilli pepper and coriander. Season with salt and pepper to taste.

Nutritional Information per Serving:

SERVES –4 | CALORIES –100KCAL | PROTEIN –8G | CARBOHYDRATES –23G | FAT –3G

PORK RIBS WITH HONEY AND GARLIC

• •

INGREDIENTS

- 1kg//2.2lb of pork spareribs
- 115g//4oz of honey
- 60ml of soy sauce
- 60g//2oz of ketchup
- 60g//2oz of brown sugar
- 30ml of rice vinegar
- 30ml of lemon juice
- 2 teaspoons of sesame oil
- 4 garlic cloves, finely chopped
- Optional: 10g//0.3oz of sesame seeds to garnish
- Optional: 30g//1oz of spring onions, finely chopped

METHOD

1. Prepare the marinade by combining the honey, soy sauce, ketchup, brown sugar, vinegar, and lemon juice in a large bowl.
2. Save about 1/3 of the marinade in a jug and refrigerate.
3. Toss the pork ribs in the bowl with the remaining 2/3 of the marinade and mix. Marinate in the refrigerator overnight.
4. Preheat the air fryer to 190C//380F. Line with a sheet of greased foil.
5. Remove the pork from the refrigerator at least 30 minutes before cooking.
6. Place the ribs in the air fryer in a single layer and cook for about 10–12 minutes at 190C//380F. Turn once during cooking.
7. Meanwhile, in a large frying pan or wok, sauté the garlic in sesame oil for about a minute, then add the saved jug of marinade to the pan. Heat gently while stirring continuously until the sauce thickens.
8. Finally, when the ribs are cooked, toss into the pan/wok with the sesame seeds, and sprinkle with spring onions to serve.

Nutritional Information per Serving:

SERVES –6 | CALORIES –429KCAL | PROTEIN –18G | CARBOHYDRATES –30G | FAT –27 G

KOREAN STYLE PORK BELLY

INGREDIENTS

- 500g//1lb of pork belly, cut into thin slices
- 4 garlic cloves, finely chopped
- 2" piece of fresh ginger, grated
- 7g//0.25oz of Korean hot pepper paste Gochujang, or to taste
- 60g//2oz of honey
- 45ml of soy sauce
- 15ml of sesame oil
- 7.5ml of apple cider vinegar
- 25g//0.8oz of toasted white sesame seeds

METHOD

1. Prepare the marinade by combining the garlic, ginger, pepper paste, honey, soy sauce, sesame oil, apple cider vinegar and sesame seeds in a large bowl.
2. Save about 1/4 of the marinade in a jug and refrigerate until needed.
3. Toss the pork belly in the bowl with the remaining 3/4 of the marinade and mix. Marinate in the refrigerator overnight.
4. Preheat the air fryer to 190C//380F. Line with a sheet of greased foil.
5. Remove the pork from the refrigerator at least 30 minutes before cooking.
6. Place the pork belly slices in the air fryer and cook for about 10–12 minutes at 190C//380F. Stir twice during cooking at regular intervals.
7. Meanwhile, gently heat the remaining ¼ of the marinade in a saucepan over a medium heat. Stir constantly until the sauce thickens.
8. Once the pork is cooked, put it in the pan with the marinade and stir.
9. Serve hot sprinkled with sesame seeds, garnished with chopped coriander and sliced spring onions.

Nutritional Information per Serving:

SERVES –4 | CALORIES –360KCAL | PROTEIN –7G | CARBOHYDRATES –9G | FAT –33G

PORK CHOPS WITH GARLIC BUTTER

INGREDIENTS

- 4 pork chops
- 15g//0.5oz of coconut butter
- 15ml of coconut oil
- 2 garlic cloves, finely chopped
- 2 teaspoons of dried parsley
- Salt and pepper to taste

METHOD

1. Combine all the seasonings, the coconut oil, butter and garlic.in a bowl together.
2. Lay the pork chops on a sheet of foil each and rub the seasoned mixture into both sides of the chop.
3. Wrap each chop up in the foil and refrigerate for 1 hour.
4. Preheat the air fryer to 175C//335F and spray with cooking oil.
5. Take the foil wrapped chops from the fridge and open the silver foil. Rub any remaining marinade into the meat.
6. Place the chops in the air fryer and cook at 175C//335F for about 7 minutes. Turn the chops over, then cook for 8 minutes on the other side.
7. Serve with salad and drizzle with olive oil.

Nutritional Information per Serving:

SERVES –4 | CALORIES –524KCAL | PROTEIN –58G | CARBOHYDRATES –2G | FAT –29G

STIR FRIED PORK AND LEEK

INGREDIENTS

- 500g//1lb of pork shoulder cut into slices
- 30ml of oyster sauce
- 30ml of soy sauce
- 15ml of sesame oil
- 1 teaspoon of garlic powder
- 1 teaspoon of onion powder
- 1 teaspoon of cornflour
- 1/2 teaspoon of black pepper
- 130g//4.5oz of leek cleaned and sliced diagonally into 1/2-inch pieces

METHOD

1. In a bowl, combine all the seasonings to create a marinade. Toss in the pork slices and mix well ensuring it's fully coated. Cover the bowl and marinate for at least 30 minutes.
2. Preheat the air fryer to 190C//380F and line with greased foil.
3. Put the marinated pork slices in the air fryer and cook for 8 minutes at 190C//380F, stirring once halfway through cooking.
4. Mix the leek into the air fryer with the pork and cook for a further 4–5 minutes at 190C//380F until the pork is cooked through.
5. Serve hot.

Nutritional Information per Serving:

SERVES −4 | CALORIES −186KCAL | PROTEIN −16G | CARBOHYDRATES −11G | FAT −9G

PAELLA WITH CHORIZO AND PRAWNS

INGREDIENTS

- 150g//5oz of paella rice
- 400g//14oz can of chopped tomatoes
- 1/2 cooked chorizo sausage ring (about 200–250g), sliced
- 1 red pepper, washed, seeded, and diced
- 150g//5oz of king prawns, ready to use
- 60g//2oz of peas
- 60g//2oz of black olives
- 1/2 teaspoon of ground paprika
- ½ teaspoon of chilli flakes
- 650ml of vegetable stock made with 1 vegetable stock cube
- One onion, peeled and diced
- 2 garlic cloves finely chopped
- 1 lemon cut into wedges
- Handful of parsley, chopped
- Cooking oil spray

METHOD

1. Preheat the air fryer to 200C//400F. Spray liberally with cooking oil.
2. Put the onions, prawns, chorizo, and peppers into the air fryer and cook for 5 minutes at 200C//400F.
3. Stir in the spices and canned tomatoes. Cook for 4 minutes at the same temperature until the tomatoes are heated through.
4. Put the paella rice into the air fryer and pour in half of the stock. Cook for 10 minutes at 200C//400F. Pour in the rest of the stock and cook for a further 10 minutes at the same temperature.
5. Add in the peas and olives and cook for another 2–3 minutes.
6. Season with salt and pepper to taste.
7. Serve garnished with fresh parsley.

Nutritional Information per Serving:

SERVES −2 | CALORIES −812KCAL | PROTEIN −20.5G | CARBOHYDRATES −84.2G | FAT −36.7G

STICKY PORK

INGREDIENTS

- 450g//1lb of pork in thin strips
- 20g//0.70z of corn flour
- 300ml passata
- 30g//1oz of tomato puree
- 30g//1oz of brown sugar
- 150ml apple juice
- 2 chopped onions
- 20ml of olive oil
- 2 garlic cloves
- 40ml of diet cola

METHOD

1. In a small bowl, blend the diet cola with the cornflour to make a paste.
2. Gradually stir in the tomato puree, apple juice, remaining diet cola, sugar, and passata. Mix thoroughly.
3. Preheat the air fryer to 200C//400F and spray with oil.
4. Put the chopped onion into the air fryer and cook for 5 minutes at 200C//400F until brown.
5. Put the pork strips in the air fryer with the onions and cook for another 5 minutes at the same temperature.
6. Finally, pour the sauce into the air fryer and stir so it fully coats the meat. Cook for 10 minutes at 200C//400F until cooked through.
7. Serve with brown rice.

Nutritional Information per Serving:

SERVES –4 | CALORIES –413KCAL | PROTEIN –53.8G | CARBOHYDRATES –26.7G | FAT –8.3G

HONEY AND MUSTARD PORK BALLS

INGREDIENTS

- 500g//1.1lb of minced pork
- 1 red onion, diced thinly
- 1 teaspoon of mustard
- 2 teaspoons of honey
- 1 teaspoon of garlic puree
- 1 teaspoon of pork seasoning
- Salt and pepper to taste
- Optional: a little plain flour

METHOD

1. In a large bowl, mix all the ingredients together until well combined.
2. Use a tablespoon to scoop the mixture out of the bowl to create meatballs. (Add a little flour to help combine the meatballs if needed).
3. Preheat the air fryer to 180C//360F and spray with cooking oil.
4. Put the meatballs in the air fryer in a single layer and cook for 10 minutes at 180C//360F. Turn the meatballs once about halfway through cooking.
5. Serve warm.

Nutritional Information per Serving:

SERVES –4 | CALORIES –357KCAL | PROTEIN –22G | CARBOHYDRATES –7G | FAT –27G

PORK AND GINGER MEATBALLS

INGREDIENTS

For the Noodles:

- 170g//6oz rice noodles
- 120ml Asian–style sesame dressing

- 1 large carrot, julienned (thin strips like long matchsticks)
- 1/2 a cucumber, julienned

- 1 spring onion, thinly sliced
- 60g//2oz of coriander chopped

For the Meatballs:

- 1 egg
- Juice and zest of 2 fresh limes
- 30g//1oz of honey
- 1 teaspoon of fish sauce
- Salt and pepper to taste

- 50g//1.7oz of breadcrumbs
- 1 garlic clove, finely chopped
- 2 spring onions, finely chopped
- 2" piece of ginger, grated

- 1 small jalapeño, seeds removed, finely chopped
- 450g//1lb of minced pork
- 60g//2oz of coriander chopped

METHOD

1. Cook the rice noodles according to the package Method, then rinse, drain and cool.
2. Transfer the noodles to a large bowl and toss with the Asian dressing, carrot, cucumber, and spring onions. Set to one side.
3. In a large bowl, whisk the egg, lime zest and lime juice, honey, fish sauce, salt and pepper until well mixed.
4. Stir in the breadcrumbs and allow to soak for one minute.
5. Next, using your hands to mix, combine the garlic, spring onions, ginger, jalapeño, minced pork and coriander.
6. Preheat the air fryer to 200C//400F and spray with cooking oil.
7. Use a tablespoon to scoop out the mixture and shape into meatballs.
8. Place the meatballs in a single layer in the air fryer and cook at 200C//400°F (in batches, if necessary, depending on the size of your air fryer) for 8 to 12 minutes.
9. Serve the noodles and meatballs topped with chopped coriander.

Nutritional Information per Serving:

SERVES –4 | CALORIES –620KCAL | PROTEIN –26G | CARBOHYDRATES –59G | FAT –31.5G

ONE–POT CURRY AND RICE

INGREDIENTS

- 500g//1lb of pork cut into 1" chunks
- 1 red onion, chopped
- 1 garlic clove, crushed
- 30g//1oz curry powder
- 30g//1oz turmeric
- 1 teaspoon of dried coriander
- 70g//2.5oz of apricot jam
- 60ml of white wine vinegar
- 170g//6oz of basmati rice
- 300ml of vegetable stock

- 255g//9oz of stir–fry vegetables
- Salt and pepper to taste

METHOD

1. Preheat the air fryer to 200C//400F. Spray with oil.
2. Put the onions and the garlic in the air fryer for about 3–5 minutes until the onion browns a little.
3. Stir in the curry, turmeric and coriander and add the meat. Cook for about 8–10 minutes at 200C//400F, stirring about halfway through cooking.
4. Next, stir in the jam, vinegar, and rice to the pot.
5. Add half the stock to the air fryer and cook for about 5 minutes at 200C//400F.
6. Add the rest of the water with the stir fry vegetables and season with salt and pepper.
7. Cook for a further 4–6 minutes until all the liquid is absorbed. Check for seasoning to taste and serve.

Nutritional Information per Serving:

SERVES –5 | CALORIES –375KCAL | PROTEIN –30.9G | CARBOHYDRATES –50.5G | FAT –5.1G

SAUSAGE AND ROSEMARY MEATBALLS

INGREDIENTS

- 30ml of olive oil
- 4 garlic cloves, finely chopped
- 1 teaspoon of curry powder
- 1 egg, beaten
- 1 jar (115g//4oz) of diced pimientos, drained
- 25g//0.8oz of dry breadcrumbs
- 50g//2oz of fresh parsley, finely chopped
- 15g//0.5oz of fresh rosemary, finely chopped
- 900g//2lb of sausage meat
- Optional: pretzel sticks

METHOD

1. Heat the olive oil in a frying pan over medium heat. Saute the garlic with the curry powder for about 1–2 minutes. Allow to cool.
2. Combine the egg, pimientos, breadcrumbs, parsley, rosemary and sauteed garlic in a bowl, then add the sausage meat. Mix thoroughly.
3. Preheat the air fryer to 200C//400F and spray with oil.
4. Use a tablespoon to scoop out the mixture to shaped into meatballs.
5. Put in the air fryer in a single layer and spray with a little more olive oil.
6. Cook for 7–10 minutes at 200C//400F until lightly browned and cooked through.
7. Serve with pretzels.

Nutritional Information per Serving:

SERVES –6 | CALORIES –601KCAL | PROTEIN –31.6G | CARBOHYDRATES –7.5G | FAT –49.1G

MAINS – CHICKEN and TURKEY DISHES

SPICY CHICKEN WINGS

INGREDIENTS

- 1kg//2lbs chicken wings
- Salt and pepper to taste
- Cooking oil spray
- 60ml of your favourite spicy sauce
- 60g//2oz of melted butter
- 1 teaspoon of Worcestershire sauce
- ½ teaspoon of garlic powder

METHOD

1. Pat the chicken wings dry if necessary and season thoroughly with salt and pepper.
2. Preheat the air fryer to 190C//380F.
3. Coat the air fryer pan with the spray cooking oil.
4. Cook the seasoned chicken wings for 12 minutes at 190C//380F.
5. Increase the heat slightly to 200C//400F and cook for a further 5 minutes.
6. In a clean bowl, whisk up your spicy sauce, butter, Worcestershire sauce, and garlic powder.
7. Toss in the chicken wings to coat with the sauce and serve immediately.
8. Spicy chicken wings are great served with cheesy dips, salad, and chips.

Nutritional Information:

SERVES –4 | CALORIES –377KCAL PER SERVING | PROTEIN –25G | CARBOHYDRATES –71G | FAT –12G

CHEESE STUFFED CHICKEN WRAPPED IN BACON

INGREDIENTS

- 6 boneless, skinless chicken thighs, or thin cut chicken breast
- 1 ½ tablespoons of barbecue seasoning
- Salt and pepper to taste
- 4 cubes of cheese about 1 ½ inches
- 12 slices of regular cut bacon (not thick cut)
- Spray cooking oil

METHOD

1. Season the chicken pieces thoroughly with salt, pepper and barbecue seasoning.
2. Put the cheese cubes in the middle of each piece of chicken.
3. Wrap the chicken around the cheese, then wrap each piece again with two slices of bacon each to create 6 neat packages. (If you struggle to wrap the cheese, just trim a little off until it fits).
4. Preheat the air fryer to 200C//400F.
5. Season the chicken pieces again with barbeque seasoning and place carefully in the air fryer.
6. Spray lightly with cooking oil.
7. Cook for 12–14 minutes at 200C//400F.
8. Open the air fryer, turn the chicken pieces, and turn again for a further 12–14 minutes.
9. Delicious served with your favourite dipping sauce.

Nutritional Information per Serving:

SERVES –6 | CALORIES –418KCAL | PROTEIN –25G | CARBOHYDRATES –19G | FAT –25G

SPINACH AND BACON STUFFED TURKEY BREAST

INGREDIENTS

- ◆ Spray cooking oil
- ◆ 2 turkey breasts about 680g//1.5lb each with bone removed
- ◆ salt and pepper to taste

For the Filling:

- ◆ 4 slices of bacon, cut into pieces
- ◆ 115g//4oz sliced mushrooms
- ◆ ½ onion, finely chopped
- ◆ 2 cloves of garlic, finely chopped
- ◆ 480g//17oz of chopped fresh spinach
- ◆ ½ teaspoon of dried thyme
- ◆ ¼ teaspoon dried sage
- ◆ Salt and pepper to taste
- ◆ 30g//1oz of crumbled feta cheese

METHOD

1. First prepare the filling:
2. Heat a pan on the hob and cook the bacon until it's lightly crisped.
3. Add the onion, garlic and mushrooms and cook until the mushrooms shrink.
4. Add the spinach and cook until softened, then stir in the dried herbs, salt and pepper.
5. Remove the pan from the heat and stir in the feta cheese.
6. Set to one side until needed.

Prepare the turkey:

1. Lightly wrap the turkey breasts in cling film, then pound each one to an even thickness of about 1 ½ cms.
2. Position each turkey breast with the skin side down and divide your bacon and spinach filling evenly between each one, in the middle of the breast.
3. Lift an edge of the turkey breast and roll it up, tying it firmly so that it stays in place. Repeat with the second turkey breast.
4. Sprinkle with salt and pepper to taste.
5. Preheat the air fryer to 180C//360F.
6. Coat the air fryer with the spray cooking oil and place the turkey breasts into the basket skin–side down with space between them. (Depending on the size of your air fryer you may need to cook them one at a time. Keep the second one in the fridge until you're ready to cook it if you don't have space for the two).
7. Cook in the air fryer at 180C//360F for 20 minutes.

8. Open the air fryer, turn the turkey breast and cook for another 10–20 minutes.
9. Allow the cooked turkey to rest before serving.

Nutritional Information per Serving:

SERVES –2 | CALORIES –295KCAL | PROTEIN –54G | CARBOHYDRATES –3G | FAT –7G

FRIED LEMON PEPPER TURKEY BREAST

INGREDIENTS

- 1.4kg//3lb boneless turkey breast
- 15ml of oil
- 15ml of Worcestershire sauce
- 1 teaspoon of lemon pepper seasoning
- Salt to taste
- Cooking oil spray

METHOD

1. Combine the oil, Worcestershire sauce, lemon pepper seasoning and salt in a large bowl. This is your turkey marinade.
2. Pat the turkey breast dry with kitchen roll, then place it in the marinade, coat thoroughly in the mixture, then leave to marinate for up to 2 hours.
3. Preheat the air fryer to 180C//350F and lightly spray with cooking oil.
4. Place the turkey breast skin side down in the air fryer basket, spritz with a little more oil and cook for about 25 minutes at 180C//350F.
5. Turn the turkey breast over, spritz with cooking oil and air fry for another 25–35 minutes until cooked through.
6. Serve hot or cold.

Nutritional Information per Serving:

SERVES –6 | CALORIES –400KCAL | PROTEIN –50G | CARBOHYDRATES –1G | FAT –21G

WHOLE ROAST CHICKEN IN BUTTERMILK MARINADE

INGREDIENTS

- 2 teaspoons of sea salt (24 hours before cooking)
- 1.4kg//3lb of trimmed whole chicken
- Salt and pepper to taste
- 475ml//1 pint 1% buttermilk

METHOD

1. 24 hours before cooking, season the chicken with 2 teaspoons of salt and let rest for 30 minutes. Tie the legs together with twine.
2. Put the salted chicken in a mixing bowl and pour over the buttermilk. Cover tightly and place in the fridge overnight. Turn it over after a few hours so both sides are marinated in the buttermilk.
3. The following day, preheat the air fryer to 180C//350F.
4. Remove the chicken from the fridge, discard all the buttermilk and put the chicken in the air fryer with its belly facing down. Season the chicken with salt and pepper.
5. Cook for 25 minutes at 180C//350F.
6. When the top of the chicken is browned, turn it over, season with salt and pepper and cook for a further 25 minutes, until the juices are funning clear and the chicken is crisp and brown all over.
7. Once cooked, remove to a meat plate, and allow to rest for 10 minutes before serving.

BREADED ADOBO CHICKEN CUTLETS WITH SEASONED AVOCADO

INGREDIENTS

For the Adobo Seasoning (can be purchased ready prepared):

- 30g//1oz of sea salt
- 15g//0.5oz of paprika
- 2 teaspoons ground black pepper
- 15g//0.5oz onion powder
- 15g//0.5oz of garlic powder
- 1 ½ teaspoons dried oregano
- 2 teaspoons ground cumin
- 1 teaspoon chilli powder

For the Sazon Seasoning (can be purchased ready prepared):

- 15g//0.5oz of cumin seeds
- 15g//0.5oz of coriander seeds
- 15g//0.5oz of achiote (annatto) seeds (turmeric or saffron make good substitues)
- 15g//0.5oz of garlic powder
- 15g//0.5oz of onion powder
- 30g//1oz of salt
- 1/2 teaspoon freshly ground black pepper

For the Chicken:

- 2 x 230g//8oz boneless chicken breasts
- 1/4 teaspoon seasoned salt (equal parts salt and adobo seasoning)
- 2 egg whites, beaten
- 1/2 teaspoon sazon seasoning
- 50g//1.7oz of breadcrumbs
- Spray cooking oil

For the Seasoned Avocado:

- 115g//4oz of avocado, cut into chunks
- 150g//5oz of cherry tomatoes, cut in half
- 15g//0.5oz of red onion, finely chopped
- 15g//0.05oz fresh coriander leaves
- Salt and pepper to taste
- 1/4 teaspoon of cumin
- Juice of 1/2 lime
- 4 lime wedges for serving

METHOD

1. Make your adobo seasoning. Combine all the ingredients in a bowl and blend together thoroughly. Store in an airtight jar for future use.
2. Make your sazon seasoning. Combine all the ingredients in a bowl and blend together thoroughly. Use a fine mesh sieve to sift the spices over a bowl to remove any husks. Store in an airtight jar for future use.
3. Cut each piece of chicken in half lengthwise so that you have 4 thinner cutlets.
4. Pat dry with kitchen towel and season with the adobo−seasoned salt.
5. Put the breadcrumbs into a bowl and set to one side.
6. In a separate bowl, beat together the egg white and the sazon seasoning.
7. Preheat the air fryer to 200C//400F and lightly spray with cooking oil.
8. First dip the chicken cutlets in the seasoned egg whites, then in the breadcrumbs. Coat thoroughly but shake off any excess.
9. Cook in batches of two for 6−7 minutes at 200C//400F until the crumbs are golden in colour and the centre of the chicken is no longer pink.
10. Prepare the seasoned avocado. Toss all the ingredients in a large bowl together.
11. Serve the chicken with the avocado over the top.
12. Enjoy!

Nutritional Information per Serving:

SERVES −2 (1 SERVING IS 1 PIECE OF CHICKEN) | CALORIES −286 KCAL | PROTEIN −31G | CARBOHYDRATES −12G | FAT −13G

FAVOURITE CHICKEN NUGGETS

INGREDIENTS

- 500g//16oz boneless chicken breast, cut into 1–inch chunks
- Salt and pepper to taste
- 2 teaspoons of olive oil
- 50g//1.7oz of seasoned breadcrumbs
- 15g//0.5oz grated parmesan cheese
- Olive oil cooking spray

METHOD

1. Put two bowls next to other, one containing olive oil, the other containing the breadcrumbs and parmesan.
2. Preheat the air fryer to 200C//400F.
3. Season the chicken pieces with salt and pepper, then add to the bowl of olive oil, turning the chicken so that each piece is coated in oil.
4. Next, coat the chicken pieces thoroughly in the breadcrumbs, and place in the air fryer in batches.
5. Spray each batch of breaded chicken with oil and cook at 200C//400F for about 8 minutes, turning them over about half way.
6. When they are crisp and golden, serve hot with chips or your favourite accompaniment.

Nutritional Information per Serving:

SERVES –4 | CALORIES –188KCAL | PROTEIN –25G | CARBOHYDRATES –8G | FAT –4.5G

CHICKEN CORDON BLEU

INGREDIENTS

- Olive oil cooking spray
- 1kg//2.25lb of skinless, boneless chicken breast, cut into 12 x 85g//3oz pieces
- Salt and pepper to taste
- 1 egg
- 2 egg whites
- 1 tablespoon of water
- 50g//1.7oz of seasoned breadcrumbs
- 30g//1oz of grated parmesan cheese
- 6 thin slices of deli ham
- 130g//4.5oz of Swiss cheese (you'll need 12 slices)

METHOD

1. Wash and pat dry the chicken and lightly pound it to thin it. Season with salt and pepper.
2. You will need two bowls. One will contain the breadcrumbs mixed with the parmesan cheese. The other will contain the eggs and egg whites, whisked, and combined.
3. Lay a piece of chicken on a clean work surface. Place a ham slice on top of the chicken, then a cheese slice on top of the ham.
4. Now roll the chicken up and put it to one side with the roll seam down. Repeat with the remaining chicken, ham, and cheese.
5. Preheat the air fryer to 200C//400F. Spray with cooking oil.
6. Taking care that it doesn't unroll, dip the chicken into the egg wash first and then into the breadcrumbs making sure it is coated thoroughly at each stage.
7. Place the chicken in the air fryer and spritz it with cooking oil.
8. Cook for 6 minutes at 200C//400F. Turn the chicken pieces over and spritz with oil again. Cook for a further 6 minutes.
9. Serve hot as part of a main meal.

Nutritional Information per Serving:

SERVES –6 (2 PIECES PER SERVING) | CALORIES –378KCAL | PROTEIN –55G | CARBOHYDRATES –8G | FAT –10G

QUICK—COOK CHICKEN AND VEGETABLES

INGREDIENTS

- 500g//1lb bone—free chicken cut into bite—size pieces
- 170g//6oz of broccoli florets (fresh or frozen)
- 1 courgette, chopped
- 115g//4oz of chopped mixed peppers
- 1/2 onion chopped
- 2 garlic cloves, finely chopped
- 30ml of olive oil
- 1/2 teaspoon of garlic powder
- 1/2 teaspoon of chilli powder
- 1/2 teaspoon of salt
- 1/2 teaspoon of pepper
- 15g//0.5oz of Italian seasoning (or your favourite spice blend)

METHOD

1. Preheat the air fryer to 200C//400F. Lightly spray with cooking oil.
2. Put the chopped vegetables and chicken pieces in a large bowl together and toss with the olive oil and seasonings to combine.
3. Put the chicken and vegetables into the air fryer, spritz with oil and cook for 10 minutes at 200C//400F. Shake the air fryer half way through cooking.
4. Plate and serve.

Nutritional Information per Serving:

SERVES —4 | CALORIES —230KCAL | PROTEIN —26G | CARBOHYDRATES —8G | FAT —10G

THE EASIEST TURKEY MEATBALLS

INGREDIENTS

- 450g//1lb of minced turkey
- 100g//3.5oz of seasoned breadcrumbs (Italian seasoning or preferred spice blend)
- 45g//1.5oz of grated parmesan cheese
- 1 egg
- Salt and pepper to taste
- Olive oil spray

METHOD

1. Put all the ingredients into a large bowl and mix thoroughly to combine.
2. Preheat the air fryer to 180C//350F and spray lightly with cooking oil.
3. Shape 14 meatballs out of the mixture and place in the air fryer.
4. Cook for 7–8 minutes at 180C//350F.
5. Serve over pasta topped with fresh chopped parsley or grated cheese.

Nutritional Information per Serving:

SERVES —4 | CALORIES —90KCAL | PROTEIN —11G | CARBOHYDRATES —6G | FAT —2G

ORANGE CHICKEN

INGREDIENTS

- 900g//2lb of skinless, boneless chicken breasts, cut into 1» pieces
- Salt and pepper to taste
- 2 eggs, beaten
- 30g//1oz of plain flour
- 60g//2oz of cornflour, plus an extra 14g//0.5oz
- Olive oil cooking spray
- 350ml of orange juice
- 45g//1.5oz packed light brown sugar
- 30ml of soy sauce
- 30ml of rice vinegar
- 2 garlic cloves, finely chopped
- 1/2–inch piece of ginger, grated
- 1/4 teaspoon of crushed red pepper flakes
- 2 teaspoons of toasted sesame oil
- Sliced spring onions and toasted sesame seeds, garnish

METHOD

1. Pat the chicken pieces dry with kitchen roll and season with salt and pepper.
2. Put the beaten eggs in one bowl, and in a separate bowl mix the flour and cornflour together.
3. Preheat the air fryer to 200C//400F and spray with cooking oil.
4. Coat the chicken in the egg, allow the excess to drain back into the bowl, then coat thoroughly in the flour.
5. Arrange the chicken in a single layer in the air fryer. You may need to cook in batches if your air fryer is small.
6. Spray the chicken with cooking oil and cook at 200C//400F for about 10 minutes until golden in colour and cooked through. Remember to turn the chicken halfway through cooking.
7. While the chicken is cooking, put the orange juice, brown sugar, soy sauce, vinegar, and remaining 14g//0.5oz of cornflour into a jug and whisk.
8. Spray a saucepan with a little oil and cook the garlic, ginger, and red pepper flakes for about 2 minutes.
9. Add the liquid for the sauce and bring to a simmer, stirring occasionally until it thickens. This will take about 10 minutes.
10. Add the oil and continue stirring to combine.
11. Transfer the cooked chicken to a plate, pour over the orange sauce, and serve with a spring onion and sesame seed garnish.

Nutritional Information per Serving:

SERVES –4 TO 6 | CALORIES –339KCAL | PROTEIN –34G | CARBOHYDRATES –32G | FAT –7G

TURKEY MEATLOAF

INGREDIENTS

- 2 teaspoons of olive oil
- 1 onion, finely chopped
- 3 garlic cloves, finely chopped
- 1/2 teaspoon of rosemary
- 500g//1lb of turkey mince
- 35g//1.2oz of breadcrumbs
- 5g//0.2oz fresh parsley, chopped
- 1 egg, beaten
- 2 teaspoons of Worcestershire sauce
- 1 teaspoon of Dijon mustard
- Salt and pepper to taste
- Olive oil cooking spray
- 60g//2oz ketchup
- 15g//0.5oz of light brown sugar

METHOD

1. Heat the oil in the pan and fry the onion for about 4 minutes until soft and golden. Add the garlic and rosemary and cook for a further minute.
2. Put the onion into a large bowl and allow to cool slightly before adding the minced turkey, breadcrumbs, parsley, egg, Worcestershire, mustard, salt, and pepper. Mix and combine thoroughly.
3. Preheat the air fryer to 180C//350F and lightly spray with cooking oil.
4. Divide the turkey mixture into two equal loaves, put in the air fryer and cook for 30 minutes at 180C//350F. Turn halfway through cooking.
5. While the meatloaf is cooking combine the ketchup and brown sugar. Turn the turkey meatloaf again and spoon the ketchup/sugar glaze over the top.
6. Cook for a further 2 minutes until the glaze is set.
7. Serve immediately.

Nutritional Information per Serving:

SERVES –2 | CALORIES –527KCAL | PROTEIN –52G | CARBOHYDRATES –36G | FAT –19G

TANDOORI CHICKEN BREAST

INGREDIENTS

- 1 split skin–on, bone–in chicken breast (about 800g//1.75lb)
- 1 ½ teaspoons of salt
- 280g//10oz of plain Greek yoghurt
- 2 garlic cloves, finely chopped
- 15g//0.5oz of sweet paprika
- 2 teaspoons of ground turmeric
- 1" piece of fresh ginger, grated
- 1 teaspoon of ground cumin
- Olive oil cooking spray

METHOD

1. Pat the chicken dry with kitchen roll, then season with 1 teaspoon of the salt (save ½ teaspoon for the marinade.) Set aside.
2. Combine the yoghurt, garlic, paprika, turmeric, ginger, cumin, and remaining 1/2 teaspoon salt together in a bowl.
3. Cover the chicken all over with the chicken mixture. Allow to stand at room temperature for about 30 minutes.
4. Preheat the air fryer to 180C//350F. Spray with cooking oil.
5. Put the marinated chicken in the air fryer and cook at 180C//350F for 35–40 minutes, turning every 10 minutes to ensure its golden brown all over and cooked through.
6. Remove the chicken from the fryer onto a plate and let rest about 10 minutes before slicing.
7. Serve as part of a main meal.

Nutritional Information per Serving:

SERVES –4 | CALORIES –350KCAL | PROTEIN –48G | CARBOHYDRATES –5G | FAT –14G

CHICKEN HIBACHI STYLE IN JAPANESE YUM YUM SAUCE

INGREDIENTS

For the Chicken and Vegetables:

- 2 raw, boneless chicken breasts cut into bite sized pieces (about 450g//16oz in total)
- 1 onion, sliced

- 230g//8oz of mushrooms cut into fourths
- 2 courgettes cut into bite sized pieces
- 1/2 teaspoon of ground ginger

- 1/4 teaspoon of of black pepper
- 15g//0.5oz of garlic powder
- 60ml of soy sauce
- 30ml of olive oil

For the Yum Yum Sauce:

- 240g//8.5oz of mayonnaise
- 60ml of water

- 1 teaspoon of tomato puree/ pesto/ketchup
- 15g//0.5oz of melted butter

- 1/2 teaspoon of garlic powder
- 1 teaspoon of sugar
- 1/4 teaspoon of paprika

METHOD

1. Preheat the air fryer to 200C//400F. Spray with cooking oil.
2. Toss the chicken, vegetables, oil, and seasonings for the chicken recipe into a bowl and give it a good stir.
3. Place the seasoned chicken and vegetables in air fryer and cook at 200C//400F for about 15 minutes.
4. While the chicken is cooking, make the sauce. Add all the sauce ingredients into a bowl and stir well.
5. Serve hot as an accompaniment to a main meal.

Nutritional Information per Serving:

SERVES −4 | CALORIES −587KCAL | PROTEIN −37.5G | CARBOHYDRATES −24.9G | FAT −38.7G

FRIED CHICKEN WITH HONEY, GARLIC, AND VEGETABLES

INGREDIENTS

- 60ml of olive oil
- 70g//2.5oz of honey
- 3 garlic cloves, finely chopped
- 15ml of soy sauce

- Salt and pepper to taste
- 500g//1.1lb of chicken breast
- 4 medium red potatoes, peeled, washed, and diced into 1" cubes

- 350g//12oz of fresh broccoli florets, chopped
- Olive oil cooking spray

METHOD

1. Whisk together 60ml of olive oil with honey, garlic, soy sauce, salt, and pepper.
2. Put the chicken in a separate bowl and pour the marinade over the top. Turn the chicken to coat it well. Cover the bowl and leave to marinate while you prepare the vegetables.
3. Preheat the air fryer to 180C//360F. Spray with cooking oil.
4. Put the chopped potatoes and broccoli in a single layer into the air fryer and spray over the top with cooking oil. Season with salt and pepper.
5. Next, place the chicken over the vegetables and pour any remaining marinade over the top.
6. Cook for 14 minutes at 180C//360F, turning the chicken and stirring the vegetables halfway through cooking.
7. Remove the chicken and continue to cook the vegetables for another 5−8 minutes.
8. Serve.

Nutritional Information per Serving:

SERVES −4 | CALORIES −518KCAL | PROTEIN −30G | CARBOHYDRATES −51G | FAT −23G

ONE–POT BALSAMIC CHICKEN WITH VEGETABLES

INGREDIENTS

For the Marinade:

- 750ml of balsamic vinegar
- 45ml of olive oil
- 30g//1oz of honey
- 1 teaspoon of dried basil
- ½ teaspoon of dried oregano
- Salt and pepper

For the Vegetables:

- 2 courgettes cut into bite sized pieces
- 2 small yellow squash cut into bite sized pieces
- 1 bell pepper, any colour, cut into bite sized pieces
- 1 head of broccoli, chopped into bite sized pieces
- 1 small red onion chopped into bite sized pieces
- 700g//1.5lb chicken cut into bite sized pieces
- 400g//14oz of cherry tomatoes, halved

METHOD

1. Mix all the marinade ingredients together in a large bowl.
2. Put all the ingredients into the bowl of marinade and stir thoroughly.
3. Cover the bowl and leave the ingredients to marinate for up to 2 hours.
4. When ready to cook, preheat the air fryer to 185C//370F and spritz with cooking oil.
5. Cook the first batch for 12 mins at 185C//370F, stirring once during cooking.
6. Turn the temperature up to 200C//400F and cook for a further 5 minutes.
7. Repeat the process with the second batch of chicken and vegetables.
8. Serve with rice or boiled potatoes.

Nutritional Information per Serving:

SERVES –3 TO 4 | CALORIES –208KCAL | PROTEIN –12G | CARBOHYDRATES –15G | FAT –12 G

HAWAIIAN COCONUT CHICKEN

INGREDIENTS

For the Hawaiian Chicken:

- 1.3kg//2.8lb of chicken thighs trimmed and halved
- 200ml of soy sauce
- 230g//8oz of brown sugar
- 60g//2oz spring onions sliced
- 1 garlic clove, finely chopped
- 1 teaspoon of sesame oil
- 1 x 400ml can of coconut milk
- Avocado oil cooking spray (other cooking sprays will work too)

For the Vegetables and Pineapple:

- 1 red pepper, sliced with stalk and seed removed
- 1 courgette, diagonally slice
- ½ pineapple, peeled, with stalk removed, and sliced

For the Coconut Rice:

- 450g//16oz of jasmine rice
- 1 x 400ml can of coconut milk
- 118ml of water
- Salt to taste

METHOD

1. Prepare the chicken and all the vegetables for cooking.
2. Put the chicken in one bowl: and the vegetables in a second clean bowl.
3. Combine the soy sauce, brown sugar, spring onions, garlic, oil, and coconut milk for the marinade. Scoop out a cup (approximately 240ml) to use with the vegetables.
4. Pour the cup of marinade over the vegetables and put to one side.
5. Put the chicken in the other bowl of marinade and put to one side.
6. Cover both bowls and leave in their respective marinades for up to 24 hours.
7. When you are ready to cook, start with the rice. In a saucepan, bring the coconut milk and water to the boil and add the salt and jasmine rice. Simmer for 15 minutes, stirring at the halfway point. Remove from the heat and leave for 5 minutes.
8. In the meantime, preheat the air fryer to 190C//380F and spray with cooking oil.
9. Place half of the chicken in the air fryer and cook for 16 minutes at 190C//380F. Halfway through cooking turn the chicken over and add half of the vegetables.
10. Remove from the air fryer and repeat for the remaining chicken and vegetables.
11. Drain the coconut rice.
12. Serve the chicken and coconut rice immediately and enjoy.

Nutritional Information per Serving:

SERVES −4 | CALORIES −1788KCAL | PROTEIN −73G | CARBOHYDRATES −156G | FAT −99G

SWEET POTATOES STUFFED WITH BBQ CHICKEN

INGREDIENTS

- 2 sweet potatoes, scrubbed clean
- 230g//0.5lb of chicken cut into bite size pieces
- 1 medium bell pepper cut into bite size pieces
- 60g//2oz of red onion cut into bite size pieces
- 85g//3oz of frozen corn kernels
- 30g//1oz of black beans
- 7ml olive oil
- ½ teaspoon of cumin
- ½ teaspoon of brown sugar
- ½ teaspoon of paprika
- ¼ teaspoon chilli powder
- Salt and pepper to taste
- Cooking oil spray

METHOD

1. Preheat the air fryer to 190C//380F. Spray with a little cooking oil.
2. Once your sweet potatoes are scrubbed clean, pierce with a fork 4–5 times, then massage oil into the skins. Sprinkle with salt.
3. Put the potatoes in the air fryer and cook for 20 minutes at 190C//380F.
4. While the potatoes are cooking, combine the chicken, corn, bell pepper, red onion and black beans in a bowl with the oil and seasonings.
5. When the air fryer beeps that the 20 minutes is done, add the chicken and vegetables to the air fryer with the potatoes.
6. Cook for a further 15 minutes at 190C//380F, stirring the vegetables once about halfway through cooking.
7. Check your potatoes are cooked through. If they are big potatoes, they may need a little longer. Adjust the time as required.
8. Once everything is cooked, remove the potatoes from the air fryer, cut them open and top with the chicken and vegetables.
9. Serve with avocado, cherry tomatoes or fresh coriander, and accompanied with BBQ sauce mixed with Greek yoghurt or sour cream.

Nutritional Information per Serving:

SERVES –2 | CALORIES –473KCAL | PROTEIN –20G | CARBOHYDRATES –72G | FAT –13G

ONE–POT KUNG PAO CHICKEN

INGREDIENTS

- 15ml of vegetable oil
- 10 dried chilli pods
- 4 garlic cloves, finely chopped

- 2 large spring onions, thinly sliced
- 30g//1oz of dry roasted peanuts

For the Chicken:

- 450g//1lb of chicken thighs, skin and bone removed, cut in 1–inch pieces

- 1 teaspoon of garlic powder
- 1 teaspoon of onion powder
- 1/2 teaspoon of salt

- 15g//0.5oz of cornflour
- 1 large red bell pepper, diced
- 1 medium courgette, diced

For the Sauce:

- 60ml of soy sauce
- 30g//1oz of granulated sugar

- 20ml of chicken stock
- 15ml of rice vinegar

- 2 teaspoons of oyster sauce

METHOD

1. In a large bowl, toss the chicken with the garlic powder, onion powder, and salt. Add the cornflour and mix with your hands until the pieces are coated. Set to one side.
2. Preheat the air fryer to 180C//350F. Spray with a little cooking oil.
3. Put the pepper and courgette in the air fryer and spray with a little cooking oil so they are coated.
4. Cook the pepper and courgette for 10–15 minutes at 180C//350F, shaking the basket every few minutes until the vegetables are tender, crisp, and starting to char. Remove from the air fryer and set to one side.
5. Increase the temperature in the air fryer to 200C//400F and spray again with a little cooking oil.
6. Add the chicken in an even layer, spray with oil to prevent it drying out, and cook for 9 minutes. Shake the basket every couple of minutes. If you have a meat thermometer, the internal temperature of the chicken will be 165F when it's cooked.
7. In a separate small bowl, whisk the soy sauce, sugar, stock, vinegar, and oyster sauce until well combined and set aside.
8. Finally, in a large pan over a high heat, add the oil, then toss in the chilli pods, garlic and spring onions. Cook for about 30 seconds stirring constantly.
9. Now it's time to add the sauce you made earlier to the pan and let it simmer for 15 seconds on a medium heat.
10. Add the cooked peppers, courgette and chicken and toss to coat in the sauce. Continue cooking until all the food is coated and the sauce has reduced. Throw in the peanuts and stir in.
11. Serve immediately with thinly sliced spring onions as a garnish.

Nutritional Information per Serving:

SERVES –4 | CALORIES –423KCAL | PROTEIN –24G | CARBOHYDRATES –22G | FAT –27G

CHICKEN POPPERS

INGREDIENTS

- 15ml of olive oil
- 200g//7oz of breadcrumbs
- 1 teaspoon salt
- 500g//1.1lb of boneless, skinless chicken breasts cut into 1–inch pieces
- 15g//0.50zg plain flour
- 1 egg, beaten with 1 teaspoon of water
- 2 teaspoons of garlic powder
- 2 teaspoons of onion powder
- 1 teaspoon of dried oregano
- Optional: a pinch of cayenne pepper
- Freshly ground black pepper to taste
- Olive oil cooking spray

METHOD

1. Lightly spray a pan with cooking oil, add the breadcrumbs and ½ teaspoon of the salt and fry for about 4 minutes until golden. Stir regularly while cooking. Transfer the toasted breadcrumbs to a plate and set to one side.
2. Pat the chicken pieces dry with kitchen towel and place in a bowl. Season with pepper and ¼ teaspoon of the salt.
3. You will need three shallow bowls.
4. Put the flour mixed with ¼ teaspoon salt in one bowl.
5. Place the beaten egg and water in the second bowl.
6. Take the bowl of breadcrumbs and add the garlic powder, onion powder, oregano, (optional cayenne pepper) and black pepper. Place near the egg bowl.
7. Preheat the air fryer to 200C//400F and spray with cooking oil.
8. Cook in 4 batches of approximately 15–30 pieces of chicken, depending on the size of your air fryer. Take the first batch and put in the bowl of flour, coating all over thoroughly.
9. Next, dip the coated chicken in the egg (allow any excess to fall off).
10. Finally press the chicken pieces firmly into the breadcrumbs, coating evenly all over. Repeat the process with all the remaining pieces and throw away any unused breadcrumbs.
11. Add your first batch of breadcrumbed chicken pieces to the air fryer, leaving space between the pieces so they crisp up nicely.
12. Cook for 5 minutes at 200C//400F and shake the basket about halfway through.
13. Serve immediately.

Nutritional Information per Serving:

SERVES –5 PEOPLE WITH 3 PIECES | CALORIES –283KCAL | PROTEIN –30G | CARBOHYDRATES –21G | FAT –8G

CHICKEN PERI PERI

INGREDIENTS

For the Sauce:

- 450g//1lb of red chillies, diced
- 8 garlic cloves, diced
- 1 teaspoon of smoked paprika
- 100g//3.50z of fresh coriander
- 5g//0.20z of fresh basil
- 120ml of olive oil
- 45ml of lemon juice
- Salt to taste
- Optional: choose a shop–bought, ready–made peri peri sauce mix

For the Chicken:

- 900g//2lb chicken (preferably drumsticks, thighs, or wings)
- 30ml of olive oil
- 1 teaspoon of sea salt
- 1 teaspoon of cracked pepper

METHOD

1. Put all the sauce ingredients into a blender and blend until smooth and liquid.
2. Put the chicken in a bowl and pour half of the sauce over the top. Toss the chicken to coat it thoroughly in the sauce.
3. Sprinkle with a little more salt and pepper to taste and leave to marinate in the fridge for up to 4 hours.
4. Preheat the air fryer at to 200C//400F. Spray lightly with cooking oil.
5. Put the chicken in the air fryer and cook for 10 minutes at 200C//400F. Discard the sauce it was marinating in.
6. Turn the chicken, baste it with the juices/sauce and leave to cook for another 10 minutes at 200C//400F.
7. If the chicken needs a little more time, baste again and cook for 5 more minutes.
8. Once cooked, remove to a plate, and allow to rest for 10 minutes before serving.
9. Serve with the remaining sauce and enjoy.

Nutritional Information per Serving:

SERVES –4 | CALORIES –593KCAL | PROTEIN –55G | CARBOHYDRATES –5G | FAT –0G

TANDOORI CHICKEN KEBABS

INGREDIENTS

- 500g//1.1lb of chicken breast diced into chunks
- 60g//2oz of Greek yoghurt, 4%
- 2 teaspoons of garlic puree
- 2 teaspoons of ginger puree
- 2 teaspoons of turmeric
- 1 teaspoon of garam masala
- 1 teaspoon of dried coriander
- 2 teaspoons of paprika
- ½ teaspoon of cayenne pepper
- Salt and pepper to taste

METHOD

1. Add all the ingredients to a large bowl and mix well.
2. Cover the bowl and leave to marinate in the fridge overnight.
3. When ready, preheat the air fryer to 190C//375F and spray lightly with cooking oil.
4. Skewer the marinated chicken chunks into kebabs and place in the air fryer.
5. Cook at 190C//375F for 15 minutes. Turn the chicken skewers over and cook for a further 15 minutes at the same temperature.
6. Serve with Greek salad and goats' cheese.

Nutritional Information per Serving:

SERVES –4 | CALORIES –167KCAL | PROTEIN –28G | CARBOHYDRATES –3G | FAT –4G

LEMON PEPPER CHICKEN

INGREDIENTS

- 3 large chicken breasts
- Juice and rind of 1 large lemon
- 1 additional medium lemon
- 1 teaspoon of garlic powder
- Salt and pepper to taste

METHOD

1. Pre heat the air fryer to 180C//360F and spray with a little cooking oil.
2. Lay the chicken breasts out flat on a clean surface.
3. Smother the chicken breasts all over in lemon juice and rind from your large lemon. Season with the sea salt, ground black pepper and garlic powder.
4. Put the chicken breasts into your air fryer. Cut the medium lemon into slices and place on top and around the chicken.
5. Cook for 15 minutes at 180C//360F.
6. Check the chicken breast and if it needs a little longer, cook for a further 3–5 minutes.
7. Slice and serve.

Nutritional Information per Serving:

SERVES –3 | CALORIES –276KCAL | PROTEIN –49 G | CARBOHYDRATES –5G | FAT –6G

ONE–POT MOROCCAN CHICKEN WITH VEGETABLES

INGREDIENTS

For the Chicken and Vegetables:

- 900g//2lb of boneless chicken thighs
- 230g//8oz of red bell peppers, seeds removed and cut into large slices
- 85g//3oz small onions, peeled and halved
- 7g//0.2oz of paprika powder
- 1 teaspoons of ground cumin
- Salt and pepper to taste
- 1 teaspoon of ground coriander
- 1 teaspoon of ground cinnamon
- 1 teaspoon of ground turmeric
- 1" piece of fresh ginger, grated
- Optional: ¼ teaspoon cayenne pepper
- 15ml of olive oil

For the Tzatziki:

- 85g//3oz grated cucumber
- 2g//0.07oz fresh mint, finely chopped or ground black pepper, to taste
- 2 garlic cloves, finely chopped
- 280g//10oz of Greek yoghurt, 4%
- Salt and pepper to taste

METHOD

1. Preheat the air fryer to 190C//380F. Spray with a little cooking oil.
2. Put the paprika, cumin, salt, coriander, cinnamon, turmeric, ginger, cayenne, and olive oil into a large bowl.
3. Add the chicken and vegetables and combine. Cover and allow to marinate in the fridge for up to 4 hours.
4. Once marinated, place the chicken and vegetables into the air fryer and cook for 15–20 minutes at 190C//380F turning halfway.
5. Meanwhile make up the tzatziki. Put the grated cucumber in a strainer with the salt and mix well. Let the liquid drain, then wrap the cucumber in a tea towel and squeeze out any remaining fluid.
6. Add the drained cucumber to a bowl with the garlic, oil, fresh mint, salt and black pepper.
7. Stir in the yoghurt, mix well and leave in the fridge for about 10 minutes before serving.
8. Serve the chicken and vegetables with a side of tzatziki.

Nutritional Information per Serving:

SERVES –4 | CALORIES –631KCAL | PROTEIN –49G | CARBOHYDRATES –8.8G | FAT –43.4G

CHICKEN TAGINE

INGREDIENTS

For the Spice Mix:

- 50g//1.7oz of sweet paprika
- 1 teaspoon of garlic powder
- 2 teaspoons of cinnamon
- 45g//1.5oz of ground coriander
- 15g//0.5oz plus 1 extra teaspoon of ground turmeric
- 15g//0.5oz ginger powder
- 8g//0.3oz of ground cardamom
- 2 ½ teaspoons ground allspice

For the Tagine:

- 8 chicken thighs, approximately 3lb in total weight
- Salt and pepper to taste
- 30g//1oz of spice mix (see Method 1* instructions)
- 80ml of olive oil
- 3 tomatoes, cored with an x cut into the bottom
- 1 head cauliflower, cut into bite-size florets
- 1 large onion, diced
- 3 garlic cloves, chopped
- 2" piece of freshly grated ginger
- 1 pinch saffron
- 15g//0.5oz of tomato paste
- 500ml of chicken stock
- 45g//1.5oz of preserved lemons (approximately 2 lemons, roughly chopped)
- 170g//6oz of green olives
- 50g//1.8oz of fresh coriander, leaves only

METHOD

1. *Sauté the spice mix ingredients for 2 minutes in a dry pan over a low heat. Transfer the toasted spices to a bowl to cool.
2. In a small bowl, combine 28.17g//1oz of the toasted spices with 30ml of olive oil and salt and pepper to taste.
3. Lay the chicken on a clean surface and rub the olive oil and spice mix all over. Set to one side.
4. Next, have a large bowl of boiling, salted water on the hob next to a large bowl of cold water.
5. First, boil the cauliflower for 3 minutes, then submerge in the cold water. Pat dry.
6. Next, boil the tomatoes for 20 seconds, and chill in the cold water too. Peel the skin off the tomatoes and cut them into quarters.
7. Finally, heat the remaining olive oil in a pan, and sear the spiced chicken thighs all over until browned. Place in a casserole dish that will fit in your air fryer.
8. Remove most of the excess fat from the pan, leaving about a tablespoon to sear the cauliflower in the same pan until brown. Add the cauliflower to the chicken.
9. Cook the onion, garlic, ginger and saffron to the same pan for about 5 minutes, add the tomato paste and chicken stock and simmer until reduced by 1/3.
10. Preheat the air fryer to 150C//300F.
11. Pour the gravy from the pan into the casserole dish over the chicken and cauliflower, cover the pot. Place in the air fryer and cook for 15–20 minutes at 150C//350F.
12. Stir in the tomatoes, preserved lemon and olives, return to the air fryer, and cook for another 15–20 minutes until the chicken is cooked through.
13. Serve with couscous, garnished with the coriander leaves.
14. Preserve any remaining spices in an airtight container for future use.

Nutritional Information per Serving:

SERVES –4 | CALORIES –1036KCAL | PROTEIN –59G | CARBOHYDRATES –35G | FAT –76G

CHINESE CASHEW CHICKEN

INGREDIENTS

- 450g//1lb boneless and skinless chicken thigh or breast (about 500g) cut into bite–size pieces

For the Marinade:

- 60ml of hoisin sauce
- 60ml of soy sauce

- 15ml of white vinegar
- 3g//0.10z of sugar

- 2" piece of ginger, grated
- 4g//0.10z of cornflour

Additional:

- 1 teaspoon olive oil
- 4 garlic cloves, finely chopped
- 30g//1oz of cooked, diced carrots

- 15g//0.5oz spring onions, sliced thinly

- 60g//2oz of roasted cashew halves

METHOD

1. Mix all the marinade ingredients together in a bowl.
2. Remove about 1/3 sauce to a jug for use later and add the chicken to the bowl with the remainder. Cover the bowl and marinate the chicken in the fridge for about an hour.
3. Preheat the air fryer to 190C//380F and line with greased foil.
4. Spread the chicken pieces out in the air fryer and cook for 10–12 minutes at 190C//380F until cooked through.
5. Spread the chicken out in the fryer basket and air fry at 380F (190C) for 10–12 minutes until the cooked through.
6. While the chicken is cooking, sauté the garlic in a frying pan with a little oil for about 1 minute. Add the marinade that you saved in a jug to the garlic and cook, stirring constantly, until the sauce thickens.
7. When the chicken is finished in the air fryer, toss into the pan with the carrots and cashew nuts until thoroughly coated with the sauce, and serve immediately, sprinkled with sliced spring onions.

Nutritional Information per Serving:

SERVES –4 | CALORIES –271KCAL | PROTEIN –29G | CARBOHYDRATES –18G | FAT –9G

CHICKEN PASTA IN CHIMICHURRI SAUCE

INGREDIENTS

- 4 chicken thighs, skin and bones removed
- 60g//2oz of bacon bits
- 30g//1oz of butter

- 8g//0.3oz of plain flour
- 160ml of milk
- 500g//1.1lb of cooked spaghetti

For the Chimichurri Sauce:

- 350g//12.5oz of chopped coriander
- 30g//1oz of spring onions, thinly sliced
- 4–6 garlic cloves, thinly sliced
- Zest and juice of 2 fresh limes

- 120ml of olive oil
- 30g//1oz of pickled jalapenos, chopped
- Salt and pepper to taste

METHOD

1. Put all the chimichurri sauce ingredients into a food processor and blend until smooth. Pour out about ¾ of the sauce into a jug and set to one side.
2. Put the remaining ¼ of the sauce into a bowl and add the chicken. Cover the bowl and place in the fridge to marinate for up to 4 hours.
3. Take the chicken out of the refrigerator 30 minutes before air frying.
4. Preheat the air fryer to 190C//380F and line with greased foil.
5. Put the chicken inside the air fryer in a single layer and cook for 10–12 minutes at 190C//380F.
6. While waiting for the chicken to cook, heat the butter and gradually add the flour, stirring continuously over a low heat until the sauce bubbles and thickens. Gradually add the milk and the jug of saved chimichurri sauce. Stir until it thickens.
7. Toss the chicken into the sauce and serve over the spaghetti, sprinkled with chopped bacon.

Nutritional Information per Serving:

SERVES –4 | CALORIES –760KCAL | PROTEIN –41G | CARBOHYDRATES –49G | FAT –45G

ROAST CURRIED CHICKEN

INGREDIENTS

For the Chicken:

* 5 chicken thighs with skin and bone

For the Marinade:

* 60g//2oz of mayonnaise
* 15g//0.5oz of brown sugar
* 2 garlic cloves, finely chopped
* 30ml of soy sauce
* 2" piece of ginger, grated
* 1 teaspoon of curry powder
* 1/4 teaspoon of paprika
* 1/4 teaspoon of cumin

Additional Dry Seasoning Mix:

* 1/2 teaspoon of curry powder
* 1/4 teaspoon of cumin
* 1/4 teaspoon of paprika
* 30g//1oz of spring onion

METHOD

1. Mix all the ingredients for the marinade in a bowl together. Add the chicken and coat thoroughly with the mixture. Cover the bowl and marinate in the fridge for up to 12 hours.
2. In a separate small container, mix the 1/2 teaspoon of curry, 1/4 teaspoon of cumin and 1/4 teaspoon of paprika. Set aside for later.
3. Remove the chicken from the fridge 30 minutes before cooking.
4. Preheat the air fryer to 190C//380F and line with greased foil.
5. Place the chicken thighs in a single layer into the air fryer, skin side down. Cook for 10 minutes at 190C//380F.
6. Turn the chicken over and sprinkle some of the additional dry seasoning mix over the skin.
7. Cook for another 6–7 minutes at 190C//360F until the meat is cooked through.
8. Serve sprinkled with sliced spring onions.

Nutritional Information per Serving:

SERVES –5 | CALORIES –101KCAL | PROTEIN –1G | CARBOHYDRATES –5G | FAT –9G

THAI CHICKEN DRUMSTICKS

INGREDIENTS

- 10g//0.40z of chopped coriander
- Extra Thai sweet chilli sauce

For the Chicken:

- 8 chicken drumsticks

For the Marinade:

- 4–6 garlic cloves, finely chopped
- 45ml of fish sauce
- 30ml of rice wine
- 1 teaspoon sesame oil
- Black pepper to taste
- Optional: 1/2 teaspoon Sriracha hot sauce
- 60g//20z of brown sugar
- Juice of one lime

METHOD

1. Blend all the marinade ingredients into a smooth sauce, either with a hand blender or a food processor.
2. Place the chicken into a large bowl and pour the marinade over the top, turning the chicken drumsticks to ensure they are thoroughly coated in the sauce. Cover the bowl and allow to marinate in the fridge for a least 3–4 hours.
3. Take the chicken out of the fridge 30 minutes before cooking.
4. Preheat the air fryer to 180C//360F and line with lightly grease foil.
5. Put the chicken into the air fryer and cook at 180C//360F for 18–20 minutes, until the chicken is cooked through.
6. Serve immediately with a drizzle of Thai sweet chilli sauce and garnished with chopped coriander.

Nutritional Information per Serving:

SERVES –4 | CALORIES –324KCAL | PROTEIN –28G | CARBOHYDRATES –16G | FAT –15G

YAKITORI CHICKEN

INGREDIENTS

- 500g//1.1lb of chicken thighs without skin or bones, cut into bite sized chunks.
- 60ml of dark soy sauce
- 60ml of Japanese mirin sauce
- 30ml of rice wine
- 30g//10z of brown sugar
- 3–4 garlic cloves, finely chopped
- 2" piece of fresh ginger, grated
- Spring onions, thinly sliced, for garnish

METHOD

1. Blend the dark soy sauce, mirin, rice wine, brown sugar, garlic, and ginger together in a bowl. Remove about 1/3 of the sauce and put aside in a jug for use later.
2. Toss the chicken thigh cubes into the bowl of sauce and mix to coat the chicken thoroughly. Cover the bowl and marinate in the fridge for a least an hour.
3. Preheat the air fryer to 190C//380F and line with lightly greased foil.
4. Skewer the chicken pieces and place in the fryer. Spray a little cooking oil over the chicken so it doesn't dry out during cooking.
5. Cook at 190C//380F for 10–12 minutes until cooked through. Turn one during cooking and spritz again with oil.
6. While the chicken is cooking, pour the saved jug of sauce into a pan and bring to the boil. Simmer, stirring continuously until it thickens. Place in a small bowl as a dipping sauce.
7. Serve the yakitori chicken skewers with the dipping sauce on the side, sprinkled with spring onions.

Nutritional Information per Serving:

SERVES –4 | CALORIES –258KCAL | PROTEIN –22G | CARBOHYDRATES –28G | FAT –5G

THAI CHICKEN WITH BASIL

INGREDIENTS

- 50g//1.8oz of chopped yellow onions
- 10g//0.4oz of Thai basil leaves
- Optional: 1 fresh jalapeno, thinly sliced
- 60ml of chicken stock

For the Chicken:

- 230g//8oz chicken thighs, skin and bone removed, thinly sliced

For the Marinade:

- 6 garlic cloves, finely chopped
- 20ml of fish sauce
- 10ml of olive oil
- 1 teaspoon of sugar
- 1 teaspoon of cornflour
- 10ml of dark soy sauce
- 1/2 teaspoon light soy sauce
- 7ml of oyster sauce
- 1/4 teaspoon of white pepper powder

METHOD

1. Using a hand blender or food processor, mix all the marinade ingredients together into a smooth sauce.
2. Place the chicken slices into a bowl and pour the sauce over the top. Mix to ensure the chicken is thoroughly coated with the sauce.
3. Cover the bowl and marinate in the fridge for a minimum of 1 hour.
4. Preheat the air fryer to 160C//320F and line with greased foil.
5. Put the chopped onion in the air fryer and cook for 3–4 minutes at 160C//320F.
6. Add the marinated chicken to the air fryer over the onion and turn the temperature up to 190C//380F. Cook for 10–12 minutes until the meat is cooked through. Give the food a stir a couple of times during cooking.
7. Stir the basil leaves, jalapeno, and chicken broth into the air fryer and cook for a further 2 minutes at 190C//380F.
8. Serve hot with rice.

Nutritional Information per Serving:

SERVES –2 | CALORIES –132KCAL | PROTEIN –13G | CARBOHYDRATES –10G | FAT –4G

CHICKEN WITH MUSHROOM
• •

INGREDIENTS

- 115g//4oz of button mushrooms
- 3 garlic cloves, finely chopped

For the Chicken:

- 500g//1.1lb of chicken thigh without skin or bone, cut into thin slices

For the Sauce:

- 45ml of oyster sauce
- 15ml of rice wine
- 15ml of soy sauce

- 1 spring onion, chopped into 1" pieces

- 15ml of soy sauce
- 15ml of rice wine

- 30ml of chicken stock
- 1" piece of fresh ginger, grated
- 1 teaspoon of sugar

- 1 teaspoon of sesame oil

- 1/4 teaspoon of black pepper
- 1 teaspoon of cornflour

METHOD

1. Put the chicken in a bowl.
2. Mix the soy sauce and rice wine and pour over the chicken slices. Marinade for at least 30 minutes.
3. In a saucepan over a low heat, combine all the ingredients for the sauce and cook slowly until the sauce thickens.
4. Preheat the air fryer to 190C//380F and spray with cooking oil.
5. Put the garlic in the bottom of the air fryer pan with the marinated chicken on top. Discard the marinade that's left over.
6. Cook the chicken for 10 minutes at 190C//380F, stirring once about halfway through.
7. Stir in the cooked sauce and chopped mushrooms. Cook for a further 4–5 minutes at the same temperature the chicken is cooked through.
8. When cooked, stir in the sesame oil, serve hot with rice and top with chopped spring onions.

Nutritional Information per Serving:

SERVES –5 | CALORIES –57KCAL | PROTEIN –2G | CARBOHYDRATES –8G | FAT –1G

TAIWANESE THREE CUP CHICKEN
• •

INGREDIENTS

- 2 teaspoon olive oil
- 5 cloves of garlic
- 6–7 slices of ginger
- Optional: red chilli pepper

For the Chicken:

- 500g//1.1lb of boneless skinless thighs cut into one inch pieces
- 30ml of sesame oil

- 1 teaspoon sesame oil
- 1 bunch of basil
- 2 spring onions cut into one– inch pieces

- 60g//2oz of soy paste
- 45ml of rice wine
- 30ml of mirin

- 2" piece of ginger, grated

METHOD

1. Mix all the seasonings in the chicken ingredients and marinate the chicken with half of the marinade for about 30 minutes.
2. Put the garlic cloves and ginger slices into the cake pan and drizzle them with 2 teaspoons of olive oil. Air fry at 400F (200C) for about 2–3 minutes.
3. Add in the chicken along with its marinade and air fry at 380F (190C) for 10 minutes, stir two times in between. Add the rest of the marinade, 3/4 of the green onion, 3/4 of the basil, and chilli pepper (optional) and stir. Air fry at 380F (190C) for 6–7 minutes stirring once in between until the chicken is cooked through.
4. When done, mix the rest of the basil and green onion and drizzle 1 teaspoon of sesame oil to serve.

Nutritional Information per Serving:

SERVES –4 | CALORIES –291KCAL | PROTEIN –24G | CARBOHYDRATES –12G | FAT –15G

CHICKEN WITH MISO MARINADE

INGREDIENTS

- 3 boneless chicken thighs
- 45g//1.5oz of miso paste
- 15ml of soy sauce
- 15ml of mirin
- 15ml of rice wine
- Optional: if you don't have mirin, then use 30ml of the rice wine, and vice versa

METHOD

1. Mix the miso, soy sauce, mirin, and rice wine together in a bowl until blended. Add the chicken to the bowl and coat it thoroughly in the marinade.
2. Cover the bowl and leave the chicken to marinate in the sauce in the fridge for at least 3 hours or overnight.
3. Remove the chicken from the fridge at least 30 minutes before cooking.
4. Preheat the air fryer to 190C//380F and line with greased foil. Place the chicken thighs skin side down into the fryer basket. Make sure you discard any remaining marinade. Do not use for basting.
5. Cook for 12 minutes at 190C//380F. Turn it over then cook for a further 6–7 minutes at 190C//380F until it's cooked through.
6. Serve with rice.

Nutritional Information per Serving:

SERVES –3 | CALORIES –225KCAL | PROTEIN –16G | CARBOHYDRATES –6G | FAT –15G

SHREDDED CHICKEN

INGREDIENTS

- 1 whole free–range chicken
- 15ml of olive oil
- 45g//1.5oz of shop–bought Italian seasoning (or make your own)
- Salt and pepper to taste

For the Italian Seasoning:

- 45g//1.5oz of dried basil
- 45g//1.5oz of dried oregano
- 45g//1.5oz of dried parsley flakes
- 15g//0.5oz of garlic powder
- 1 teaspoon of dried thyme
- 1 teaspoon of dried, crushed rosemary
- ¼ teaspoon of pepper
- ¼ teaspoon of crushed red pepper flakes

METHOD

1. Combine all ingredients for the Italian seasoning in a bowl, and grind/crush to a powder. Store any unused seasoning in an airtight container for future use.
2. Preheat the air fryer to 180C//360F and spray with oil.
3. Prepare the chicken and place breast side down in the air fryer.
4. Rub half of the olive oil onto the skin and season with salt, pepper, and Italian seasoning.
5. Cook at 180C//360F for about 25 minutes. Turn the chicken over so that it is breast side up, oil and season again and cook for a further 20 minutes at 180C//360F.
6. Remove to safe surface, cover and allow to cool.
7. Use clean hands to shred the chicken from the carcass, taking care to ensure any small bones are removed.
8. Use for sandwiches and rolls or add to recipes. The prepared chicken can be stored in the fridge if being used quickly, or freezer for use at your convenience.

Nutritional Information per Serving:

SERVES −4 TO 6 | CALORIES −444KCAL | PROTEIN −36G | CARBOHYDRATES −1G | FAT −32G

MARINADED FILIPINO BARBECUE CHICKEN

INGREDIENTS

- 1.4kg//3lb of chicken, butterflied to an even thickness
- 120ml of soy sauce
- 60ml of lemon juice
- 115g//4oz of brown sugar
- 1 head of garlic, peeled and finely chopped
- 1 teaspoon of salt
- 1 teaspoon of pepper
- Spray cooking oil

METHOD

1. Combine the soy sauce, lemon juice, brown sugar, garlic, salt and pepper in a bowl and mix thoroughly to make the marinade. Remove about 1/3 of the marinade and set aside to use later.
2. Add the chicken to the bowl and rub all over with the marinade to ensure it's thoroughly coated. Cover the bowl and leave the chicken to marinate for at least 4 hours in the fridge.
3. Remove from the fridge at least 30 hours before cooking.
4. Preheat the air fryer to 180C//360F and line with lightly greased foil.
5. Drain the chicken and discard any marinade. Place the chicken in the air fryer and spray with cooking oil so it doesn't dry out while cooking.
6. Place the saved marinade in a small pan and bring to the boil. Simmer gently for a few minutes.
7. Cook for about 15 minutes on 180C//360F. Turn the chicken, spray with a little more oil and cook for another 15−20 minutes until cooked through.
8. Remove to a platter, pour over the remaining marinade/sauce and allow to rest for 10 minutes before serving.

Nutritional Information per Serving:

SERVES −4 TO 6 | CALORIES −409KCAL | PROTEIN −23G | CARBOHYDRATES −21G | FAT −25G

CHICKEN AND POTATOES SEASONED WITH ROSEMARY AND LEMON

INGREDIENTS

- 1 whole chicken
- 2 large potatoes, peeled, washed, and cut for roast potatoes
- 1 small lemon
- 2 teaspoons of olive oil
- 7g//0.3oz of dried rosemary
- Salt and pepper to taste

METHOD

1. Slice the lemon into 3 pieces cut as a small piece from the end and then in half.
2. Prepare the chicken and place the 2 large pieces of lemon inside it.
3. Working with the chicken breast side up, rub 1 teaspoon of olive oil all over the skin, then season with salt, pepper, and rosemary.
4. Preheat the air fryer to 180C//360F and spray with cooking oil.
5. Place the chicken breast side down in the air fryer and oil and season the other side in the same way.
6. Cook the chicken at 180C//360F for about 25 minutes.
7. Season the chopped potatoes with salt, pepper, olive oil and rosemary. Squeeze the little lemon piece over the potatoes and mix, so that the potatoes are well coated with all the seasonings.
8. When the air fryer beeps after 25 minutes, turn the chicken over and add the potatoes wherever you can in the spaces. Spritz with a little more cooking oil.
9. Cook at 180C//360F for another 25 minutes.
10. Serve.

Nutritional Information per Serving:

SERVES –4 TO 6 | CALORIES –1162KCAL | PROTEIN –137GG | CARBOHYDRATES –62G | FAT –39G

CHICKEN SOUVLAKI

INGREDIENTS

- 1 chicken breast cut into 1" bites
- Juice and rind of 1 small lemon
- 3 garlic cloves, peeled and finely chopped
- 1 teaspoon of coconut oil
- 1 teaspoon of Greek yoghurt
- 3g//0.1oz of dried oregano
- A pinch of dried thyme
- Salt and pepper to taste

METHOD

1. Put the garlic, seasonings, and lemon into a mixing bowl. Add the chicken pieces and mix well with your hands.
2. Cover the bowl or transfer to a container and allow to rest in the seasonings in the fridge overnight.
3. Remove the chicken at least 30 minutes before cooking.
4. Toss the seasoned chicken in the coconut oil and Greek yoghurt.
5. Preheat the air fryer to 180C//350F and lightly spray with cooking oil.
6. Push the chicken onto skewers, place in the air fryer in a single layer so they are not touching and cook at 180C//350F for about 9 minutes.
7. Optional: you can push chunks of lemon onto the skewers with the chicken to give a lemonier flavour.
8. Turn the chicken with tongs at about halfway to ensure it cooks thoroughly all over.
9. Serve with fresh oregano.

Nutritional Information per Serving:

SERVES –4 TO 6 | CALORIES –79KCAL | PROTEIN –7G | CARBOHYDRATES –8G | FAT –3G

WARM CHICKEN COBB SALAD

INGREDIENTS

- 85g//3oz of cooked chicken strips
- 1 hardboiled egg, cut into large pieces
- 10 cherry tomatoes, cut in half
- 3 spring onions, finely sliced
- 70g//2.5oz of cucumbers, sliced
- 150g//5oz of shredded lettuce
- Optional: 30g//1oz of cheese, cut into cubes
- Ranch dressing or catalina dressing

METHOD

1. Preheat the air fryer to 180C//350F and spray with a little cooking oil.
2. Put the chicken strips in the air fryer and cook for 12 minutes at 180C//350F.
3. While the chicken is cooking, combine all the salad ingredients in a bowl and place on a place.
4. Put the cooked chicken strips on the top and serve with your choice of dressing.

Nutritional Information per Serving:

SERVES –2 | CALORIES –536KCAL | PROTEIN –29G | CARBOHYDRATES –28G | FAT –36G

THAI CHICKEN CURRY

INGREDIENTS

- 500g/1.1lb of chicken breast, diced into 1–inch chunks
- 1 red pepper, deseeded and cut into thin strips
- 1 green pepper, deseeded and cut into thin strips
- 1 courgette, cut into thin slices
- 1 garlic clove, finely chopped
- 1 red chilli, finely chopped
- 100ml of coconut milk
- 100ml of water
- 20ml of olive oil
- 1" piece of fresh ginger grated
- 15g//0.5oz of cornflour
- 9g//0.3oz of green curry paste
- Optional: 10ml of fish sauce
- 20g//0.7oz of coriander
- Salt and pepper

METHOD

1. In a pan, combine the coconut milk, water, curry paste and cornflour over a gentle heat stirring continuously until the sauce thickens.
2. Preheat air fryer to 200C//400F and spray with oil.
3. Put the garlic, chilli, ginger and coriander at the bottom of the pan.
4. Pour the prepared sauce into the pan, and layer the chicken, courgettes and peppers over the top.
5. Spray with olive oil and cook for 25 minutes on 200C//400F.
6. Check about halfway through and give a gentle stir/shake.
7. When the chicken is cooked through, serve with your choice of sides, and enjoy!

Nutritional Information per Serving:

SERVES –4 | CALORIES –253KCAL | PROTEIN –36G | CARBOHYDRATES –14.6G | FAT –8.3G

CHICKEN CHOW MEIN

INGREDIENTS

- 2 chicken breasts, sliced into thin pieces
- 1 onion, finely chopped
- 2 garlic cloves, finely chopped
- 15ml of dark soy sauce
- 15ml of light soy sauce
- 15ml of cooking oil or cooking oil spray
- 300g//10.6oz of egg noodles
- 1 handful beansprouts
- Extra 30ml of dark soy sauce
- Extra 15ml of light soy sauce
- Optional: 2 spring onions, thinly sliced

METHOD

1. Combine the garlic, and 15ml each of light soy sauce and dark soy sauce in a large bowl. Add the onion and stir in.
2. Toss the chicken pieces into the soy and garlic mixture and coat thoroughly. Cover the bowl and marinate in the fridge for about an hour.
3. Preheat the air fryer to 200C//400F and spray with cooking oil.
4. Put the chicken in the air fryer and cook for 8 minutes at 200C//400F.
5. Add the handful of beansprouts, the egg noodles, and the remainder of the light and dark soy sauce. Give the mixture a good stir.
6. Cook for a further 5 minutes.
7. Serve immediately topped with chopped spring onion.

Nutritional Information per Serving:

SERVES –2 | CALORIES –417KCAL | PROTEIN –45G | CARBOHYDRATES –28G | FAT –13G

CARIBBEAN CHICKEN WITH PINEAPPLE SALSA

INGREDIENTS

- 115g//4oz of diced pineapple
- 30ml of lime juice
- 1 jalapeno pepper, diced into small pieces
- 50g//1.8oz of chopped coriander
- 30g//1oz of red onion, chopped
- 2 x 170g//6oz chicken breasts
- 30ml of olive oil
- 30g//1oz of jerk seasoning

METHOD

1. In a bowl, combine the diced pineapple, onion, coriander, lime juice, jalapeno pepper, and lime juice to create your pineapple salsa. Set to one side.
2. Place the chicken on a clean surface and coat it with the olive oil and jerk seasoning.
3. Preheat the air fryer to 190C//370F and spray with cooking oil.
4. Place the chicken in the air fryer and cook at 190C//370F for 7 minutes.
5. Turn the chicken over, and cook for a further 7 minutes at the same temperature until cooked through.
6. Serve topped with pineapple salsa and enjoy!

Nutritional Information per Serving:

SERVES –2 | CALORIES –320KCAL | PROTEIN –27G | CARBOHYDRATES –13G | FAT –18G

PAPRIKA CHICKEN

INGREDIENTS

- 6 bone-in, skin-on chicken thighs
- 2 garlic cloves, finely chopped
- 45g//1.5oz of ground paprika
- 1 teaspoon ground oregano
- ½ teaspoon ground onion powder
- Salt and pepper to taste

METHOD

1. Combine the garlic, paprika, oregano, onion powder, salt and pepper in a large bowl until thoroughly blended.
2. Preheat the air fryer to 190C//380F and spray with cooking oil.
3. Toss the chicken thighs into the spice mix and turn until thoroughly coated.
4. Put the chicken thighs in the air fryer, skin side down and spray with cooking oil. Cook at 190C//380F for 10 minutes.
5. Turn the chicken thighs over so that they are skin side up and spray again with some cooking oil.
6. Cook at 190C//380F for a further 10 minutes until the chicken is cooked through.
7. Serve as part of a main meal.

Nutritional Information per Serving:

SERVES –6 | CALORIES –322KCAL | PROTEIN –24G | CARBOHYDRATES –2G | FAT –24G

SATAY CHICKEN FRIED RICE

INGREDIENTS

- 2 chicken breasts, diced
- 30g//1oz of peanut butter
- 45ml of soy sauce
- 15ml of fish sauce
- Zest and juice of 2 fresh limes
- 4 spring onions, finely chopped
- 2 carrots thinly sliced
- 2 fresh red chillies, thinly sliced
- 2 garlic cloves, finely chopped
- 1 red pepper, diced
- 2 handfuls of frozen peas
- 255g//9oz of brown rice, already cooked
- 140ml water
- 2 teaspoons of sesame oil
- Fresh coriander garnish

METHOD

1. Wash and prepare the vegetables for cooking and dice the chicken breasts.
2. In a large bowl, whisk the peanut butter, soy sauce, lime juice, zest, and fish sauce until blended.
3. Toss the chicken into the bowl, coating it thoroughly with the sauce.
4. Grease the air fryer with the sesame oil and preheat to 190C//380F.
5. Place the chicken in the air fryer and cook at 190C//380F for 7 minutes, stirring once halfway through to prevent the chicken clumping.
6. Stir in the carrots, spring onion, garlic, red pepper, and half of the red chilli. Cook for a further 7 minutes at 190C//380F, again stirring halfway through.
7. Add the rice and water and cook for another 6 minutes. Check about half way through and add a little more water for the rice if necessary so the rice doesn't go crispy.
8. Serve with chopped vegetables, topped with the rest of the chilli and fresh coriander.

Nutritional Information per Serving:

SERVES –2 | CALORIES –416KCAL | PROTEIN –36.4G | CARBOHYDRATES –35.6G | FAT –16G

CHICKEN SHAWARMA

INGREDIENTS

- 500g//1.1lb of boneless, skinless chicken breasts
- 1 teaspoon of ground cumin
- 1 teaspoon of ground nutmeg
- 1 teaspoon of ground cardamom
- 1 garlic clove, finely chopped
- 1 small onion, finely chopped
- 40ml of vinegar
- 10ml of olive oil
- Salt and pepper to taste

METHOD

1. Cut the chicken into thin slices and set to one side while you prepare the marinade.
2. Mix the remaining ingredients into a large bowl and combine until thoroughly blended.
3. Toss the chicken slices into the bowl and make sure it's thoroughly coated with the marinade. Cover the bowl and allow to marinate for 12 hours in the fridge.
4. Remove the chicken from the marinade at least 30 minutes before cooking.
5. Preheat the air fryer to 190C//380F, and spray with cooking oil.
6. Remove the chicken from the bowl and discard the remaining marinade.
7. Put the chicken in the air fryer, spray again with oil and cook for 10–12 minutes, stirring once or twice during cooking.
8. Serve topped with chopped parsley.

Nutritional Information per Serving:

SERVES –4 | CALORIES –228KCAL | PROTEIN –36.8G | CARBOHYDRATES –3.7G | FAT –6.5 G

STIR FRY TURKEY WITH 3 PEPPERS

INGREDIENTS

- 3 peppers, 1 each of red, green and yellow, diced
- 40ml of olive oil
- 2 garlic cloves, finely chopped
- 1 red onion, sliced thinly
- 80ml of port
- 10ml of cider vinegar
- 1 teaspoon of cornflour
- 500g//1.1lb of turkey breast, skin and bone removed, sliced into thin strips
- Salt and pepper to taste

METHOD

1. Preheat the air fryer to 190C//380F and spray with cooking oil.
2. Put the peppers into the air fryer, drizzle with the oil and cook for 5 minutes.
3. Add the onion and garlic and cook for a further 5 minutes.
4. Next stir in the port, vinegar and cornflour until thoroughly combined.
5. Add the turkey breast strips to the air fryer with the port mixture.
6. Cook at 190C//380F for 10 to 15 minutes until the turkey is tender and cooked through.
7. Season to taste with salt and pepper.

Nutritional Information per Serving:

SERVES –4 | CALORIES –333KCAL | PROTEIN –37.1G | CARBOHYDRATES –5.4G | FAT –15.8G

CHICKEN TIKKA MASALA

INGREDIENTS

- 500g//1.1lb of chicken breasts cut in 2cm cubes
- 100g//3.5oz of tikka masala curry paste
- 2 x 150g//5oz pots of natural low-fat yoghurt
- 20ml of vegetable oil
- 1 large onion, finely chopped
- 1 x 390g//14oz can of chopped tomatoes
- 150ml of water
- 1/2 teaspoon of sugar
- 2 teaspoons of lemon juice

METHOD

1. In a large bowl blend 57g//2oz of natural yoghurt with the tikka masala paste.
2. Put the chicken into the bowl and coat thoroughly with the tikka masala sauce. Cover and leave to marinate in the fridge for up to 2 hours.
3. Preheat the air fryer to 190C//380F and spray with cooking oil. Add the onion and cook for 5 minutes at 190C//380F.
4. Remove the chicken from the marinade and discard the rest of the sauce. Add the chicken to the air fryer. Cook for a further 10 minutes at 190C//380F.
5. Stir in the chopped tomatoes and water. Cook for 10 minutes then stir in the rest of the yoghurt, the sugar and lemon juice.
6. Serve with basmati rice and naan.

Nutritional Information per Serving:

SERVES −6 | CALORIES −364KCAL | PROTEIN −32.3G | CARBOHYDRATES −16.8G | FAT −17.8G

JERK CHICKEN

INGREDIENTS

For the Pumpkin Couscous:

- 170g//6oz of couscous (double the liquid to cook)
- 100g//3.5oz pumpkin, with seeds removed, diced into small cubes
- 240ml of coconut water
- 1 red onion, peeled and diced
- 1 teaspoon of dried parsley
- Salt and pepper to taste

For the Jerk Chicken:

- 4 large chicken breasts about the same weight
- 15ml of olive oil
- 30g//1oz of jerk chicken seasoning

METHOD

1. Preheat the air fryer to 200C//400F and spray with oil.
2. Place your cubed pumpkin into a bowl and season with salt and pepper, then place in the air fryer. Cook for 10 minutes on 200C//400F.
3. In a large saucepan, add the couscous, along with the red onion, seasonings, and the coconut water. When the pumpkin has finished cooking, add that too and stir the mixture. Stir.
4. Boil a kettle of water and pour 470ml of boiling water into the saucepan with the couscous and vegetables. Put the lid on the pan and securely and leave it to stand for 10 minutes – no extra heat needed. When you take the lid off it will be ready to eat.
5. Meanwhile, put the chicken breasts on a clean chopping board and drizzle with olive oil. Rub in the jerk seasoning thoroughly so that the chicken is covered all over.
6. Place the chicken in the air fryer and cook at 180C//360F for 15 minutes.
7. Turn the temperature up to 200C//400F and cook for a further 3 minutes.
8. Serve the jerk chicken over the pumpkin couscous.

Nutritional Information per Serving:
SERVES –4 TO 6 | CALORIES –487KCAL | PROTEIN –55G | CARBOHYDRATES –41G | FAT –10G

MEDITERRANEAN CHICKEN COUCOUS
• •

INGREDIENTS

- 500g//1.1lb chicken, boneless, skinless, cut into chunks about 1 1/2–inches
- 15ml of olive oil
- 1 teaspoon of dried oregano

- 1 teaspoon of ground sumac (lemon pepper seasoning can be used instead)
- Salt and pepper to taste
- 280g//10oz of cherry tomatoes, cut in half
- 1 onion, chopped

- 180g//6.5oz of couscous (double the liquid to cook)
- Zest and juice from 1 lemon
- 8g//0.3oz of fresh dill
- Optional: Lemon wedges
- Optional: Crumbled feta

METHOD

1. Preheat the air fryer to 200C//400F and spray with oil.
2. Put the oregano sumac, salt, and pepper into a large bowl. Toss in the chicken, tomatoes and onions and make sure everything is well coated with the seasoning mix.
3. Place in a single layer in the greased air fryer and cook for 15–20 minutes at 200C//400F, making sure to shake occasionally during cooking.
4. While the chicken is cooking, combine the couscous with the lemon zest add double the quantity of boiling water. Cover with a lid and leave to stand, no heat, for 10 minutes. Once cooked, fold in the lemon juice and half of the dill and fluff up with a fork.
5. Serve the chicken and vegetables over the couscous, with any leftover juice from the fryer spooned over the top.
6. Sprinkle with crumbled feta and the remaining dill, with lemon wedges on the side.

Nutritional Information per Serving:
SERVES –2 TO 4 | CALORIES –475KCAL | PROTEIN –43G | CARBOHYDRATES –53G | FAT –9.5G

LEMON AND PEA RISOTTO SERVED WITH DICED CHICKEN

INGREDIENTS

- 300g//10.6oz chicken breasts, boneless, skinless and diced
- Optional: 12g//0.4oz of Mediterranean seasoning (shop bought or make your own)
- Spray cooking oil

- 1 onion, finely chopped
- 1litre of stock, vegetable, or chicken
- 200g//7oz of arborio rice
- 30g//1oz of butter, melted
- 60ml of dry white wine

- 30ml of lemon juice
- 70g//2.5oz of frozen peas
- 45g//1.5oz of grated parmesan cheese
- 130ml of double cream

For the Mediterranean Seasoning:

- 9g//0.3oz of dried oregano
- 9g//0.3oz of sesame seeds

- 2 teaspoons of salt
- 1 teaspoon of red chilli flakes

METHOD

1. If you're making your own Mediterranean seasoning, place all the spices in a small bowl, then grind and blend to a powder. Store in an airtight container and set aside for future use.
2. Preheat the air fryer to 200C//400F and spray with oil.
3. Bring the stock to a boil, then reduce to a simmer while you prepare the other ingredients.
4. In a separate bowl, toss the olive oil, the seasoning and the chicken, and sprinkle with salt and pepper. Ensure the chicken is thoroughly coated.
5. Next, cook the onion in the air fryer for 2–3 minutes.
6. Add the diced chicken and cook for another 3 minutes at 200C//400F.
7. Add the rice to another bowl containing the melted butter and coat thoroughly, then add the buttered rice and half the stock to the air fryer.
8. Cook at 200C//400F for another 5 minutes.
9. Add the remaining stock and cook for another 5 minutes, giving it a good stir before and after.
10. Stir in the wine, peas, lemon juice, cream, and parmesan (leaving a little parmesan as a topping) and cook for a final 2 minutes. Check the rice. It should be tender, but firm to the bite. Most of the liquid should be absorbed, but it should remain creamy.
11. Serve topped with the remaining parmesan.

Nutritional Information per Serving:

SERVES –4 TO 6 | CALORIES –876KCAL | PROTEIN –74.1G | CARBOHYDRATES –49.7G | FAT –39.4G

CHICKEN AND BROCCOLI IN LEMON PEPPER

INGREDIENTS

- 500g//1.1lb boneless skinless chicken breasts cut into 1.5–inch pieces
- 700g//1.5lb of broccoli crown, cut into 1.5–inch pieces
- 15ml of olive oil
- 2 teaspoons of lemon pepper seasoning
- 1 teaspoon of dried basil

- ¼ teaspoon of salt
- Cooking oil spray

METHOD

1. In a large bowl containing the olive oil, toss the chicken and broccoli and add the lemon pepper, basil, and salt, ensuring they are completely coated.
2. Preheat the air fryer to 200C//400F and spray with cooking oil.
3. Arrange the chicken and broccoli in a single layer with space between in the air fryer. You may need to cook in batches.
4. Cook for 5 minutes at 200C//400F.
5. Turn the pieces over in the air fryer and cook for another 5–7 minutes until the chicken is cooked through and no longer pink in the middle.

Nutritional Information per Serving:

SERVES –4 | CALORIES –194KCAL | PROTEIN –27G | CARBOHYDRATES –7G | FAT –7G

ALMOND CHICKEN
• •

INGREDIENTS

- 1 large egg
- 60ml of buttermilk
- 1 teaspoon of garlic salt
- 1/2 teaspoon of pepper

- 115g//4oz of slivered almonds, finely chopped
- 2 x 170g//6oz chicken breasts without skin

- Optional: Ranch salad dressing, barbecue sauce or honey mustard

METHOD

1. Preheat air fryer to 180C//350F and spray with cooking spray.
2. Whisk the egg, buttermilk, garlic salt and pepper together in a bowl, and place the almonds in a second bowl nearby.
3. Dip the chicken breasts first into the egg mixture, and then into the almonds. Pat to help the almonds stick to the chicken.
4. Place the chicken in a single layer in the air fryer, spray with cooking oil and cook for 15–18 minutes at 180C//350F.
5. Serve with your choice of dressing.

Nutritional Information per Serving:

SERVES –4 | CALORIES –353KCAL | PROTEIN –41G | CARBOHYDRATES –6G | FAT –18G

MAINS – BEEF DISHES

MEAT FEAST – THE COMPLETE AIR FRIED BARBECUE!

INGREDIENTS

- 4 burgers
- 6 standard size sausages
- 3 pork steaks
- 3 thin beef steaks
- 500g//1.1lb of baby potatoes
- 500g//1.1lb of Mediterranean vegetables (e.g. courgette, pepper, mushroom etc)
- 30ml of olive oil (as 2 x 15ml)
- 6g//0.2oz of dried oregano
- 6g//0.2oz of dried parsley
- Salt and pepper to taste

METHOD

1. Preheat the air fryer to 180C//360F and spray with cooking oil.
2. In a large bowl, toss the potatoes with 15ml of the olive oil and half of the seasonings. Ensure the potatoes are coated well.
3. Place the potatoes in the air fryer and cook for 17 minutes at 180C//360F.
4. Take the baby potatoes out of the air fryer and keep them warm.
5. Put the 4 burgers and 4 sausages into the air fryer and cook for 10 minutes at 180C//360F. Remove and keep warm once cooked.
6. Put the remaining 2 sausages, the pork steaks and however many of the beef steaks that will fit without overcrowding. Cook for 10 minutes at 180C//360F.
7. Meanwhile, add the Mediterranean vegetables to a bowl with the remaining oil and seasoning and coat well. Once the steaks are cooked, remove them from the air fryer and load with the vegetables. Cook for another 12 minutes at 180C//360F.
8. Finally, when the vegetables are cooked, transfer them to a warmed bowl and add the last of the steaks. Cook for 6 minutes at 180C//360F.
9. Plate up and serve!

Nutritional Information per Serving:

SERVES –4 | CALORIES –1282KCAL | PROTEIN –114G | CARBOHYDRATES –41G | FAT –71G

EASY BOLOGNESE SAUCE

INGREDIENTS

- 15ml of cooking oil
- 1 medium onion, peeled and chopped
- 2 garlic cloves, peeled and crushed
- 500g//1.1lb of minced beef
- 15g//0.5oz of tomato puree
- 3g//0.1oz of mixed herbs
- 400g//14oz can of chopped tomatoes
- Optional: a splash of red wine
- Salt and pepper to taste

METHOD

1. Preheat your air fryer to 190C//375F and spritz lightly with cooking oil.
2. Add the 15ml of cooking oil to the air fryer, followed by the garlic, onion, and minced beef.
3. Give it a stir, then cook for 4–5 minutes at 190C//375F. Stir once or twice during cooking to prevent the meat clumping.
4. Stir in the wine, mixed herbs, and tomato puree. (If you prefer not to use wine, then add a little of the tomato juice from the can instead). Cook for a further 5 minutes at 190C//375F.
5. Finally, mix in the can of chopped tomatoes and cook for a further 20 minutes at the same temperature.
6. Serve with cooked spaghetti or cooked pasta or your choice and top with grated cheese.

Nutritional Information per Serving:

SERVES –4 | CALORIES –304KCAL | PROTEIN –39.5G | CARBOHYDRATES –7.1G | FAT –11.5G

STEAK WITH HERB BUTTER

INGREDIENTS

- 60g//2oz butter, softened
- 2 cloves of minced garlic
- 2 teaspoons of freshly chopped parsley
- 1 teaspoon of freshly chopped chives
- 1 teaspoon of freshly chopped thyme
- 1 teaspoon of freshly chopped rosemary
- 900g//2lb bone–in ribeye steak
- Coarse sea salt
- Freshly ground black pepper

METHOD

1. Mix the softened butter and fresh herbs together in a bowl. Roll the butter mixture in cling film to create a sausage shape, then place in the refrigerator for about 15–20 minutes until firm.
2. Season the steak with salt and pepper to taste.
3. Put the steak in the air fryer and cook for 12–14 minutes at 200C//400F (adjust according to your preferred tenderness).
4. Turn the steak halfway through cooking.
5. Serve immediately with a wedge of herby butter.

Nutritional Information per Serving:

SERVES –2 | CALORIES –1114KCAL | PROTEIN –164.4 | CARBOHYDRATES –1.8 G | FAT –45.8G

JUICY MEATBALLS

INGREDIENTS

For the Meatballs:

- 450g//1lb of lean minced beef
- 225g//0.5lb of lean minced pork
- 30g//1oz seasoned breadcrumbs
- 1 egg
- 30ml of milk
- 8g//0.3oz of fresh parsley
- 15g//0.5oz of parmesan cheese grated
- ½ teaspoon of Italian seasoning
- ½ teaspoon of onion powder
- ½ teaspoon of salt
- ¼ teaspoon of black pepper

For the Italian Seasoning:

- 30g//1oz of marjoram
- 30g//1oz of oregano
- 30g//1oz of rosemary
- 30g//1oz of thyme
- 30g//1oz of basil

METHOD

1. If you're making your own Italian seasoning, then combine all the ingredients together, and put them in a food processor or grind them by hand into a powder. Store in an airtight container.
2. Combine the Italian seasoning in with all the ingredients except for the beef and pork in a large bowl together.
3. Add the beef and the pork and mix well.
4. Preheat the air fryer to 200C//400F and spray with cooking oil.
5. Divide the mixture to create 16 meatballs of equal size.
6. Put the meatballs into the air fryer in a single layer (you may need to cook in batches of 8 depending on the size of your air fryer).
7. Reduce the temperature to 190C//380F and cook for 12–14 minutes.
8. Allow to rest for 3 minutes before serving.

Nutritional Information per Serving:

SERVES –3 TO 4 (ABOUT 16 MEATBALLS) | CALORIES –114KCAL | PROTEIN –8G | CARBOHYDRATES –2 G | FAT –8G

HAMBURGERS

• •

INGREDIENTS

- ◆ 450g//1lb of lean minced beef
- ◆ ½ teaspoon of salt
- ◆ ½ teaspoon of pepper
- ◆ ½ teaspoon of onion powder
- ◆ ¼ teaspoon of garlic powder
- ◆ Optional: 60g//2oz of barbecue sauce
- ◆ 4 hamburger buns
- ◆ Optional: toppings as desired

METHOD

1. Combine the meat and seasonings together in a bowl and mix thoroughly.
2. Preheat the air fryer to 190C//375F and spritz with cooking oil.
3. Form the meat mixture into 4 hamburger shapes about 1/2" thick. Make a small indent in the middle of the burger with your thumb.
4. Brush the burgers with barbecue sauce if you're using it.
5. Put the burgers in a single layer into the basket with a little space between each.
6. Cook for about 6 minutes at 190C//375F. Turn the burgers over and cook for a furth 3–5 minutes until cooked through.
7. Serve on buns with a slice of cheese.

Nutritional Information per Serving:

SERVES –SERVES 4 (BASED ON 1 HAMBURGER PER SERVING WITHOUT TOPPINGS) | CALORIES –365KCAL | PROTEIN –25G | CARBOHYDRATES –22G | FAT –19G

ONE–POT – ASIAN BEEF WITH VEGETABLES

• •

INGREDIENTS

For the Beef and Vegetables:

- ◆ 450g//1lb sirloin steak cut into thin strips
- ◆ ½ onion, sliced thinly
- ◆ 1 medium red pepper, sliced into strips
- ◆ 70g//2.5oz of sugar snap peas

For the Marinade:

- 3 garlic cloves finely chopped
- 2" piece of fresh ginger, grated
- ¼ teaspoon of red chilli flakes
- 265ml of soy sauce
- 18g//0.6oz of cornflour
- 60ml of rice vinegar
- 1 teaspoon of sesame oil
- 70g//2.5oz of brown sugar
- 60ml of water
- Optional:1 teaspoon of Chinese 5 spice

METHOD

1. Combine all the marinade ingredients in a bowl together and blend to form a sauce.
2. Add the steak and vegetables to the bowl and ensure they are thoroughly coated in the mixture. Cover the bowl and leave to marinate in the fridge for at least an hour.
3. Preheat the air fryer to 200C//400F and spray with cooking oil.
4. Once marinaded, use tongs to transfer the beef and vegetables to the air fryer and discard any leftover marinade.
5. Cook for 8 minutes in the air fryer at 400°F/204C.
6. Serve with rice topped with finely sliced spring onions and sesame seeds.

Nutritional Information per Serving:

SERVES –4 | CALORIES –299KCAL | PROTEIN –29G | CARBOHYDRATES –30G | FAT –6G

LIVER AND ONIONS

INGREDIENTS

- 680g//1.5lb of beef liver
- 2 large onions sliced into rings
- Salt and pepper to taste
- 1 teaspoon of smoked paprika
- 1 teaspoon of garlic powder
- 1 teaspoon of onion powder
- 1 teaspoon of dry mustard

METHOD

1. Preheat the air fryer to 185C//370F and spritz with cooking oil.
2. Put the onion rings in a bowl with all the seasonings and coat them thoroughly.
3. Put the onions into the air fryer.
4. Next toss the liver in the bowl with the salt, pepper, garlic powder, onion powder, dry mustard, and smoked paprika. Turn it over so that both sides are covered.
5. Put the liver into the air fryer on top of the onions.
6. Cook for 7 minutes at 185C//370F.
7. Check to see if the liver and onions are fully cooked and set the air fryer for a further 4 minutes if necessary.
8. Serve and enjoy!

Nutritional Information per Serving:

SERVES –2 | CALORIES –537KCAL | PROTEIN –72G | CARBOHYDRATES –30G | FAT –13G

BEEF POT ROAST

INGREDIENTS

- 1.1 kg//2.5lb of top round roast/ topside beef
- 15ml of soy sauce
- 60ml of Worcester sauce
- 4 large carrots, peeled and diced
- 5 medium potatoes, peeled and cut for roast potatoes
- 60ml of maple syrup
- 15ml of olive oil

METHOD

1. Put the soy sauce and 30ml of the Worcester sauce into a bowl.
2. Use a sharp knife to gently score the beef roast.
3. Preheat the air fryer to 180C//360F and spritz with cooking oil.
4. Turn the beef in the sauce so it is thoroughly coated, then season with salt and pepper, making sure it gets into the scored areas.
5. Put the beef joint into the air fryer and cook for 15 minutes at 180C//360F. Discard the sauce that's left in the bowl.
6. In a clean bowl, put the remaining 30ml of Worcester sauce, the maple syrup, olive oil and a pinch more salt and pepper. Toss in the carrots and potatoes ensuring that they are fully coated with the mixture.
7. Add the carrots and potatoes into the gaps around the beef joint.
8. Cook for a further 45 minutes at 160C//320F.
9. Once cooked, rest the beef for 5 minutes before slicing and serving with the potatoes and carrots.

Nutritional Information per Serving:

SERVES –4 | CALORIES –546KCAL | PROTEIN –68G | CARBOHYDRATES –23G | FAT –19G

ONE–POT BURGER IN A BOWL

INGREDIENTS

- 230g//8oz of minced beef
- 1 teaspoon of garlic puree
- ½ small onion, peeled and sliced
- 15g//0.5oz of mixed herbs
- Salt and pepper to taste

For the Sauce:

- 20g//0.7oz of fromage frais
- 1 teaspoon of mustard powder
- 20g//0.7oz of Greek yoghurt
- 20g//0.7oz of tomato puree
- ½ teaspoon of paprika
- ½ teaspoon of gherkin juice

For the Burger Salad:

- 1/3 of a crisp iceberg lettuce, cut into thin slices
- 3 tomatoes, sliced
- ½ onion, sliced
- 10 gherkin slices

METHOD

1. Preheat the air fryer to 180C//360F and spritz with cooking oil spray.
2. Combine all the burger ingredients into a bowl until they're well mixed and form into 2 burger shapes. Press your thumb into the centre of each to form a slight indent.
3. Put the burgers into the air fryer and cook for 15 minutes at 180C//360F.
4. Make your burger sauce by putting all the ingredients into a bowl and blending thoroughly.
5. While you're waiting for the burgers to finish cooking, place a layer of lettuce in your salad bowl, following by a layer of sliced tomatoes, sliced gherkins, and sliced onion.
6. Once cooked, remove the burgers from the air fryer and cut into chunks.
7. Load the burger chunks on top of your salad bowl and drizzle with your sauce.
8. Serve!

Nutritional Information per Serving:

SERVES –2 | CALORIES –407KCAL | PROTEIN –26G | CARBOHYDRATES –20G | FAT –26G

STICKY KOREAN BEEF STIR FRY

INGREDIENTS

For the Sauce:

- 85g//3oz of packed brown sugar
- 125ml of soy sauce
- 2" piece of fresh ginger, grated
- 2 garlic cloves, finely chopped
- 15ml of sesame oil
- 1/4 teaspoon crushed red pepper flakes (or to taste)

For the Stir Dry:

- 500g//1.1lb of minced beef
- 1 teaspoon cornflour
- 60g//2oz Korean BBQ sauce (shop bought or homemade)
- 45g//1.5oz of courgette sliced into thin strips
- 45g//1.5oz of carrots, cut into thin strips
- 9g//0.3oz of sesame seeds
- 30g//1oz of spring onions, finely sliced into strips

METHOD

1. If you are making your own Korean sauce, combine all the sauce ingredients into a blender and mix thoroughly. Keep the sauce handy for the next step.
2. In a large bowl combine the minced beef, cornflour and the Korean BBQ sauce. Marinate for about 5 minutes.
3. Preheat the air fryer to 190C//380F and spritz lightly with cooking oil.
4. Add the carrots and courgettes to the bowl, and gently mix.
5. Transfer the mixture to the air fryer and spread it out a little with a spatula.
6. Cook at 190//380F for 8–10 minutes, stirring twice so that the stir fry doesn't clump too much.
7. When the beef is cooked through, transfer to a plate and serve with sesame seeds and sliced spring onions.

Nutritional Information per Serving:

SERVES –4 | CALORIES –189KCAL | PROTEIN –11G | CARBOHYDRATES –7G | FAT –5G

BEEF STROGANOFF

INGREDIENTS

- 600g//1.3lbs of tender beef, sliced into thin strips
- 200g//7oz of chopped onions
- 7g//0.2oz of paprika
- 200ml of sour cream
- Salt and pepper to taste
- Spray cooking oil

METHOD

1. Put the slices of beef into a bowl with the paprika and toss until thoroughly covered.
2. In a hot pan, sauté the onions in a little vegetable oil until translucent.
3. Add the beef strips and sauté for 5 minutes.
4. Preheat the air fryer to 200C//400F and spritz with oil.
5. Add the beef and the onions to the air fryer, add salt and pepper to taste, and spritz with a little more oil.
6. Cook at 200C//400F for 3 to 4 minutes.
7. Stir in the sour cream and cook for another 2–3 minutes until piping hot.
8. Season, and serve.

Nutritional Information per Serving:

SERVES –4 | CALORIES –353KCAL | PROTEIN –40.5G | CARBOHYDRATES –10.3G | FAT –15.7G

STIR FRIED STEAK IN HOISIN SAUCE

INGREDIENTS

- 400g//14oz rump steak cut 1.5 cm thick
- 40ml of toasted sesame oil
- 600g//1.3lb of mixed stir fry vegetables
- 90ml of hoisin sauce
- 250g//9oz fine egg noodles cooked

METHOD

1. Trim the fat off the beef and cut into thin strips 6mm thick. Bring your steak to room temperature before cooking.
2. Add 20ml of oil to the air fryer and preheat to 200C//400F.
3. Cook the beef for 5 minutes at 200C//400F, or until just about pink remains in the centre, stirring to make sure the meat doesn't clump together.
4. Remove from the air fryer and keep warm while you cook the vegetables.
5. Put the stir fry vegetables in the air fryer and drizzle over the remaining 20ml of oil. Cook at 200C//400F for 5 minutes or until vegetables are cooked and still crunchy.
6. In a bowl mix the hoisin sauce and 28ml of water.
7. Add the sauce to the vegetables in the air fryer, then stir in the beef.
8. Cook for a further 3–4 minutes at 200C//400F until hot.
9. Serve with cooked fine egg noodles.

Nutritional Information per Serving:

SERVES –4 | CALORIES –659KCAL | PROTEIN –43.8G | CARBOHYDRATES –66.2G | FAT –22.8G

KOREAN BULGOGI

INGREDIENTS

- 450g//1lb of beef rib–eye, thinly sliced
- 15g//0.5oz of onion, thinly sliced
- 85g//3oz of Korean BBQ Sauce
- 2" piece of fresh ginger, grated
- 30g//1oz of spring onions, thinly sliced
- 2 teaspoons of sesame seed

METHOD

1. Toss the meat in a large bowl with the onion, Korean BBQ sauce, and ginger. Mix well then cover the bowl and marinate for at least 30 minutes.
2. Preheat the air fryer to 190C//380F and lightly spray with oil.
3. Line the air fryer with greased foil and spread the meat out in a layer.
4. Cook for 8–10 minutes at 190C//380F, stirring once about halfway through cooking.
5. Serve topped with spring onions and sesame seeds.

Nutritional Information per Serving:

SERVES –4 | CALORIES –283 KCAL | PROTEIN –24G | CARBOHYDRATES –9G | FAT –17G

MONGOLIAN BEEF

INGREDIENTS

For the Beef:

- 500g//1.1lb beef flank, trimmed and cut into 1/4 inch pieces
- 2 teaspoons of soy sauce
- 1 teaspoon of sesame oil
- 40g//1.4oz of cornflour

For the Sauce:

- 30ml of olive oil
- 2" piece of fresh ginger, grated
- 3 garlic cloves, finely chopped
- 30ml of soy sauce
- 50g//1.7oz of brown sugar
- 3–4 green onion spring onions, cut into 1–2-inch pieces
- Optional: 1–2 teaspoon sesame seeds

METHOD

1. Toss the steak into a bowl with the soy sauce, sesame oil, and cornflour and make sure it is covered thoroughly. Marinate for a at least 15 minutes.
2. Preheat the air fryer to 200C//400F and line it with greased foil.
3. Place the steak pieces in a single layer and cook for about 8 minutes at 200C//400F. Turn about halfway through.
4. While the meat is cooking, fry the garlic and grated ginger in the olive oil for about 1–2 minutes. Stir in the soy sauce and brown sugar and stir constantly until the sauce thickens.
5. Toss the beef and green onion into the sauce, making sure it is all heated through, then serve.
6. Serve hot, sprinkled with sesame seeds.

Nutritional Information per Serving:

SERVES –4 | CALORIES –306KCAL | PROTEIN –26G | CARBOHYDRATES –19G | FAT –14G

TRADITIONAL CHILLI CON CARNE

INGREDIENTS

- 1 onion, thinly sliced
- 400g//14oz can of Mexican tomatoes (shop bought or make your own)
- Optional: 1 fresh red chilli with seeds removed and finely chopped
- 350ml of hot beef stock
- 30g//1oz of tomato puree
- Salt and pepper to taste
- Chilli powder to taste; a little goes a long way, so start at ½ teaspoon!
- 1 teaspoon of ground coriander
- 1 teaspoon of ground cumin
- 500g//1.1lb of lean minced beef
- 15ml of olive oil
- 1 pepper, seeds removed and diced
- 400g//14oz can of red kidney beans, drained and rinsed
- 150g//5oz of sweetcorn

METHOD

1. Preheat the air fryer to 180C//350F and spray with cooking oil.
2. Place the onion, red pepper and chillies into the air fryer, drizzle with oil and cook for 5 minutes at 180C//350F.
3. Stir in the minced beef, breaking up any large chunks with a fork. Cook for another 5 minutes or until the meat is no longer pink.
4. In a small bowl, mix the spices and seasoning into the tomato puree and add to 200 ml of the beef stock. Keep the extra 150ml extra beef stock for use later.
5. Add your spiced stock to the air fryer along with the canned tomatoes. Stir well and cook for 25 minutes at 180C//350F, stirring at regular intervals.
6. Mix in the canned beans and the saved 150 ml of hot beef stock and stir well.
7. Cook for a further 5–10 minutes, stirring halfway through.
8. Serve with boiled rice, topped with a little sour cream.

Nutritional Information per Serving:

SERVES –6 | CALORIES –153KCAL | PROTEIN –8.2G | CARBOHYDRATES –23.8G | FAT –3.5G

BEEF WELLINGTON

INGREDIENTS

- 15g//0.5oz butter
- 60g//2oz of fresh mushrooms
- 2 teaspoons of plain flour
- 125ml of double cream
- 1 egg yolk
- 7g//0.2oz of onion, finely chopped
- Salt and pepper to taste
- 230g//0.5lb of minced beef
- 1 tube 115g//4oz of refrigerated crescent rolls
- Optional: 1 egg, beaten
- 1 teaspoon of dried parsley flakes

METHOD

1. In a pan on a medium heat, melt the butter, add the mushrooms and cook for about 5–6 minutes until tender.
2. Stir in the flour slowly until blended and add salt and pepper to taste.
3. Continue stirring as you gradually add the cream, then bring to the bowl and stir for about 2 minutes until the sauce thickens. Remove from the heat and set to one side.
4. Combine the egg yolk, onion, 2 tablespoons of mushroom sauce, salt and pepper to taste. Crumble the minced beef into the mixture and mix thoroughly.
5. Shape the beef mixture into 2 loaves.
6. Unroll the dough into 2 rectangles and seal any pre–cut perforations.
7. Place one meatloaf on each dough rectangle, bring the edges together and seal. Brush with the egg wash.
8. Preheat the air fryer to 150C//300F. Spray with cooking oil.
9. Place the beef wellingtons on a greased tray in the air fryer in a single layer.
10. Cook for 22 minutes at 150C//300F until golden brown.
11. While waiting warm the remaining sauce gently over a low heat and stir in the parsley flakes.
12. Serve the beef wellington with the sauce as part of a main meal.

Nutritional Information per Serving:

SERVES –4 | CALORIES –585KCAL | PROTEIN –29G | CARBOHYDRATES –30G | FAT –38G

ONE–POT BEEF AND VEGETABLE CASSEROLE

INGREDIENTS

- 45ml of olive oil
- 40g//1.4oz of small onions, chopped
- 1 garlic clove, finely chopped
- 450g//1lb of lean minced beef
- 1 medium carrot, diced
- 200g//7oz of potatoes, peeled and diced
- 1 celery stalk, diced
- 15g//0.5oz of fresh coriander chopped
- 60g//2oz of grated cheddar cheese
- 60g//2oz of shredded mozzarella cheese
- Salt and pepper to taste

METHOD

1. Stir fry the shallots and garlic in a pan with about 1 tablespoon of the olive oil for 3 minutes.
2. Stir in the minced beef and cook for about 10 minutes until the meat is no longer pink. Stir at intervals to stop the meat clumping. Remove from the pan and set aside on a plate.
3. Heat the remaining olive oil in a pan and add the carrot, potatoes, and celery. Cook, stirring for 20 minutes or until tender. Stir in the coriander and season with salt and pepper to taste. Remove from heat.
4. Preheat your air fryer to 200C//400F and spritz with oil.
5. Place the beef mixture in a casserole dish that will fit your air fryer and spread evenly in a thin layer. Top with the vegetables, cheddar, and mozzarella.
6. Cook at 200C//400F for a further 15–20 minutes.
7. Serve and enjoy.

Nutritional Information per Serving:

SERVES –6 | CALORIES –336KCAL | PROTEIN –28G | CARBOHYDRATES –21G | FAT –15G

BASIC BEEF AND TOMATO BASE RECIPE

INGREDIENTS

- 400g//14oz of minced beef
- 300g//11oz of canned tomatoes

METHOD

1. Preheat the air fryer to 180C//360F and spritz with oil.
2. Add the minced beef and tomatoes.
3. Cook at 180C//360F for about 10 minutes.
4. (This is a base recipe for bolognese, chilli con carne and other meals. This is the point at which you would add your other ingredients.)
5. Stir and cook for a final 4 minutes at the same temperature.
6. Serve and enjoy!

Nutritional Information per Serving:

SERVES −4 | CALORIES −278KCAL | PROTEIN −18G | CARBOHYDRATES −5G | FAT −20G

MAINS – LAMB

MEDITERRANEAN LAMB CHOPS

INGREDIENTS

- 8 lamb loin chops bone−in, trimmed
- 3 garlic cloves, crushed
- 1 teaspoon of olive oil
- Juice of half a fresh lemon
- 6g//0.2oz of salt
- 15g//0.5oz of za'atar (or combine equal parts of thyme, sesame and salt)
- Fresh ground pepper, to taste

METHOD

1. Mix the garlic and oil together in a small bowl and allow to steep for about 30 minutes.
2. Preheat the air fryer to 200C//400F and spray with oil.
3. Rub the oil and garlic mix all over the lamb chops.
4. Squeeze the lemon over both sides of the chops, then season with salt, za'atar and black pepper.
5. Place in the air fryer and cook for 4−5 minutes at 200C//400F. Turn the lamb chops over and cook for a further 4−5 minutes.
6. Serve and enjoy.

Nutritional Information per Serving:

SERVES −4 | CALORIES −206KCAL | PROTEIN −29G | CARBOHYDRATES −1.5G | FAT −8G

LAMB KEBABS

INGREDIENTS

- 500g//1.1lb of minced lamb
- 1 teaspoon of coriander
- 1 teaspoon of mixed spice
- 1 teaspoon of chilli flakes
- 1 teaspoon of turmeric
- 1 teaspoon of cumin
- 1 teaspoon of mixed herbs
- ½ teaspoon of tandoori seasoning

METHOD

1. Put all the ingredients into a large bowl, and using your hands, mix thoroughly until it's all combined.
2. Take out small handfuls at a time to shape into kebab sausage shapes. Use floured hands if you find the mixture too sticky.
3. Preheat the air fryer to 180C//360F and spray with cooking oil.
4. Skewer the kebabs and place in the air fryer in a single layer, ensuring they are not touching each other. Cook at 180C//360F for about 8 minutes.
5. Turn the kebabs over in the air fryer and cook for a further 8 minutes at the same temperature.
6. Serve with a favourite dipping sauce.

Nutritional Information per Serving:

SERVES –4 | CALORIES –362KCAL | PROTEIN –21G | CARBOHYDRATES –1G | FAT –30G

GREEK–STYLE LAMB CHOPS

INGREDIENTS

- 6 lamb shoulder chops (size depends on what fits in your air fryer)
- 500g//1.1lb of medium potatoes, peeled, rinsed, and cut into large roast potato pieces
- 1 large lemon, sliced
- Salt and pepper to taste

For the Marinade:

- 15ml of olive oil
- Juice and zest of 1 lemon
- 10 whole garlic cloves, peeled
- 15g//0.5oz of oregano

METHOD

1. Put all your marinade ingredients into a large bowl and mix well.
2. Toss the potatoes and lamb chops into the bowl and so they are well covered in the marinade. Cover the bowl and place in the fridge for at least two hours to marinate, or overnight if possible.
3. Preheat the air fryer to 180C/360F and spray with cooking oil.
4. Place the roast potatoes in a single layer in the air fryer and fill any gaps with the garlic cloves and the sliced lemon from the marinade. Place the lamb chops on top of the potatoes.
5. Cook for 25 minutes at 180C//360F, turning the lamb and potatoes once or twice during the cooking.
6. Serve.

Nutritional Information per Serving:

SERVES –4 | CALORIES –652KCAL | PROTEIN –32 G | CARBOHYDRATES –22G | FAT –49G

FAMILY FAVOURITES ROAST LAMB

INGREDIENTS

- 1.2kg//2.6lb lamb joint, prepared for cooking
- 300g//11oz of potatoes, peeled, washed, and cut for roast potatoes
- 15ml of olive oil
- 2 teaspoons of rosemary
- 1 teaspoon of thyme
- 1 teaspoon of bouquet garni
- Salt and pepper to taste

METHOD

1. Preheat the air fryer to 160C//320F and spray with oil.
2. Use a sharp knife to score the lambs skin and season with the salt, pepper, bouquet garni and thyme, paying extra attention to the score marks.
3. Put the joint in the air fryer and cook at 160C//320F for about 30 minutes.
4. Toss the potatoes in a separate bowl with salt, pepper, rosemary, and olive oil. Use your hands to mix well and ensure the potatoes are well coated.
5. Turn the lamb after the 30 minutes and place the seasoned potatoes in the gaps around the lamb joint. Cook for another 25 minutes at 160C//320F.
6. Check the lamb at the end of cooking, and if it looks too pink in the middle, cook for a few minutes longer.
7. Finally, remove the potatoes and keep warm while the lamb 'rests' for 10 minutes.
8. Carve the lamb and serve with roast potatoes and seasonal vegetables.

Nutritional Information per Serving:

SERVES −4 | CALORIES −464KCAL | PROTEIN −63G | CARBOHYDRATES −1G | FAT −21G

EASY ROAST LEG OF LAMB

INGREDIENTS

- 1.4kg//3lb leg of lamb
- 500g//1.1lb of potatoes, peeled, rinsed and cut for roast potatoes
- Salt and pepper to taste
- 15ml of juices from the lamb or 15ml of olive oil

METHOD

1. Preheat the air fryer to 180C//360F and spray with cooking oil.
2. With a sharp knife, score the lamb and season all over with salt and pepper.
3. Cook in the air fryer for 30 minutes at 180C//360F.
4. In a bowl, toss the potatoes with salt, pepper and either the juices of the lamb roast or the olive oil. Ensure the potatoes are well covered.
5. Put the seasoned roast potatoes in the gaps around the lamb and cook for a further 25 minutes, or until the meat is cooked through.
6. Carve and enjoy.

Nutritional Information per Serving:

SERVES −6–8 | CALORIES −512KCAL | PROTEIN −66.9G | CARBOHYDRATES −13.1G | FAT −19.6G

MORROCAN SPICED LAMB BURGERS

INGREDIENTS

For the Lamb Burgers:

- 650g//1.4lb of minced lamb
- 2 teaspoons of garlic puree
- 1 teaspoon of harissa paste (or tomato puree if too spicy)
- 15g//0.5oz of Moroccan spice
- Salt and pepper to taste

For the Greek Dip:

- 60g//2oz of Greek yoghurt
- 1 teaspoon of Moroccan spice
- ½ teaspoon of oregano
- Juice of one small lemon

METHOD

1. Use your hands to mix all the lamb burger ingredients together in a bowl until well combined.
2. Preheat the air fryer to 180C//360F and spray with cooking oil.
3. Scoop out spoonfuls of the lamb mixture to create burger shapes and make an indent in the top of each one with your thumb.
4. Put the burger shapes into the air fryer and cook at 180C//360F for 18 minutes.
5. Meanwhile, make your Greek dip by blending all the ingredients together in a small dish until blended into a sauce.
6. Remove the burgers from the air fryer and serve with Greek salad and the yoghurt dip.

Nutritional Information per Serving:

SERVES –4 | CALORIES –478KCAL | PROTEIN –28G | CARBOHYDRATES –3G | FAT –38 G

LAMB MEATBALLS

INGREDIENTS

- 500g//1.1lb of minced lamb
- ¼ teaspoon of salt
- ¼ teaspoon of black pepper
- ½ teaspoon of garlic powder
- ½ teaspoon of onion powder
- 20g//0.7oz of fine breadcrumbs
- 5g//0.2oz of fresh parsley (chopped)
- Cooking oil spray

METHOD

1. Preheat the air fryer to 190C//380F. Spray with cooking oil.
2. In a large bowl use your hands to combine all the ingredients (except the oil) until they are thoroughly mixed.
3. Use a tablespoon to scoop spoonfuls of mixture and roll to create the meatballs.
4. Put the meatballs into the air fryer in an even, single layer and spray over the top with more cooking oil.
5. Cook for 15 minutes at 380F//190C turning the meatballs halfway through.
6. Serve with your favourite pasta sauce over cooked pasta.

Nutritional Information per Serving:

SERVES –4 | CALORIES –119KCAL | PROTEIN –7G | CARBOHYDRATES –2G | FAT –9G

MAINS – DUCK

BREAST OF DUCK

INGREDIENTS

- 2 duck breasts
- 1 teaspoon of parsley
- Salt and pepper to taste

For the Marinade:

- 15ml of olive oil
- 1 teaspoon of garlic powder
- ½ teaspoon of balsamic vinegar
- ½ teaspoon of French mustard
- 2 teaspoons of honey

METHOD

1. Preheat the air fryer to 180C//350F and spray with cooking oil.
2. Use a sharp knife to gently make cuts in the duck breasts and season with salt, pepper, and parsley.
3. Put all the marinade ingredients into one bowl and mix until thoroughly blended.
4. Brush the marinade over the duck breasts, paying attention to the cuts.
5. Place the duck breasts in the air fryer, pour the marinade over the top, and cook at 180C//360F for about 20 minutes.
6. Slice and serve.

Nutritional Information per Serving:

SERVES –2 | CALORIES –693KCAL | PROTEIN –49G | CARBOHYDRATES –45G | FAT –35G

DESSERTS AND SWEET TREATS – AIRFRYER COOKBOOK

DESSERTS AND SWEET TREATS

CARAMELISED BANANA

INGREDIENTS

- 2 large yellow bananas, peeled and cut into thick circular slices
- Coconut oil spray (other light cooking oils can be used)
- ½ teaspoon of coconut sugar (coconut sugar adds a lovely caramel flavour, but white granulated, brown or demerara sugar can be used)
- Optional: ¼ teaspoon of cinnamon

METHOD

1. Preheat the air fryer to 200C//390F.
2. Mix the sugar and cinnamon together in a bowl.
3. Roll the banana pieces in the sugar and put them into the air fryer basket.
4. Cook at 200C//390F for between 5–8 minutes.
5. Serve immediately with ice cream or cream.

Nutritional Information per Serving:

SERVES –2 | CALORIES –117KCAL | PROTEIN –1G | CARBOHYDRATES –31.2G | FAT –0.3G

CRISPY APPLE DESSERT

INGREDIENTS

<u>For the Crispy Apple:</u>

- 255g//9oz of apple, peeled, cored, and diced

<u>For the Oaty Topping:</u>

- 30g//1oz of jumbo rolled oats
- 30g//1oz of brown sugar
- 40ml of water
- 7g//0.25oz of sugar

- 30g//1oz of plain flour
- 15g//0.5oz of melted butter
- ½ teaspoon of ground cinnamon (optional)

METHOD

1. Preheat the air fryer to 175C//350F.
2. Butter an ovenproof dish (check it fits your air fryer first).
3. In a separate bowl, combine the remaining ingredients and transfer them to the buttered dish. Cover tightly with foil.
4. Put the dish inside the air fryer and cook at 175C//350F for 10 minutes.
5. Remove the foil, stir the ingredients, replace the foil, and cook for a further 10 minutes.
6. In a clean bowl, mix the oats, sugar, flour, and butter together with a fork to make a crumbly topping.
7. Remove and discard the foil from the cooked apple, sprinkle the oaty topping over the top, and return to the air fryer for a further 5 minutes.
8. Allow to cool before serving with cream, ice cream, or yoghurt.

Nutritional Information per Serving:

SERVES −2 | CALORIES −207KCAL | PROTEIN −3.2G | CARBOHYDRATES −38.8G | FAT −4.9G

TASTY COCONUT BALLS

INGREDIENTS

- 200g//7oz of desiccated coconut
- 150g//5oz of sugar
- 300g//11oz of plain flour
- Pinch of salt
- 1.5 level teaspoons of baking powder
- 75ml of coconut milk
- 75ml of milk
- 3 medium eggs
- Pinch of salt
- Spray cooking oil

METHOD

1. Put all the dry ingredients together in a bowl and mix thoroughly.
2. Add the wet ingredients and mix with a fork into a dough.
3. Preheat the air fryer to 160C//320F.
4. Spray the air fryer with a light coat of cooking oil.
5. Scoop the mixture into small 30g balls and place in the air fryer, leaving plenty of space between each one.
6. Don't overfill the air fryer but cook in batches of about 6−12 pieces depending on the size of your fryer.
7. Cook at 160C//320F for 10−12 minutes or until golden brown.
8. Serve on their own or with a sweet dip.
9. Optional: dip in a bowl of melted chocolate to half coat the coconut ball and allow to set for an indulgent treat.

Nutritional Information per Serving:

SERVES −6 | CALORIES −345KCAL PER SERVING (EXCLUDING CHOCOLATE DIP) | PROTEIN −8.6G | CARBOHYDRATES −66G | FAT −5.5G

DOUGHNUTS/DONUTS

INGREDIENTS

- 125ml milk, lukewarm
- 60g//2oz caster sugar, plus 1 teaspoon for the yeast
- 15g//0.5oz packet of dried yeast
- 280g//10oz plain flour
- 45g//1.5oz of melted butter, cooled to lukewarm
- 1 egg
- 1 teaspoon vanilla extract
- Optional: ½ teaspoon of ground cinnamon
- Cooking spray
- Melted butter, extra sugar, and cinnamon for dusting

METHOD

The dough can be mixed by hand. Alternatively, you can use a stand mixer; or if you have a bread maker, use the dough feature.

This method will take you through 'by hand' Method which you can adapt accordingly.

1. Add 1 teaspoon of sugar to the lukewarm milk and stir until dissolved.
2. Add the dried yeast and leave to stand for 8–10 minutes, or until frothy.
3. In a separate bowl, whisk the sugar, butter, egg, and vanilla until combined, then mix in the yeast and milk mixture.
4. Add the flour (and cinnamon if using) and mix to a sticky dough.
5. Transfer the dough to a clean, lightly floured surface and knead until you have a smooth, elastic dough.
6. Lightly spray a large bowl with cooking oil, put the ball of dough in the greased bowl and cover.
7. Leave to prove in a warm place for about 60–90 minutes. The dough should double in size.
8. When the dough is ready, roll out onto a floured surface to a depth of 1.5cms.
9. Either used a dedicated doughnut cutter, or 2 standard cookie cutters (1 large and 1 small) to cut out your doughnut shapes. Keep the doughnut 'holes' as they made great bitesize doughnut pieces.
10. Put your doughnut pieces onto a lined greaseproof tray, cover, and place in the fridge to prove for a further 40–60 minutes.
11. Preheat the air fryer to 180C//350F, then add the doughnut pieces 2 or 3 at a time.
12. Prepare a tray with a layer of caster sugar and cinnamon and keep close to hand.
13. Cook at 180C//350F for about 6 minutes until golden brown.
14. When golden, use tongs to remove the doughnuts from the air fryer, brush lightly with melted butter, and turn over in the sugar–filled tray.
15. Leave to cool on a wire rack while you cook your next batch.
16. Optional: delicious coated with sugar (and cinnamon) or dipped in melted chocolate or a glaze of your choice. You may want to add sprinkles, coconut flakes or even chopped nuts to your glaze. Be creative!

Nutritional Information per Serving:

SERVES –MAKES 6-8 DOUGHNUTS | CALORIES –290KCAL | PROTEIN –6G | CARBOHYDRATES –51G | FAT –7G

CHURROS

INGREDIENTS

For the Coating:

◆ 100g//3.50z of granulated sugar   ◆ ¾ teaspoon of cinnamon

For the Churros:

◆ 235ml water
◆ 75g//2.60z of unsalted butter
◆ 30g//1oz of sugar
◆ ¼ teaspoon of salt
◆ 130g//4.50z plain flour
◆ 2 eggs
◆ 1 teaspoon of vanilla extract
◆ Spray cooking oil

METHOD

1. Mix the cinnamon and granulated sugar for the churros coating in a wide shallow bowl and set to one side.
2. Put the water, butter, sugar, and salt in a saucepan, and bring to a slow boil over a medium heat.
3. Add the flour to the saucepan. Keep stirring the mixture until it forms a smooth dough.
4. Remove from the heat and transfer the dough to a bowl, leaving to cool for a few minutes.
5. Once cooled, add the eggs and vanilla to the dough and combine until smooth. You can use an electric stand or hand mixer at this stage if you prefer.
6. Preheat the air fryer to 190C//375F.
7. Press balls of the dough mixture into a piping bag and use a large star–shaped tip to pipe out traditional 10cms lengths onto greaseproof paper.
8. Place the prepared churros in a refrigerator for about an hour. Refrigeration will make them easier to handle when cooking.
9. Transfer the churros in batches to the air fryer. Don't overcrowd as they will increase slightly in size, and you don't want them to clump together.
10. Cook at 190C//375F for 10–12 minutes until golden brown.
11. When ready, transfer immediately to the prepared sugar and cinnamon plate and coat thoroughly with the mixture.
12. Serve dipped in melted chocolate or with your favourite sweet dipping sauce.

Nutritional Information per Serving:

SERVES –4 TO 6 | CALORIES –204KCAL | PROTEIN –3G | CARBOHYDRATES –27G | FAT –9G

DELICIOUS APPLE FRITTERS WITH APPLE CIDER GLAZE

INGREDIENTS

- 2 large crisp apples
- 255g//9oz plain flour
- 65g//2.3oz sugar
- 15g//0.5oz of baking powder
- 1 teaspoon of salt

- 1 teaspoon cinnamon
- 1/2 teaspoon ground nutmeg
- 1/4 teaspoon ground cloves
- 175ml apple cider or apple juice (not apple cider vinegar)

- 2 eggs
- 70g//2.5oz of melted butter
- 1 teaspoon vanilla essence

For the Apple Cider Glaze:

- 255g//9oz icing sugar
- 60ml apple cider or apple juice
- 1/2 teaspoon cinnamon
- 1/4 teaspoon nutmeg

METHOD

1. Peel the apples and remove the cores.
2. Chop the apple into pieces of about ½ cm.
3. Pat the apple pieces dry with kitchen roll; excess moisture will make your fritters soggy.
4. Mix all the dry ingredients together in a bowl and stir in the apples.
5. Whisk the apple cider, eggs, melted butter, and vanilla in a separate bowl, then add to the flour mixture. Combine all the ingredients together.
6. Preheat the air fryer to 200C/392F.
7. Being careful not to overfill the air fryer, scoop 3–4 dollops of the dough into the air fryer basket.
8. TIP – an ice cream scoop makes this task a little easier.
9. Spray a light coating of oil over the fritters in the basket.
10. Cook for 6 minutes at 200C//392F, then flip over and cook for another 4 minutes. Remove from the air fryer and let them cool.
11. Whisk together the glaze and drizzle over the top, allowing a few minutes for it to set before serving.

Nutritional Information per Serving:

SERVES –12 TO 14 APPLE FRITTERS | CALORIES –221KCAL | PROTEIN –3G | CARBOHYDRATES –46G | FAT –3G

GOOEY BROWNIES

INGREDIENTS

- 115g/4oz of butter
- 30g//1oz of 100% dark chocolate
- 85g//3oz of dark cocoa powder
- 85g//3oz of plain flour
- 130g//4.5oz of sugar
- 1/4 teaspoon salt
- 2 eggs
- 1 teaspoon vanilla extract

METHOD

1. Lightly spray a 6–inch square cake pan with cooking spray.
2. Preheat the air fryer to 155C//311°F.
3. Melt the butter and chocolate together in a heatproof bowl.
4. Stir in the dry ingredients, the egg, and the vanilla extract to create a batter mixture.
5. Pour the batter into the cake pan.
6. Place the pan in the air fryer and cook at 155C//311F for 18–22 minutes.
7. Leave to cool for 15–20 minutes before cutting into squares and serve with a dollop of extra thick double cream for a delicious gooey treat.

Nutritional Information per Serving:

SERVES –MAKES 8–10 BROWNIES, 1 PER SERVING | CALORIES –255KCAL | PROTEIN –4G | CARBOHYDRATES –30G | FAT –14G

EASY CHOCOLATE CUPCAKES

INGREDIENTS

- 70g//2.5oz dark cocoa powder
- 120ml hot water
- 70g//2.5oz sugar
- 60ml vegetable oil
- 120ml milk
- 1 egg
- 1 teaspoon vanilla extract
- 70g//2.5oz flour
- 3/4 teaspoon baking powder
- 3/4 teaspoon baking soda
- 1/2 teaspoon salt

METHOD

1. Due to the size and shape of most air fryers, individual silicone cupcake holders are a more practical choice than cupcake trays.
2. Preheat the air fryer to 155C//310F.
3. Lightly spray 12 silicone cupcake holders with cooking oil. Or, if preferred, individually line with paper cupcake holders.
4. Whisk the hot water and cocoa powder together in a large bowl.
5. Whisk in the sugar, oil, milk, egg, and vanilla extract into a batter.
6. Sift the flour, baking powder, and baking soda into the batter, add the salt and stir thoroughly.
7. Pour the batter equally between the cupcake holders.
8. Cook at 155C//310F for 10–12 minutes until firm to touch. Poke a skewer gently into the cupcake; if it comes away clean then the cakes are ready.
9. Place the cupcakes on a cooling rack, dust with sieved icing sugar, or spread with frosting of your choice.

Nutritional Information per Serving:

SERVES –MAKE 12–14 CUPCAKES, 1 PER SERVING | CALORIES –278KCAL | PROTEIN –3G | CARBOHYDRATES –40G | FAT –12G

BANANA FRITTERS

INGREDIENTS

- 4 bananas, cut in half
- 130g//4.5oz plain flour
- 2 whisked eggs
- 130g//4.5oz desiccated coconut (replace with ground almonds if preferred)
- 1 teaspoon of cinnamon
- 2 teaspoons of melted butter

METHOD

1. Roll the bananas in the flour, then dip in the whisked egg so they are coated in the mixture.
2. Mix the coconut, cinnamon, and melted butter in a separate bowl.
3. Roll the banana halves in the coconut mix.
4. Preheat the air fryer to 180C//350F.
5. Roll the banana halves in the coconut mix and put in the air fryer.
6. Cook at 180C//355F for 5–8 minutes until the fritters are a golden colour.
7. Serve with ice cream or yoghurt.

Nutritional Information per Serving:

SERVES –2 | CALORIES –389KCAL | PROTEIN –8G | CARBOHYDRATES –59G | FAT –4G

OAT–TOPPED BAKED APPLES

INGREDIENTS

- 2 medium–sized apples
- A large knob of butter, melted
- ½ teaspoon of cinnamon

For the Topping:

- 30g//1oz of rolled oats
- 15g//0.5oz of butter
- 20ml of maple syrup (honey can be used as an alternative)
- 1 teaspoon of flour (use wholemeal if you have it otherwise, plain flour will do)
- ½ teaspoon of cinnamon

METHOD

1. Wash the apples thoroughly. Use a corer to take out the middle, then cut them in half through the stem. Scrape out any remaining seeds or core.
2. Spread a teaspoon of the butter evenly over the cut part of the apples, then sprinkle over ½ teaspoon of cinnamon.
3. In a bowl, mix the remaining ingredients thoroughly, and spoon evenly onto the apple halves.
4. Preheat the air fryer to 180C//350F.
5. Place the apple halves in the air fryer and cook for 15 minutes at 180C//350F. The apples should soften.
6. Delicious served warm with vanilla ice cream or cream.

Nutritional Information per Serving:

SERVES −2 | CALORIES −247KCAL | PROTEIN −3G | CARBOHYDRATES −43G | FAT −9G

APPLE PIE ROLL—OVERS

INGREDIENTS

For the Egg Rolls:

- 20 egg roll wrappers
- 350g//12.3oz of peeled, cored and chopped apples
- Spray cooking oil
- 1/2 teaspoon ground cinnamon

For the Cinnamon Yoghurt Dip:

- 280g//10oz of plain Greek yoghurt
- 2 teaspoon brown sugar
- 1/2 teaspoon ground cinnamon
- 1/4 teaspoon vanilla extract

METHOD

1. Steam the apple pieces on the stove for about 4–5 minutes until the apples are firm, but tender when pierced with a knife.
2. Drain the steamed apple pieces and toss in a bowl with the cinnamon.
3. Prepare the rolls by spreading the apple mixture over the wrap in a thin layer. Start one side of the wrap and roll up into a sausage shape. Preheat the air fryer to 180C//360F.
4. Arrange the apple roll–overs in a single layer in the air fryer with the seam side down. Leave space in between each one.
5. Spritz with cooking oil spray and cook for 6 minutes at 180C//360F.
6. Pause the cooking, turn the rolls over and cook for a further 2 minutes at the same temperature.
7. While the egg rolls are cooking, mix the remaining ingredients in a small bowl until smooth.
8. Optional: serve the egg rolls with the yoghurt dip, or cream.

Nutritional Information per Serving:

SERVES −2 EGG ROLLS PER SERVING | CALORIES −111KCAL | PROTEIN −5G | CARBOHYDRATES −20G | FAT −1G

GINGERBREAD DESSERT BITES

INGREDIENTS

- 1 can of crescent rolls
- 230g//8oz of cream cheese, room temperature
- 15g//0.5oz of sugar, plus an additional 100g//3.52oz sugar
- 1" piece of fresh ginger, grated
- 20g//0.7oz of ground cinnamon
- ½ teaspoon of allspice
- ¼ teaspoon of ground nutmeg
- ¼ teaspoon of ground cardamom
- ½ teaspoon ground cloves
- Spray cooking oil

METHOD

1. Mix all the spices together in one bowl, together with 100g of the sugar. Set to one side.
2. In a separate bowl, combine the 1 tablespoon of sugar with the cream cheese.
3. Open the can of crescent dough and unroll.
4. Follow the pre–cut perforations in the dough to separate the individual rolls and add 15g//0.5oz of the cream cheese mixture to the top corner of the triangle.
5. Fold the dough to cover the cream cheese and use your hands to gently shape into a round disc.
6. Preheat the air fryer to 175C//350F. Spray with cooking oil.
7. Dip the bites into the spice mixture ensuring they are covered all over.
8. Put the bites in the air fryer and cook at 175C//350F for 8–9 minutes.
9. Serve immediately.

Nutritional Information per Serving:

SERVES –4 | CALORIES –246KCAL | PROTEIN –4.6G | CARBOHYDRATES –14.1G | FAT –20.1G

APPLE WONTONS

INGREDIENTS

- 1 package of Wonton wrappers
- 1 x 425g//15oz can of apple pie filling
- 100g//3.5oz of sugar
- 1 teaspoon of cinnamon
- Spray cooking oil
- Caramel sauce
- Icing sugar

METHOD

1. Combine the apple pie filling, sugar and cinnamon in a bowl.
2. Lay the wonton wrappers open near the air fryer and place a large teaspoon of fill in the middle.
3. Squeeze some caramel sauce over the top.
4. Bring the sides of the wonton wrapper over the filling and seal at the top.
5. Preheat the air fryer to 180C//350F.
6. Put the Wontons in the air fryer and spray lightly with the cooking oil.
7. Cook for 7 minutes at 180C//350F.
8. When cooked, drizzle with the caramel sauce and sprinkle with icing sugar.

Nutritional Information per Serving:

SERVES –MAKES 50 WONTONS | CALORIES –46KCAL | PROTEIN –10G | CARBOHYDRATES –10G | FAT –1G

PUMPKIN BITES

INGREDIENTS

- 115g//4oz pumpkin puree
- 60g//2oz of softened cream cheese
- 1 egg
- 60g//2oz granulated sugar
- 1 teaspoon of pumpkin pie spice
- 1 teaspoon of vanilla extract
- Salt to taste
- 2 x 425g//15oz cans of crescent roll dough sheets

For the Topping:

- 115g//4oz melted butter
- 60g//2oz of granulated sugar
- 1 teaspoon of pumpkin pie spice

METHOD

1. Preheat the air fryer to 180C//350F.
2. In a mixing bowl combine the pumpkin puree, cream cheese, egg, sugar, 1 teaspoon of pumpkin pie spice, vanilla, and salt with an electric mixer until smooth and creamy.
3. Unroll the crescent dough and cut into squares – 8 per roll.
4. Put 14g//0.5oz of pumpkin filling in the centre of each dough square, bring the corners up and pinch the seams closed.
5. Line the air fryer with baking paper, spray with oil spray and place the dough balls inside in a single layer with space between each one.
6. Cook for 4–5 minutes at 180C//350F until the dough is golden brown.
7. Meanwhile, make the topping by mixing the sugar and the remaining pumpkin pie spice together until blended. Set the melted butter in a dish to one side.
8. Once cooked, take the pumpkin bites out of the air fryer, and dunk each one first Remove the pumpkin pie bombs from the air fryer and dunk each one first in the melted butter and then into the sugar–spice mixture.
9. Serve immediately.

Nutritional Information per Serving:

SERVES –4 | CALORIES –345KCAL | PROTEIN –5.6G | CARBOHYDRATES –36.4G | FAT –23G

GOLDEN PINEAPPLE

INGREDIENTS

- 1 fresh pineapple
- 50g//1.7oz brown sugar
- 2 teaspoons of ground cinnamon
- Pinch of salt
- 30g//1oz of melted butter

METHOD

1. Peel the pineapple and cut off the stalks. Cut the pineapple flesh into spears.
2. Mix the brown sugar, cinnamon, and salt in a small bowl.
3. Preheat the air fryer to 200C//400F.
4. Brush butter over the pineapple sprinkle with cinnamon sugar.
5. Place pineapple in the air fryer basket, leaving space between each piece for air to flow.
6. Cook for 10 minutes at 200C//400F until golden brown.
7. Serve warm.

Nutritional Information per Serving:

SERVES –4 | CALORIES –118KCAL | PROTEIN –2.3G | CARBOHYDRATES –63.9G | FAT –6.3G

PEAR CRISP

● ●

INGREDIENTS

- 2 large pears, peeled, cored, and diced
- 1 teaspoon lemon juice
- ¾ teaspoon ground cinnamon
- 2 tablespoons quick–cooking oats
- 15g//0.5oz of plain flour
- 15g//0.5oz of brown sugar
- 15g//0.5oz of salted butter at room temperature

METHOD

1. Mix the pears, lemon juice, and 1/4 teaspoon of the cinnamon together in a bowl.
2. Make sure the pears are thoroughly coated in the lemon juice and cinnamon, then divide the mixture evenly between two ramekins.
3. In a clean bowl, combine the oats, flour, brown sugar, and remaining 1/2 teaspoon cinnamon in a small bowl. Add the butter and mix with a fork until the mixture is crumbly. Sprinkle over the pears.
4. Preheat the air fryer to 180C//360F.
   Put the ramekins in the air fryer and cook at 180C~//200F for 18–20 minutes. The pears should be soft and bubbling.
5. Serve hot or cold.

Nutritional Information per Serving:

SERVES –2 | CALORIES –234KCAL | PROTEIN –2G | CARBOHYDRATES –46.3G | FAT –6.4G

SUMMER PEACHES

● ●

INGREDIENTS

- 4 peaches
- 50g//1.7oz of brown sugar
- 1 teaspoon of cinnamon
- 70g//2.5oz butter, room temperature

METHOD

1. Cut the peaches in half and remove the stone.
2. Combine the cinnamon and brown sugar in a bowl, then fold the butter into the mixture. It should resemble coarse breadcrumbs.
3. Preheat the air fryer to 180C//350F and spritz with cooking oil.
4. Place the peaches in the air fryer on its peel side with the fleshy side facing up.
5. Divide the sugar evenly between the peach halves, scooping it carefully into the hollow of each peach.
6. Cook for 7–12 minutes at 180C//350F. When the sugar begins to caramelise the peaches are cooked.
7. Serve with vanilla ice cream or cream.

Nutritional Information per Serving:

SERVES –4 | CALORIES –197KCAL | PROTEIN –1.6 G | CARBOHYDRATES –23.4 G | FAT –11.9G

BAKED PEARS

INGREDIENTS

- 2 medium pears
- 15g//0.5oz of granulated sugar
- 1/2 teaspoon ground cinnamon
- 30g//1oz of melted butter, unsalted

For the Topping:

- 15g//0.5oz of honey
- 15g//0.5oz of butter

METHOD

1. Wash the pears, remove the cores and slice in half from top to bottom. Place on a lightly oiled tray with the flesh side facing upwards.
2. Mix the cinnamon and sugar in a bowl together and sprinkle a little over the pear halves.
3. Add 14g//0.5oz of the melted butter to each pear cavity and sprinkle the rest of the sugar and cinnamon over the top.
4. Put the pears into the air fryer and cook at 185C//370F for 10 minutes.
5. Baste the pears with the butter a couple of times during the cooking.
6. Drizzle with the butter and honey and serve.

Nutritional Information per Serving:

SERVES −4 | CALORIES −152KCAL | PROTEIN −0.4G | CARBOHYDRATES −20.2G | FAT −8.8G

CRISPY THAI BANANA BITES

INGREDIENTS

- 4 ripe bananas, peeled
- 15g//0.5oz of plain flour
- 15g//0.5oz of rice flour
- 15g//0.5oz of corn flour
- 15g//0.5oz of desiccated coconut
- 1 pinch of salt
- 1/2 teaspoon of baking powder
- Water to mix
- Optional: 1/2 teaspoon of cardamom powder
- Spray cooking oil

For the Coating:

- 30g//1oz of rice flour
- Sesame seeds

METHOD

1. In a large bowl, mix the plain, rice and corn flours, baking powder, salt and coconut together.
2. Whisk in the water a little at a time to make a thick, smooth batter that coats the back of a spoon.
3. Put the rice flour, and the sesame seeds in two separate bowls and set to one side.
4. Cut the bananas in half lengthways; if you have large bananas, the pieces to about 4 inches in length.
5. Line the air fryer with foil and spritz with a little cooking oil. Preheat the 200C//400F.
6. Dip the banana slices in the batter mix so they are well coated, then roll them in the dry rice flour and then the sesame seeds.
7. Put the coated banana pieces on the greased oil in the air fryer and cook at 200C//400F for about 10−15 minutes.
8. Turn the banana pieces about halfway through cooking so they brown evenly.
9. Serve with ice cream or cream.

Nutritional Information per Serving:

SERVES −4 | CALORIES −371KCAL | PROTEIN −4.7G | CARBOHYDRATES −67.4G | FAT −10.7G

STRAWBERRY SHORTCAKE

INGREDIENTS

- 400g//14oz of fresh strawberries, washed, stalks removed and sliced
- 15g//0.5oz + 2 teaspoon granulated sugar
- 150g//5oz of plain flour
- 1 teaspoon of baking powder
- ¼ teaspoon of baking soda
- ¼ teaspoon of salt
- 45g//1.5oz of butter, refrigerated and diced
- 120ml of low-fat buttermilk
- Whipped cream for serving

METHOD

1. Mix the strawberries and 1 tablespoon of sugar together in a bowl and set to one side.
2. Preheat the air fryer to 150C//300F. Spray a baking pan with cooking oil.
3. In a separate bowl, combine the flour, remaining sugar, baking powder, baking soda and salt; next, add the butter into the mixture and with your hands, break it up into small pieces.
4. Pour the buttermilk into the mixture gradually and mix to a sticky dough.
5. Spread the shortcake mixture evenly over the baking tray.
6. Cook at 150C//300F for 15 minutes until golden brown. Allow to cool.
7. Serve with strawberries and a dollop of whipped cream.

Nutritional Information per Serving:

SERVES -4 | CALORIES -244KCAL | PROTEIN -5 G | CARBOHYDRATES -31G | FAT -12G

BAKED CARAMELISED PLANTAIN

INGREDIENTS

- 2 ripe plantains yellow/black
- 30g//1oz of melted coconut oil
- 30g//1oz of coconut sugar
- 1 teaspoon of ground cinnamon
- 1/4 teaspoon of fine grain sea salt
- Spray cooking oil

METHOD

1. Cut the ends off the plantains and peel them.
2. Preheat the air fryer to 180C//350F.
3. Cut the plantains round, ¼ inch slices.
4. Toss the slices in a bowl with the melted coconut oil.
5. Line a baking tray with greaseproof paper and lightly spritz it with cooking oil.
6. Spread the plantains in a single layer across the tray.
7. Next, mix the coconut sugar, cinnamon, and salt together in a bowl, then sprinkle evenly over the plantains.
8. Cook for 25 minutes at 180C//350F, turning after 15 minutes.
9. Serve warm.

Nutritional Information per Serving:

SERVES -4 | CALORIES -383KCAL | PROTEIN -2.4G | CARBOHYDRATES -70G | FAT -14.3G

FRIED ICE CREAM!

INGREDIENTS

- 1 litre carton of vanilla ice cream
- 150g//5oz of crunchy cinnamon cereal
- Optional: chocolate syrup for topping
- Optional: whipped cream for topping
- Optional: maraschino cherries for topping

METHOD

1. Line a baking tray with greaseproof paper.
2. Seal the cereal inside a plastic bag and crush thoroughly. Transfer the crushed cereal to a large plate.
3. Working quickly, scoop out a large ball of ice cream, shape it quickly with clean hands and immediately roll each ice cream ball one at a time in the crushed cereal. Press firmly into the cereal so that it coats the ice cream thoroughly, like a crust.
4. Place the tray of ice cream balls in the freezer for 3–4 hours.
5. Preheat the air fryer to 200C//400F.
6. Transfer the ice cream balls straight from the freezer to the preheated air fryer and cook for 2 minutes at 200C//400F.
7. Serve immediately with your favourite toppings.

Nutritional Information per Serving:

SERVES –4 | CALORIES –650 KCAL | PROTEIN –13G | CARBOHYDRATES –94G | FAT –27G

BAKED DULCE DE LECHE CHEESECAKE

INGREDIENTS

- 385g//14oz of wafers, crushed
- 60g//2oz of unsalted butter melted
- 455g//16oz of softened cream cheese, at room temperature
- 2 eggs
- 1 egg yolk
- 1 tablespoon cornflour
- 1 x 425g//15oz can of dulce de leche (set aside 160g//5.5oz for the topping)

METHOD

1. Prepare the crust by crushing the wafers into small pieces and mixing them with the melted butter in a bowl until well combined.
2. Press the wafer mixture into a greased 7-inch pan and place in the freezer.
3. Prepare the filling by mixing the cream cheese and cornflour until creamy. Use a stand mixer on a low speed for the best result.
4. Gradually add the 2 eggs to the mixture while continuing mixing on a low speed.
5. Add the contents of the can of dulce de leche and continue mixing on a low speed until all the ingredients are combined.
6. Remember to reserve a small quantity from the can of dulce de leche for the topping.
7. Preheat the air fryer to 165C//325F.
8. Retrieve the crust from the freezer and pour in the filling, spreading it evenly across the pan with a spatula.
9. Cover the cheesecake with foil and cook at 165C//325F for about 35 minutes.
10. Allow the cheesecake to cool, then chill in the fridge for at least 8 hours before serving.
11. Top with the remainder of the dulce de leche and serve.

Nutritional Information per Serving:

SERVES −8 | CALORIES −272KCAL | PROTEIN −5G | CARBOHYDRATES −3 G | FAT −27G

APPLE ROSE DESSERT

INGREDIENTS

- 3 red dessert apples
- 15ml of lemon juice
- 2 prepared sheets of puff pastry
- Flour to sprinkle
- 45g//1.5oz of cinnamon

For the Topping:

- Icing sugar for sprinkling
- Honey drizzle

METHOD

1. Wash and core the apples then cut slices as thinly as possible.
2. In a saucepan, cover the apples with water just enough so they float, and drizzle some lemon juice over the top.
3. Bring to the boil and simmer gently until the apple slices have softened, but not turned mushy.
4. On a floured surface, roll out one layer of puff pastry just enough to even it out and flatten the individual sheets. Cut the rolled pastry sheet into six slices.
5. Remove the apples from the water and drain them in a colander.

How to make the apple roses:

1. Put one of the cut pastry slices on a floured counter with the long side nearest to you.
2. Lay overlapping slices of semi–circular pieces of apple in a line along the top edge, overlapping slightly.
3. Take the long edge of the pastry nearest to you and fold it carefully up to meet the opposite edge. There should be a line of curved apples peeping above the edge as you bring the two sides of the pastry together.
4. Repeat the process with your next slice of pastry and continue until it's all used up. Sprinkle with ½ teaspoon of cinnamon.
5. Take the short end of the apple–filled pastry sheet, and with your hands, carefully roll it up, pinching the ends to seal.
6. Preheat the air fryer to 190C//375F.
7. Place the apple roses into prepared silicone cupcake liners and place in the air fryer.
8. Cook at 190C//375F for about seven minutes until the pastry is baked.
9. Serve warm, dusted with icing sugar, or drizzled with honey or syrup.

Nutritional Information per Serving:

SERVES –12 | CALORIES –262KCAL | PROTEIN –3G | CARBOHYDRATES –27G | FAT –16G

BREAD AND BUTTER PUDDING

INGREDIENTS

- 4 slices of stale thick sliced bread
- 3 eggs
- 240ml of double cream
- 75g//2.6oz of caster sugar
- 1 teaspoon of cinnamon
- 1 teaspoon of vanilla essence
- 120ml semi–skimmed milk
- 200g//7oz of raisins
- 30g//1oz butter
- Olive oil cooking spray
- Optional: icing sugar

METHOD

1. In a bowl that will fit your air fryer, whisk the eggs, cream, sugar, vanilla, and cinnamon.
2. Cut the bread into big chunks and add to the bowl.
3. Stir well until the bread is drenched in the batter mixture.
4. Preheat the air fryer to 190C//380F and spray with olive oil cooking spray.
5. Put the bread mixture in the air fryer and cook for 5 minutes at 190C//380F for about 5 minutes.
6. Now add the raisins and milk to the bread pudding mixture and mix well. Top with small knobs of butter.
7. Increase the air fryer temperature to 200C//400F and return the bowl to the air fryer.
8. Cook for a further 5 minutes at 200C//400F.
9. Sprinkle with the icing sugar before serving.

Nutritional Information per Serving:

SERVES –4 | CALORIES –514KCAL | PROTEIN –9G | CARBOHYDRATES –67G | FAT –26G

CHRISTMAS CAKE

INGREDIENTS

- 230g//8oz of butter
- 230g//8oz caster sugar
- 20g//0.7oz of golden syrup
- 4 eggs
- 60g//2oz ground rice
- 255g//9oz plain flour
- ¼ teaspoon of baking powder
- 455g//16oz currants
- 115g//4oz of raisins
- 115g//4oz of sultanas
- 60g//2oz of glace cherries
- Optional: 50ml brandy
- Silicone cake mould that fits your air fryer

METHOD

1. Use a hand mixer to combine the butter and sugar in a mixing bowl until pale and creamy.
2. Fold in the eggs and golden syrup and use a slow setting on the hand mixer to combine.
3. Next, add the baking powder, ground rice, and half (about 127g//4.5oz) of the flour. Combine, then add the rest of the flour bit by bit and stir it in.
4. Fold in all the dried fruit and the cherries. The mixture will become stiff and sticky, but the more blended the ingredients, the better the cake, so stay with it!
5. Preheat the air fryer to 150C//300F.
6. Transfer the cake mix to the silicone cake mould which has been pre-sprayed with cooking oil. Place in the air fryer.
7. Cook for 40 minutes at 150C//300F.
8. Turn up the temperature to 160C//320F and cook for a further 10 minutes.
9. Allow to cool on a wire rack.
10. Optional: brush the cake all over with brandy and leave to stand overnight.

Nutritional Information per Serving:

SERVES –8 | CALORIES –387KCAL | PROTEIN –5G | CARBOHYDRATES –65G | FAT –13G

HOMEMADE APPLE PIE
• •

INGREDIENTS

- 400g//14oz of ready prepared shortcrust pastry
- 325g//11.5oz of apples, peeled, cored, and cut into small pieces
- 50g//1.8oz of caster sugar
- Zest and freshly squeezed juice of 1 lemon
- 2 teaspoons of cinnamon
- ½ teaspoon of nutmeg
- 1 teaspoon of mixed spice
- 1 small beaten egg for egg wash
- Caster sugar for sprinkling

METHOD

1. Roll out your pie crust and place it into the bottom of your pie pan.
2. Press your peeled and diced apples, along with the lemon, cinnamon, and nutmeg into the pie pan making sure there are no gaps.
3. Add the second layer of pie crust over your apples and press down. Make a small slit in the middle to allow the pie room to breathe, and using a pastry brush, add a layer of egg wash.
4. Put in the air fryer and cook for 30 minutes at 180C//360F.
5. Serve with either cream, ice cream, or custard.

Nutritional Information per Serving:

SERVES –6 | CALORIES –384KCAL | PROTEIN –5G | CARBOHYDRATES –51G | FAT –18G

FRUIT SCONES
• •

INGREDIENTS

- 230g//8oz of self–raising flour
- 50g//1.7oz butter
- 50g//1.7oz sultanas
- 25g//0.8oz caster sugar
- 1 egg, beaten
- Milk to mix

METHOD

1. In a bowl, rub the butter and the flour between your fingers until the mixture resembles coarse breadcrumbs.
2. Add the sultanas, then the caster sugar, and mix in.
3. Add the beaten egg and use a fork to mix until combined.
4. Add the milk a little at a time continuing to mix with a fork until you have a light, smooth scone dough.
5. Preheat the air fryer to 180C//360F, and lightly spritz with cooking oil.
6. Roll out the dough on a floured surface to about 1 inch thick. Don't press too hard with the roller or your scones will be heavy. Cut out your scone shapes.
7. Place the scones in the air fryer and cook for 8 minutes at 180C//360F.
8. Serve warm or cold with butter, cream and jam.

Nutritional Information per Serving:

SERVES – MAKES 6–8 SCONES | CALORIES –370KCAL | PROTEIN – 8G | CARBOHYDRATES –57G | FAT –12G

FRUITY ROCK CAKES

INGREDIENTS

- 230g//8oz of self–raising flour
- 100g//3.50z of butter
- 50g//1.80z of caster sugar
- 1 egg, beaten
- 75g//2.50z of raisins and sultanas
- Zest and juice of 1 lemon
- Zest and juice of 1 orange
- 20g//0.70z of honey
- Milk

METHOD

1. In a bowl, use your fingertips to rub the butter and flour together to create a coarse breadcrumb mix. Add the sugar, raisins, and sultana and mix in.
2. Add the honey, the grated zest, and freshly squeezed juice of the orange and the lemon and give it all a good mix with a fork.
3. Add the egg, then add the milk a little at a time and combine with a fork until you have a soft dough.
4. Preheat the air fryer to 180C//360F, and spritz with cooking oil spray.
5. On a floured surface, roll the dough out lightly to about 1 inch thick, and cut out some scone shapes.
6. Cook in the air fryer for 10 minutes at 180C//360F.
7. Serve warm.

Nutritional Information per Serving:

SERVES –MAKES 6–8 CAKES | CALORIES –270KCAL | PROTEIN –4G | CARBOHYDRATES –39G | FAT –11G

CHEWY FRUITY GRANOLA BARS

INGREDIENTS

- 255g//9oz of rolled oats
- 60g//2oz of butter, melted
- 30g//1oz of brown sugar
- 60g//2oz of honey
- 1 dessert apple, peeled, cored and steamed until tender
- 15ml of olive oil
- 1 teaspoon of vanilla essence
- 1 teaspoon of cinnamon
- A handful of raisins, or your preferred dried fruit

METHOD

1. Blend the rolled oats until smooth, then add the remaining dry ingredients to the mixture.
2. In a separate bowl, add all the wet ingredients and mix well.
3. Combine the wet and dry ingredients and use a fork to mix well.
4. Preheat the air fryer to 180C//360F. Lightly spritz a rimmed baking tray with cooking oil.
5. Press the mixture into the baking tray with the back of a spoon.
6. Cook at 160C//320F for 10 minutes.
7. Increase the temperature to 180C//360F then cook for a further 5 minutes.
8. Allow to cool and place in the fridge for an hour to firm up.
9. Cut into granola bars and serve.

Nutritional Information per Serving:

SERVES −6 TO 8 | CALORIES −320KCAL | PROTEIN −5G | CARBOHYDRATES −46G | FAT −13G

FLAPJACKS

INGREDIENTS

- 100g//3.5oz of butter
- 100g//3.5oz brown sugar
- 45g//1.5oz of honey
- 255g//9oz rolled oats

METHOD

1. Melt the butter, honey, and brown sugar in a saucepan on low heat and stir.
2. Preheat the air fryer to 160C//320F, and lightly spritz a rimmed baking sheet with cooking oil.
3. Add the oats making sure the mixture is thoroughly combined. (Put the oats in the blender first if you prefer a smoother mixture.)
4. Cook for 10 minutes at 160C//320F.
5. Increase the temperature and cook for a further 5 minutes at 180C//320F.

Nutritional Information per Serving:

SERVES −6 | CALORIES −543KCAL | PROTEIN −8G | CARBOHYDRATES −75 G | FAT −24G

DELICIOUS CHOCOLATE BANANA BREAD

INGREDIENTS

- 20g//0.7oz of cocoa powder
- 3 ripe bananas
- 3 eggs
- 85ml coconut oil
- 40//1.4oz of honey
- 30g//1oz of banana flour
- 20g//0.7oz rolled oats
- 15ml of vanilla essence

METHOD

1. Mash the bananas in a mixing bowl with the eggs, vanilla essence, coconut oil and honey. Mix well until smooth.
2. Add the banana flour, oats and cocoa and combine.
3. Preheat the air fryer to 180C//360F.
4. Spritz a baking pan with cooking oil spray and pour in the banana bread mixture spreading it evenly with the back of a spoon.
5. Put the pan into the air fryer and cook for 18 minutes at 180C//360F.
6. Serve cold, or hot with chocolate sauce or custard.

Nutritional Information per Serving:

SERVES –8 | CALORIES –204KCAL | PROTEIN –3G | CARBOHYDRATES –17G | FAT –14G

PINEAPPLE CAKE

• •

INGREDIENTS

- 230g//8oz of self–raising flour
- 100g//3.5oz of butter, chilled and cut into cubes
- 100g//3.5oz of caster sugar
- 200g//7oz of fresh pineapple chopped into chunks
- 100ml pineapple juice
- 50g//1.8oz of dark chocolate, grated
- 1 egg
- 30ml of milk

METHOD

1. In a bowl, rub the butter and flour between your fingertips until it resembles coarse breadcrumbs.
2. Add the sugar, pineapple chunks, pineapple juice (save the juice from the pineapple when you chop it up) and dark chocolate. Stir in thoroughly and put the mixture to one side.
3. Whisk the egg and milk together in a jug.
4. Preheat the air fryer to 200C//400F. Grease a cake tin.
5. Combine all the ingredients in one large bowl and mix well.
6. Cook at 200C//400F in the air fryer for 40 minutes.
7. Allow to cool for 10 minutes, slice, and serve.

Nutritional Information per Serving:

SERVES –8 | CALORIES –612KCAL | PROTEIN –9G | CARBOHYDRATES –81G | FAT –27G

INDULGENT PROFITEROLES

• •

INGREDIENTS

For the Profiteroles:

- 100g//3.5oz of butter
- 200g//7oz plain flour
- 6 eggs
- 300ml water

For the Cream Filling:

- 2 teaspoons of vanilla essence
- 5g//0.2oz of icing sugar
- 300ml whipped cream

For the Chocolate Sauce:

- 100g//3.5oz of milk chocolate broken into chunks
- 30ml of whipped cream
- 50g//1.8oz butter

METHOD

1. Put the water and butter together in a large pan and bring to the boil slowly.
2. Remove from the heat and stir in the flour a little at a time.
3. Return to a low heat until it thickens to form a dough in the pan. Set the dough to one side to cool.
4. Once the dough has cooled, add the eggs and mix well until the mixture is smooth and combined.
5. Preheat the air fryer to 180C//350F and spritz lightly with olive oil cooking spray.
6. Create the profiterole balls, place them in the air fryer and cook at and cook for 10 minutes on 180C//350F.
7. While the profiteroles are cooking, in a bowl, whisk the vanilla essence, whipped cream, and icing sugar together until you have a nice, thick cream. Set to one side.
8. For the chocolate topping, melt the chocolate, butter, and cream together by placing a glass boil over a pan of boiling water.
9. When the cream, chocolate sauce and profiteroles are ready, cut a small cross in the side of the profiterole bun and using a piping bag, fill it with cream. Repeat the process until all the buns are filled.
10. Finish your profiteroles with melted chocolate on top and serve. Delicious!

Nutritional Information per Serving:

SERVES –4–6 | CALORIES –390KCAL | PROTEIN –7G | CARBOHYDRATES –28G | FAT –27 G

STRAWBERRY PUFF PASTRY TWISTS

INGREDIENTS

* 1 puff pastry sheet defrosted and cut into two equal pieces
* 60-70g//2-2.5oz of strawberry preserve

METHOD

1. First, spread one side of one puff pastry sheet with the strawberry preserve. Place the other puff pastry sheet over the top to create a 'sandwich.'
2. Cut into strips of ½ inch thick.
3. Preheat the air fryer to 180C//360F, line with baking paper and spritz with cooking oil.
4. Twist each pastry strip and place in the air fryer.
5. Cook at 180C//360F for 9–10 minutes, turning once, halfway through cooking.
6. Cool before serving.

Nutritional Information per Serving:

SERVES –8 TO 10 | CALORIES –393KCAL | PROTEIN –5G | CARBOHYDRATES –41G | FAT –23G

MINI MAPLE SPONGE CAKES

INGREDIENTS

* 50g//1.7oz of self–raising flour
* 1/2 teaspoon of baking powder
* 35g//1.2oz of melted butter, cooled to room temperature
* 30ml of milk
* 35ml of maple syrup
* 1/4 teaspoon of vanilla extract
* 3 eggs

METHOD

1. Break the eggs into one bowl and separate the egg whites, putting yolks into a second bowl.
2. In the bowl with the egg yolks, mix the cooled butter, maple syrup and vanilla extract until combined.
3. Mix the flour and the baking powder together in another large bowl, then add the egg yolk mixture and whisk to combine the wet and dry ingredients into a thick batter. Set to one side.
4. Now, beat the egg whites (use an electric whisk if you prefer) until it forms stiff white peaks.
5. Pour into the cake batter and combine with a spatula.
6. Put the empty muffin tins inside the air fryer. Preheat the air fryer to 200C//400F.
7. Pour the cake batter evenly between the preheated muffin tins, and air fry at for 13–15 minutes at 130C//260F.
8. Turn the temperature up to 190C//380F and cook for a further 2 minutes until the muffins are a lovely golden brown.

Nutritional Information per Serving:

SERVES –4 TO 6 | CALORIES –195KCAL | PROTEIN –6G | CARBOHYDRATES –18G | FAT –11G

STRAWBERRY CREAM FRENCH TOAST

INGREDIENTS

- 4 pieces wheat toast
- 200g//7oz of cream cheese
- 60g//2oz of strawberries, washed and sliced
- 15g//0.5oz of sugar
- 1/2 teaspoon of lemon zest
- 15g//0.5oz of melted butter
- 1 egg
- 60ml of milk

METHOD

1. Mix the butter, milk, and egg together in a large bowl.
2. In a separate bowl, mix the cream cheese, sugar, and lemon zest.
3. Spread the mixture on one side of each piece of toast.
4. Lay the strawberry slices over the top of the mixture and put another piece of toast on top to create a sandwich. Press lightly together.
5. Preheat the air fryer to 200C//400F.
6. Dip the toasted sandwich into the egg wash ensuring both sides are covered.
7. Place in the air fryer for 8 minutes at 200C//400F. Turn once during cooking.
8. When both sides of the toast are golden, remove from the air fryer and serve.

Nutritional Information per Serving:

SERVES –4 | CALORIES –235KCAL | PROTEIN –7.1G | CARBOHYDRATES –18.4G | FAT –15.2G

APPLE FRENCH TOAST

INGREDIENTS

- 1 apple, washed, peeled, cored and chopped into small pieces
- 15g//0.5oz of butter
- 170g//6oz of bread, cut into 1–inch cubes
- 70g//2.5oz brown sugar
- 1 teaspoon of cornflour
- 3 eggs
- 160ml of milk
- 1/2 teaspoon of vanilla extract
- 1/2 teaspoon of cinnamon
- 30ml of maple syrup

METHOD

1. Microwave the butter and the apple pieces together in a bowl for about 3 minutes. The apple should be tender when you remove it.
2. Mix the bread, sugar, and cornflour together in a large mixing bowl.
3. In a separate bowl, whisk the eggs, milk, vanilla, cinnamon, apple and maple syrup together, and pour into the bread bowl. Mix thoroughly until combined.
4. Preheat the air fryer to 160C//320F.
5. Transfer the mixture to a lightly greased cake tin and cook 160C//320F for 12–14 minutes until golden brown.
6. Serve.

Nutritional Information per Serving:

SERVES –6 | CALORIES –336KCAL | PROTEIN –10G | CARBOHYDRATES –55 G | FAT –9G

STREUSEL CAKE
• •

INGREDIENTS

- 120ml of oil
- 1 egg, beaten
- 1/2 teaspoon of vanilla extract
- 120ml of milk

- 100g//3.5oz of sugar
- 180g//6.3oz of self–raising flour
- 1 1/2 teaspoons of baking powder
- Pinch of salt

- 115g//4oz of brown sugar
- 1 teaspoon cinnamon
- 60g//2oz of melted butter

METHOD

1. This recipe makes two streusel cakes.
2. In a medium bowl, combine the brown sugar and cinnamon (this is the streusel) and divide into two equal portions.
3. In a large bowl, combine the oil, eggs, vanilla, and milk. Add the sugar, flour, baking powder, and salt and mix well.
4. Divide the mixture equally between two mixing bowls.
5. Preheat the air fryer at 160C//320F. Lightly grease two loaf tins that will fit in the air fryer.
6. Put a layer of batter in each of the loaf tins, and sprinkle each one with the streusel, saving some to sprinkle over the top.
7. Pour the remaining batter over each sugary layer and sprinkle the remaining streusel on top. Drizzle with the melted butter.
8. Cook in the air fryer at 160C//320F for about 30 minutes. Cool, then serve!

Nutritional Information per Serving:

SERVES –6-8 | CALORIES –379KCAL | PROTEIN –4G | CARBOHYDRATES –44G | FAT –21G

CINNAMON ORANGE SLICES
• •

INGREDIENTS

- 4 oranges
- 1/2 teaspoon of cinnamon
- 2 teaspoons of brown sugar (or honey if you prefer)

METHOD

1. Mix the cinnamon and sugar together in a small bowl and set aside.
2. Cut each orange in half.
3. Preheat the air fryer to 200C//400F.
4. Sprinkle the cinnamon and sugar over the fleshy part of the orange.
5. Place in the air fryer and cook at 200C//400F for about 4–5 minutes.
6. Serve warm by itself or over ice cream.

Nutritional Information per Serving:

SERVES –4 | CALORIES –70KCAL | PROTEIN –1G | CARBOHYDRATES –18G | FAT –1G

CREAM CHEESE AND BLUEBERRY MUFFINS

INGREDIENTS

- 180g//6.3oz of plain flour
- 100g//3.5oz of white sugar
- Pinch of salt
- 2 teaspoons baking powder
- 60ml of vegetable oil
- 230g//8oz of softened cream cheese at room temperature
- 1 egg
- 1/2 teaspoon vanilla extract
- 80ml of milk
- 170g//6oz of fresh blueberries

METHOD

1. Prepare muffin tins.
2. Combine the flour, sugar, salt, and baking powder in a large bowl.
3. In a separate bowl, mix the vegetable oil, cream cheese, egg, and vanilla extract to a creamy texture, then stir in the milk.
4. Pour the batter mixture into the dry ingredients and mix until thoroughly combined.
5. Preheat the air fryer to 160C//320F.
6. Fold in the fresh blueberries, then use a tablespoon to scoop the mixture into the muffin tins to about ¾ full.
7. Cook at 160C//320F for about 12–14 minutes.
8. Serve with coffee as a sweet treat.

Nutritional Information per Serving:

SERVES –6 | CALORIES –421KCAL | PROTEIN –7G | CARBOHYDRATES –47G | FAT –24G

APPLE AND RASPBERRY MINI PIES

INGREDIENTS

- 2 dessert apples, peeled, cored, and diced into ¼ inch pieces
- 125g//4.4oz of raspberries
- 30g//1oz of light brown sugar
- 15g//0.5oz of granulated sugar, plus additional for sprinkling
- 1/4 teaspoon of ground cinnamon
- Pinch of salt
- 15ml of apple juice or cider
- 1 teaspoon of cornflour mixed with 1 teaspoon of water (for thickening)
- 2 prepared pie crust rounds
- 1 egg yolk beaten with 1 teaspoon water as egg wash

METHOD

1. Put the apples, raspberries, sugars, cinnamon, salt, and apple juice/cider in a saucepan together, and bring to a gentle simmer.
2. Cook for about 15 minutes, occasionally stirring, until the apples soften but remain firm, not mushy.
3. Add the thickening cornflour mixture to the saucepan, turn the heat up, and cook for about 1–2 minutes. Remove from the heat, set to one side, and allow to cool.
4. Now, roll out the prepared pastry and cut 12 circles with a 4–inch cookie cutter.
5. Put a tablespoon of the fruit filling in the centre of each circle and fold the pastry into a semi–circle over the top. Brush the edge of the pastry with water and seal. Use a fork to crimp the sealed edges.
6. Note: Don't overfill the pie, or it will burst during cooking.
7. Preheat the air fryer to 160C//320F.
8. Brush the tops of the pies with egg wash and cut two small slits on the top of each. Sprinkle sugar over the top.
9. Lightly spray the air fryer with oil, then add the pies in a single layer.
10. Bake for 15 minutes at 160C//320F until golden, then place on a wire rack to cool.

Nutritional Information per Serving:

SERVES –6 | CALORIES –131KCAL | PROTEIN –1.4G | CARBOHYDRATES –23.5G | FAT –3.8G

LEMON CREAM COOKIES

INGREDIENTS

For the Cookies:

- 330g//12oz flour
- 1/2 teaspoon of baking powder
- Pinch of salt

- 230g//8oz of unsalted butter, at room temperature
- 150g//5oz granulated sugar
- 1 egg

- 1 teaspoon of pure almond extract
- 1 teaspoon of pure vanilla extract

For the Buttercream and Decorating:

- 115g//4oz of unsalted butter, room temperature
- 255g//9oz of icing sugar
- Pinch of salt
- 1 teaspoon of pure almond extract
- 1 x 310g//11oz jar of lemon curd

METHOD

1. For the Cookies:
2. Whisk together the flour, baking powder, and salt in a bowl and set aside.
3. In a separate bowl, beat the butter and sugar to a creamy, pale–yellow mixture. Use an electric mixer if you have one.
4. Fold in the egg, then add the almond and vanilla extracts.
5. Gradually add the flour and stir in slowly until you can form a dough.
6. Roll the dough out between 2 sheets of waxed paper to about ⅛ inch thick, and place in the fridge for 30 minutes until firm.
7. Heat the air fryer to 180C//350F.
8. Line baking sheets with baking paper and using a floured 1 ½ inch round cookie cutter, cut out your cookie shapes.
9. Using a smaller round cookie cutter, cut out the centres of about half the cookies. Place on the lined baking sheet.
10. Bake for 10 to 12 minutes at 165C//325F until golden brown and allow to cool for a few minutes before transferring to wire racks. Let cool on sheets 5 minutes before transferring to wire racks to cool completely.

For the Buttercream:

1. Use an electric mixer if you have one. Beat butter, icing sugar, almond extract and salt together until smooth and creamy.
2. Working with one cookie at a time, spread the cookies without the holes with buttercream. Top each cookie with the cutout with the holes.
3. Dust with icing sugar and fill the holes with lemon curd.

Nutritional Information per Serving:

SERVES –24 | CALORIES –244KCAL | PROTEIN –2.2G | CARBOHYDRATES –28.6G | FAT –14.5G

CANNELONI RICOTTA DESSERT

INGREDIENTS

For the Filling:

- 450g//1lb container of ricotta cheese
- 130g//4.5oz of mascarpone cheese

- 60g//2oz of icing sugar
- 180g//6.3oz of double cream
- 1 teaspoon of pure vanilla extract
- 1 teaspoon of orange zest

- Pinch of salt
- 85g//3oz mini chocolate chips to decorate

For the Shells:

- 240g//8.5oz of plain flour
- 50g//1.8oz of granulated sugar
- Pinch of salt
- ½ teaspoon of cinnamon

- 60g//2oz of cold butter, cut into cubes
- 90ml of white wine
- 1 egg

- 1 egg white for brushing
- Spray cooking oil
- Cannelloni moulds

METHOD

For the Filling:

1. Allow the ricotta to drain overnight in the fridge.
2. In a bowl, beat the cream and half of the icing sugar together to form stiff peaks. Set to one side.
3. In a separate bowl, combine the ricotta, mascarpone, remaining icing sugar, vanilla, orange zest, and salt.
4. Fold in the whipped cream you prepared earlier and refrigerate for at least an hour before using.

For the Shells:

1. Whisk together the flour, sugar, salt, and cinnamon in a large bowl.
2. Cut butter into flour mixture with your hands until pea sized.
3. Add the wine and egg to the mixture and combine until a dough forms. Knead a few times in bowl to help dough come together.
4. Pat the dough into a flat circle, wrap in cling film, then refrigerate at least 1 hour .
5. When the dough is ready to use, on a lightly floured surface, divide the dough into two equal parts and roll one half out to ⅛" thick. Use a 4" round cookie cutter to cut out shapes. Repeat with remaining dough.
6. Wrap the dough around your cannoli moulds and brush egg whites where the dough will meet to seal the ends.

For the Cooking:

1. Work in batches. Preheat the air fryer to 180C//350F and lightly spray with cooking oil.
2. Place the dough covered moulds in the air fryer and cook at for 12 minutes at 180C//350F until golden.
3. Allow to cool before twisting the cannelloni shells off the moulds.
4. Use a piping bag to fill the shells, then dip the ends into a bowl filled with the mini chocolate chips.
5. Serve and enjoy!

Nutritional Information per Serving:

SERVES –20 | CALORIES –239KCAL | PROTEIN –5G | CARBOHYDRATES –21G | FAT –15G

CINNAMON BREAD CURLS

INGREDIENTS

- 120g//4.2oz of plain flour
- 1 teaspoon of baking powder
- Pinch of salt
- 150g//5oz of fat free Greek yoghurt
- 30g//1oz of butter
- 30g//1oz of granulated sugar
- 1–2 teaspoons of ground cinnamon, to taste

METHOD

1. In a bowl, combine the flour, baking powder, and salt. Add the Greek yoghurt and use a fork to stir everything together to form a crumbly dough.
2. On a floured surface, knead the dough until it's a smooth ball, then divide into 6 pieces of approximately 45g//1.5oz each.
3. Roll the dough into thin strips about 8 inches long.
4. Preheat the air fryer to 180C//350F.
5. Form a ribbon shape by folding one end of each strip over to create a 'bow.'
6. Place in the air fryer and spray lightly with cooking oil.
7. Cook at 180C//350F for about 15 minutes.
8. While the bread twists are cooking, in a pan over a low heat, melt the butter with the granulated sugar and cinnamon and stir.
9. Remove the bread twists and brush immediately with the cinnamon sugar butter.
10. Serve warm with your favourite sweet dipping sauce.

Nutritional Information per Serving:

SERVES –MAKES 6 BREAD TWISTS | CALORIES –105KCAL | PROTEIN –5G | CARBOHYDRATES –16G | FAT –5G

BEIGNETS

INGREDIENTS

- 120g//4.2oz of self raising flour
- 280g//10oz of Greek yoghurt
- 15g//0.5oz of sugar
- 1 teaspoon of vanilla essence
- 30g//1oz of butter, melted
- 60g//2oz of icing sugar

METHOD

1. Put the yoghurt, sugar, and vanilla in a bowl together and mix thoroughly.
2. Add the flour and mix to form a dough.
3. On a floured surface, gently knead the dough by folding it over a couple of times and pushing it into shape.
4. Form a rectangle shape about 1 inch thick and cut into 9 pieces. Dust the pieces with flour and let them rest of 15 minutes.
5. Preheat the air fryer to 180C//350F. Spray lightly with cooking oil.
6. Brush the top of the dough pieces/beignets with butter, and place butter side down in the air fryer. Brush the other side with butter.
7. Cook for 6–7 minutes at 180C//350F.
8. Turn the beignets over and cook for a further 6–7 minutes.
9. Remove from the air fryer and dust with icing sugar.

Nutritional Information per Serving:

SERVES –9 | CALORIES –123KCAL | PROTEIN –4 G | CARBOHYDRATES –20G | FAT –3G

SHORTBREAD

INGREDIENTS

- 255g//9oz of self–raising flour
- 175g//6oz of butter, cut into cubes
- 75g//2.7oz of sugar

METHOD

1. In a bowl, use your fingertips to rub together the butter, flour, and sugar until it resembles coarse breadcrumbs.
2. Combine until it forms a shortbread dough.
3. On a clean, floured surface, roll out your shortbread and use shaped cookie cutters to cut into shapes.
4. Add a layer of foil into the air fryer and preheat to 180C//360F.
5. Place the shortbread on the foil in the air fryer and cook for 8 minutes at 180C//360F.
6. Allow to cool, and ice and decorate if you wish.

Nutritional Information per Serving:

SERVES –12 | CALORIES –408KCAL | PROTEIN –5G | CARBOHYDRATES –43G | FAT –24G

CINNAMON TORTILLAS WITH FRUITY SALSA

INGREDIENTS

For the Fruit Salsa:

- 170g//6oz, finely chopped
- 2 kiwis, finely chopped
- 1 medium apple, finely chopped
- 15ml of lemon juice
- 30g//1oz of sugar

For the Cinnamon Tortilla Chips:

- 8 Flour tortillas (8" diameter)
- 30g//1oz of melted light butter
- 30g//1oz of sugar
- 1/2 teaspoon ground cinnamon

METHOD

1. Mix the mango, kiwis, apple, lemon juice and 2 tablespoons of sugar in a bowl together and refrigerate.
2. Preheat the air fryer to 200C//400F.
3. Slice the tortilla into triangular tortilla chips and add to a sealed bag with the sugar, butter, and cinnamon. Shake to coat the tortillas.
4. Remove the coated tortillas from the bag and spread evenly into the air fryer.
5. Cook for 4 minutes at 200C//400F.
6. Serve with the fruity salsa dip.

Nutritional Information per Serving:

SERVES –4 | CALORIES –299KCAL | PROTEIN –4G | CARBOHYDRATES –55.4G | FAT –8.6G

EASY BANANA ROLLS

INGREDIENTS

- 4 ripe bananas
- 115g//4oz brown sugar
- 8 lumpia wrappers (spring roll wrappers are a suitable substitute)
- 30ml of coconut oil

METHOD

1. Peel and cut each banana into 4 pieces. You should have 16 pieces in total.
2. Sprinkle the banana slices in brown sugar and wrap 2 pieces together in a lumpia wrapped. Repeat.
3. Preheat the air fryer to 200C//400F.
4. Brush each package with coconut oil.
5. Put them in the air fryer and cook for 15 minutes at 200C//400F.
6. Serve warm with cream or ice cream.

Nutritional Information per Serving:

SERVES –8 | CALORIES –286KCAL | PROTEIN –7.7G | CARBOHYDRATES –57.3G | FAT –4.1G

ROAST MANGO AND PINEAPPLE

INGREDIENTS

- ⅔ of a pineapple
- 1.5 peeled mangos
- Juice of 1 lemon
- 20ml of honey
- 20g//0.7oz of brown sugar
- 1 pinch of cinnamon

METHOD

1. Cut off the top and bottom of the pineapple, peel, core and chop into 1cm cubes.
2. Peel the mangoes, remove the stone and cut into 1cm cubes.
3. Preheat the air fryer to 220C//425F.
4. Put the pineapple in a pan, place in the air fryer and pour in the honey.
5. Cook for 8 minutes at 220C//425F.
6. Add the mango, lemon juice, brown sugar and cinnamon to the pineapple and cook for a further 4 minutes at 220C//425F.
7. Serve with natural Greek yoghurt.

Nutritional Information per Serving:

SERVES −4 | CALORIES −81KCAL | PROTEIN −0.6G | CARBOHYDRATES −24.3G | FAT −0.5G

SIMPLE APPLES WITH CINNAMON

INGREDIENTS

- 4 dessert apples
- 85g//3oz of dried apricots, finely chopped
- 1/2 teaspoon of ground cinnamon
- 40g//1.4oz sugar
- 20ml sunflower oil

METHOD

1. Peel and core the apples. Cut each apple into 8 apple equal wedges.
2. Preheat the air fryer to 200C//400F.
3. In a bowl, toss the apples with the oil so they are coated, then put in the air fryer and cook at 200C//400F for 12−15 minutes.
4. Add the chopped apricots and cook for a further 3 minutes.
5. Meanwhile, mix the sugar and cinnamon in a bowl.
6. Serve warm, sprinkled with cinnamon sugar. Add a dollop of double cream!

Nutritional Information per Serving:

SERVES −4 | CALORIES −211KCAL | PROTEIN −0.9G | CARBOHYDRATES −43.4G | FAT −5.8G

BANANA PASTRY PARCELS

INGREDIENTS

- 4 bananas
- 20g//0.7oz of cocoa nibs
- 9 sheets brick pastry
- 60g//2oz of dark chocolate
- 30ml milk

METHOD

1. Cut each banana into 9 pieces of 1cm thick. Cut the pastry sheets into quarters.
2. Onto each pastry sheet, put a pinch of cocoa nibs, topped with a slice of banana.
3. Preheat the air fryer to 190C//375F.
4. Fold the pastry into a parcel with the banana inside, and seal. Tie with kitchen string if needed.
5. Cook in the air fryer for 10 minutes at 190C//375F.
6. While cooking, heat the milk and the chocolate in a saucepan, and blend to a smooth sauce.
7. Serve the banana parcels warm with the chocolate sauce.

Nutritional Information per Serving:

SERVES –4 | CALORIES –550KCAL | PROTEIN –7.8G | CARBOHYDRATES –64.8G | FAT –31.1G

HONEYED FIG AND PINEAPPLE

INGREDIENTS

- 1 pineapple
- 4 fresh figs
- 15ml of lemon juice
- 70g//2.5oz of honey
- 1 pinch of ground cinnamon

METHOD

1. Preheat the air fryer to 180C//350F.
2. Cut off the top and bottom of the pineapple, peel, core and chop into cubes.
3. Put the pineapple cubes into the air fryer. Drizzle about 40g//1.5oz of the honey over the top and cook for 10 minutes at 180C//350F.
4. Wash the figs and cut each one into quarters.
5. Add the figs to the air fryer, drizzle over the rest of the honey with the lemon juice and cinnamon. Cook at 180C//350F for further 4 to 5 minutes.
6. Serve warm with vanilla ice cream.

Nutritional Information per Serving:

SERVES –4 TO 6 | CALORIES –174KCAL | PROTEIN –1.7G | CARBOHYDRATES –45.7G | FAT –0.4G

APPLE CAKE

INGREDIENTS

- 230g//8oz brown sugar
- 3 eggs
- 115g//4oz peeled, cored, and chopped
- 120g//4.2oz of plain flour

METHOD

1. Combine the sugar and eggs together until you have a smooth mixture, then add the flour and mix well.
2. Stir in the chopped apples so they are spread evenly throughout the mixture.
3. Preheat the air fryer to 160C//320F.
4. Spray the cake tin with cooking oil and pour the cake batter into it.
5. Place the tin in the air fryer and cook for 12–15 minutes at 160C//320F.
6. Check your cake, and if it's not quite ready, then cook for another 2–3 minutes.
7. Serve and enjoy!

Nutritional Information per Serving:

SERVES –6 | CALORIES –237 KCAL | PROTEIN –5G | CARBOHYDRATES –44.9G | FAT –3GG

WALNUT CAKE

INGREDIENTS

- 180g//6.3oz of plain flour
- 110g//4oz of ground walnuts
- 150g//5oz of caster sugar
- 2 eggs
- 120ml of milk
- 2 teaspoons of baking powder
- 80ml of vegetable oil
- 1 teaspoon pure vanilla extract

METHOD

1. Whisk the flour, sugar, and baking powder together in a mixing bowl, then fold in the eggs and vanilla to make a thick cake mixture.
2. Now at the vegetable oil and the milk and whisk to a smooth batter.
3. Add the walnuts and stir gently to distribute through the mixture.
4. Preheat the air fryer to 170C//340F.
5. Grease a 7-inch baking tin and line with baking paper. Pour the batter in.
6. Place the cake tin in the air fryer and cook for about 40 minutes at 170C//340° F.
7. Allow to cool and serve. (You can decorate with frosting and chopped walnuts if you prefer.)

Nutritional Information per Serving:

SERVES −6 | CALORIES −477KCAL | PROTEIN −10.8G | CARBOHYDRATES −52.1G | FAT −26.5G

RED VELVET CAKE

INGREDIENTS

For the Red Velvet Cake:

- 245ml of buttermilk
- 1 teaspoon pure vanilla extract
- 1 teaspoon white vinegar
- 245ml of vegetable oil
- 2 eggs
- ½ a teaspoon of red food colouring
- 400g//14oz of granulated sugar
- 300g//11oz of self-raising flour
- 30g//1oz cocoa powder
- 1 teaspoon of baking powder

For the Cream Cheese Frosting:

- 455g//16oz full fat cream cheese at room temperature
- 170g//6oz of unsalted butter at room temperature
- 625g//22oz of icing sugar
- 1 teaspoon of pure vanilla extract

METHOD

1. Combine the buttermilk, pure vanilla extract, vinegar, oil, eggs, and food colouring.
2. In a separate mixing bowl combine the sugar, cake flour, cocoa powder, and baking powder.
3. Pour the milk and egg mixture into the flour and sugar and mix thoroughly.
4. Preheat the air fryer to 160C//320F.
5. Grease two shallow cake tins and line with baking paper. Pour the mixture evenly between the two tins.
6. Put the pans into the air fryer and cook at 160C//320F for 10−15 minutes. Depending on the size of your air fryer you may need to cook each cake separately. Check your cakes and if necessary, give them a couple of minutes longer. Let the cake cool, while you prepare the frosting.
7. To make the frosting, mix the cream cheese, butter, icing sugar and vanilla extract together to a smooth consistency. Use an electric mixer if you have one.
8. Spread the frosting on the flat side of one of the cakes and place the second cake on top so the frosting lies between the two like a sandwich. Spread frosting over the top of the cake too.
9. Refrigerate for at least two hours before serving.

Nutritional Information per Serving:

SERVES –8 | CALORIES –607KCAL | PROTEIN –6.9G | CARBOHYDRATES –83.2G | FAT –29.3G

LEMON CUPCAKES

INGREDIENTS

- 80g//2.8oz of plain flour
- 200g//7oz of caster sugar
- 2 teaspoons of lemon zest
- 1/2 teaspoon of baking soda
- 1 teaspoon baking powder
- 1/2 teaspoon of salt
- 170g/6oz of unsalted butter, room temperature
- 2 eggs
- 120ml of sour cream, room temperature
- 60ml of milk
- 60ml of fresh lemon juice
- 230g//8oz of buttercream frosting

METHOD

1. In a bowl, combine the sugar, lemon zest, flour, baking powder, baking soda.
2. In a separate bowl, combine the butter, eggs, sour cream, milk, and lemon juice.
3. Gradually pour the wet ingredients into the dry. Mix thoroughly.
4. Preheat the air fryer to 160C//320F.
5. Spritz the muffin tin with cooking oil, or line with cupcake liners.
6. Distribute the muffin mix among the muffin tins evenly, filling to about ⅔ for each one.
7. Place in the air fryer and cook for 10–12 minutes at 160C//320F. Add on a few minutes cooking time at the end if required.
8. Decorate and serve.

Nutritional Information per Serving:

SERVES –6 | CALORIES –528KCAL | PROTEIN –7G | CARBOHYDRATES –62G | FAT –29.3G

BLUEBERRY DESSERT

INGREDIENTS

For the Blueberry Layer:

- 330g//12oz of fresh blueberries
- 100g//3.5oz sugar

For the Batter:

- 120g//4.2oz plain flour
- 100g//3.5oz sugar
- 2 teaspoons of baking powder
- 1 teaspoon of salt
- 180ml whole milk
- Optional: vanilla ice cream

METHOD

1. Put the fresh blueberries and sugar into a bowl, stirring gently to coat the blueberries.
2. Spray 2 ramekins with cooking oil and pour in the blueberry mixture.
3. In a separate bowl, combine the flour, sugar, baking powder, salt, and milk.
4. Preheat the air fryer to180C//350F.
5. Pour the topping over the blueberries and sugar.
6. Put the ramekins into the air fryer and cook for 8–10 minutes at 180C//350F.
7. Optional: Serve with a scoop of ice cream.

CARROT CAKE

INGREDIENTS

- 180g//6.3oz flour
- ¾ teaspoon of baking soda
- 1 teaspoon of baking powder
- 1 teaspoon of ground cinnamon
- ¼ teaspoon of ground nutmeg
- ¼ teaspoon of ground ginger

- Pinch of salt
- 135g//5oz of shredded carrot
- 125ml of vegetable oil
- 2 eggs
- 130g//4.5oz of light brown sugar, packed

- 85g//3oz of unsweetened applesauce
- 1 teaspoon of vanilla extract
- 50g//1.8oz of chopped pecans for decoration

For the Frosting:

- 115g//4oz of cream cheese, softened to room temperature

- 30g//1oz of butter, room temperature

- 100g//3.5oz of icing sugar
- 1 teaspoon of vanilla extract

METHOD

1. In a bowl, mix the flour, baking soda, baking powder, cinnamon, nutmeg, ginger, and salt.
2. One by one, add the carrots, oil, eggs, brown sugar, applesauce, and vanilla extract and stir well until just combined.
3. Preheat the air fryer to 160C//320F.
4. Prepare a loaf tin by spritzing with cooking oil and lining with baking paper.
5. Pour the batter into the loaf tin and place in the air fryer.
6. Cook for 20–30 minutes at 160C//320F, or until a toothpick inserted in the centre comes out clean.
7. For the frosting, beat together the cream cheese and butter until creamy and smooth. Add the icing sugar and vanilla and mix until combined. Set to one side.
8. Once cooked, cool the carrot cake on a wire rack before frosting over the top. Decorate with chopped pecan nuts and serve.

CRANBERRY CAKE

INGREDIENTS

- 115g//4oz of butter at room temperature
- 200g//7oz of granulated sugar
- 120ml of full cream Jersey milk (Gold top)
- 1 egg
- 1 teaspoon of vanilla extract
- 1 teaspoon salt
- 250g//9oz of plain flour
- 2 teaspoons of baking powder

- 240g//8.5oz of cranberries, fresh or frozen

METHOD

1. In a large mixing bowl, beat the butter and sugar until pale and fluffy.
2. Fold in the eggs, vanilla extract, and milk.
3. Gradually stir in the flour, salt, and baking powder, then add the cranberries. Mix well until combined.
4. Preheat the air fryer to 160C//320F.
5. Spritz a cake tin with cooking oil, line with baking paper and pour the mixture in.
6. Sprinkle some sugar over the top and place the filled cake tin in the air fryer.
7. Cook at 160C//320F for 12–15 minutes.
8. Allow to cool, serve, and enjoy.

Nutritional Information per Serving:

SERVES –8 | CALORIES –355KCAL | PROTEIN –4.5G | CARBOHYDRATES –52.7G | FAT –14.1G

SPICE CAKE

● ●

INGREDIENTS

- 300g//10.6oz of plain flour
- 1 teaspoon of baking powder
- 1 teaspoon of baking soda
- 1 teaspoon of salt
- 1 teaspoon of ground cinnamon
- 1 teaspoon of all–spice
- 1/2 teaspoon of ground nutmeg
- 115g//4oz of butter
- 200g//7oz of granulated sugar
- 150g//5oz of light brown sugar
- 3 eggs
- 330ml of buttermilk

METHOD

1. Mix all the dry ingredients in a bowl together and set to one side.
2. In a separate bowl, mix the cream, butter, granulated sugar, and brown sugar.
3. Gradually fold in the eggs and add the buttermilk. Stir in flour and mix until well combined.
4. Next, blend the dry mix with the wet mix until your cake batter is thoroughly combined.
5. Preheat the air fryer to 160C//320F. Spritz a cake tin with cooking oil and line with baking paper.
6. Pour the cake mixture into the cake tin, place in the air fryer and cook for 15–20 minutes at 160C//320F.
7. Allow to cool before slicing and serving.

Nutritional Information per Serving:

SERVES –8 | CALORIES –443KCAL | PROTEIN –7.5G | CARBOHYDRATES –70.8G | FAT –15.2G

GINGERBREAD CAKE

● ●

INGREDIENTS

- 315g//11oz of plain flour
- 1 teaspoon of salt
- 1 teaspoon of baking soda
- 1 teaspoon of ginger
- 280g//10oz of molasses
- 1 large egg
- 50g//1.8oz of granulated sugar
- 240ml of buttermilk
- 45g//1.5oz of butter, melted

METHOD

1. First combine the flour, baking soda, salt, and ground ginger in a large mixing bowl.
2. Gradually add, and stir in, the egg, molasses, sugar, buttermilk, and butter.
3. Preheat your air fryer to 160C//320F.
4. Spray your baking pan with olive oil spray and pour the batter in.
5. Put your cake in the air fryer and cook at 160C//320F for 20 minutes.
6. Check to see if it's fully cooked. If not, cook for an extra 10 minutes.
7. Plate, serve, and enjoy.

Nutritional Information per Serving:

SERVES –8 | CALORIES –320KCAL | PROTEIN –6G | CARBOHYDRATES –69G | FAT –2G

DEVILS FOOD CAKE

INGREDIENTS

- 255g//9oz of plain flour
- 1 teaspoon of baking powder
- 2 teaspoons of baking soda
- 1 teaspoon of salt
- 100g//3.5oz of unsweetened cocoa powder
- 450g//1lb of sugar
- 2 eggs
- 235ml of vegetable oil
- 235ml of buttermilk
- 235ml of hot coffee
- 2 teaspoons vanilla extract
- Frosting: buttercream frosting

METHOD

1. Mix the eggs and sugar together, then gradually add and stir in the rest of the ingredients. Mix until well combined.
2. Preheat the air fryer to 160C//320F and spray with cooking oil.
3. Grease the cake pan that fits your air fryer and pour in your cake batter.
4. Cook in the air fryer for 12 minutes at 160C//320F. If it's not cooked when the time is up, give it a few more minutes cooking time.
5. Remove your cake from the air fryer and allow to cool completely before adding your frosting.
6. Plate, serve, and enjoy!

Nutritional Information per Serving (without frosting):

SERVES –8 | CALORIES –593KCAL | PROTEIN –7.2G | CARBOHYDRATES –80.2G | FAT –30G

COFFEE CAKE

INGREDIENTS

For the Coffee Cake:

- 255g//9oz of butter at room temperature
- 200g//7oz of brown sugar
- 2 eggs
- 1 teaspoon vanilla extract
- 180ml of sour cream
- 310g//11oz of plain flour
- 1 teaspoon of baking powder

For the Brown Sugar Topping:

- 115g//4oz of lour
- 170g//6oz of brown sugar
- 1 teaspoon ground cinnamon
- 100g//3.5oz of melted butter

METHOD

1. Grease your cake pan for the air fryer.
2. Cream the butter and brown sugar together until the mixture is fluffy, then gradually fold in the eggs, vanilla extract, sour cream, flour, and baking powder.
3. Pour the cake batter into your greased cake pan.
4. Preheat your air fryer to 160C//320F.
5. In a separate bowl combine the brown sugar topping ingredients and sprinkle on the cake.
6. Cook at 160C//320F for 12 minutes. If the cake isn't cooked when the time is up, try 5–10 minutes more.
7. Plate, serve and enjoy!

Nutritional Information per Serving:

SERVES –8 | CALORIES –627 KCAL | PROTEIN –7.3G | CARBOHYDRATES –68.5G | FAT –36.8G

EASY APPLE PIE CAKE

INGREDIENTS

- 1kg//2.2lb of apple pie filling
- 470g//16.6oz of packet cake mix (yellow sponge)
- 120g//4.2oz of butter, melted

METHOD

1. Spray an air fryer safe pan lightly with cooking oil and spread the apple pie filling evenly over the bottom.
2. Preheat your air fryer to 140C//320F.
3. In a small bowl, combine the cake mix and melted butter thoroughly.
4. Pour the cake mix evenly over the apple pie filling and put the cake into the air fryer.
5. Cook for 20 minutes at 140C//320F. Cook another couple of minutes if it's not quite done at the end of the 20 minutes.
6. Allow to cool and enjoy!

Nutritional Information per Serving:

SERVES –8 | CALORIES –373 KCAL | PROTEIN –3G | CARBOHYDRATES –88G | FAT –2 G

ITALIAN RICOTTA CAKE

INGREDIENTS

- 3 egg whites
- 3 egg yolks
- 1 teaspoon of salt
- 170g//6oz of sugar
- 280g//10oz of melted butter
- 150g//5oz of flour
- 15g//0.5oz of baking powder
- 250g//9oz ricotta cheese
- Zest of two lemons

METHOD

1. In a bowl, whisk the egg whites into firm peaks.
2. In a separate bowl, mix the yolks, salt, and sugar until combined. Add the melted butter, flour, baking powder, ricotta cheese, and lemon zest.
3. Finally, stir in the egg whites.
4. Grease an air fryer safe pan and pour the batter in.
5. Put the cake in the air fryer and cook at 160C//320F for 20 minutes. Give it another 5 minutes if it's not quite cooked.
6. Allow to cool, plate, and enjoy.

Nutritional Information per Serving:

SERVES –8 | CALORIES –467KCAL | PROTEIN –7.5G | CARBOHYDRATES –33.3G | FAT –34.9G

BERRY COBBLER

INGREDIENTS

- 130g//4.5oz of fresh blackberries washed and dried
- 130g//4.5oz of fresh raspberries washed and dried
- 130g//4.5oz of fresh blueberries washed and dried
- ¾ teaspoon of lemon juice
- 100g//3.5oz of granulated sugar
- 180g//6.3oz of melted butter, cooled
- 90g//3.1oz plain flour
- 170g//6oz of brown sugar
- 170ml milk
- 115g//4oz old fashioned oats
- Optional: serve with vanilla ice cream and fresh mint leaves

METHOD

1. Grease 6 ramekins ready for the mixture.
2. Toss all the berries with the granulated sugar in a mixing bowl, making sure that they are thoroughly coated.
3. In a separate bowl, combine the flour, butter, brown sugar, and milk.
4. Add about 60ml of batter to each ramekin then heap each with about 41.5g//2oz berries.
5. Preheat your air fryer to 200C//400F.
6. Stir the oats into the remaining batter, then share equally between the ramekins, pouring over the top of the berries.
7. Put the filled ramekins into the air fryer and cook for 15 minutes at 200C//400F.
8. Remove from the air fryer, allow to cool and serve with ice cream, garnished with mint leaves.

Nutritional Information per Serving:

SERVES –6 | CALORIES –538KCAL | PROTEIN –6G | CARBOHYDRATES –71G | FAT –27G

MONKEY BREAD FOR ONE

INGREDIENTS

- 3 frozen rolls defrosted
- 30g//1oz of granulated sugar
- 1 teaspoon of ground cinnamon
- 1 teaspoon of unsalted butter, melted
- 1 teaspoon of brown sugar

METHOD

1. Defrost your bread rolls, then cut them each into 4 pieces.
2. In a separate bowl, blend the sugar and ground cinnamon thoroughly.
3. In a second bowl, mix the melted butter with the brown sugar.
4. Preheat your air fryer to 170C//330F and spray with cooking oil.
5. Roll your dough pieces (the cut bread rolls) into a ball and dip in the cinnamon sugar mix. Place in a greased ramekin.
6. Pour the melted butter and ground cinnamon sugar over the top.
7. Put in air fryer and cook for 7 to 10 minutes at 170C//330F.
8. Plate, serve, and enjoy!

Nutritional Information per Serving:

SERVES –1 | CALORIES –473KCAL | PROTEIN –11G | CARBOHYDRATES –94G | FAT –6G

BUTTERSCOTCH PUDDING WITH SAUCE

INGREDIENTS

- 170g//6oz of brown sugar (dark brown or light brown)
- 150g//5oz of self–raising flour
- 100g//3.5oz of butter, melted
- 1 egg
- 120ml of milk
- 85g//3oz of golden syrup
- 1 tablespoon of corn flour
- 350ml of boiling water

METHOD

1. Grease a heat proof dish that will fit in your air fryer.
2. In a bowl, combine the flour and about a 1/3 of the sugar, then add the melted butter, egg, milk, and half of the golden syrup. Mix well.
3. Transfer to your greased dish.
4. In another bowl, mix the remaining brown sugar and corn flour together, and sprinkle over the top of the pudding and set to one side for a moment.
5. Preheat the air fryer to 180C//350F.
6. In a jug, blend the remaining golden syrup with the boiling water, then pour over the top of your pudding.
7. Put the pudding bowl into the air fryer and cook for 40–45 minutes at 180C//350F.
8. Allow to cool slightly before serving with double cream or ice cream.

Nutritional Information per Serving:

SERVES –6 | CALORIES –346KCAL | PROTEIN –4.5G | CARBOHYDRATES –50G | FAT –15G

STRAWBERRY DESSERT CASSEROLE

INGREDIENTS

- 200g//7oz of white bread, crumbled
- 100g//3.5oz of white sugar
- 30ml of sour cream
- 150ml of milk, warmed
- 2 eggs
- 200g//7oz of strawberries, washed and cut into halves quarters
- Extra 15g/0.5oz of breadcrumbs for sprinkling

METHOD

1. Soak the breadcrumbs in warm milk, add the sour cream, eggs and sugar. Mix well.
2. Add sour cream, sugar, eggs and mix well.
3. Preheat the air fryer to 150C//300F.
4. Grease a cake mould with butter and sprinkle with breadcrumbs. Spread the mixture evenly over the breadcrumbs and spread the strawberries over the top.
5. Cook in the air fryer for 30 minutes at 150C//300F.
6. Serve with ice cream or cream.

Nutritional Information per Serving:

SERVES –6 | CALORIES –346KCAL | PROTEIN –4.5G | CARBOHYDRATES –50G | FAT –15G

PAVLOVA

INGREDIENTS

- 4 egg whites
- 200g//7oz of caster sugar
- 1 teaspoon of vanilla extract
- 1 teaspoon of cornflour
- ½ teaspoon of white vinegar

METHOD

1. Whisk the egg whites in a bowl with the caster sugar until it forms stiff peaks. An electric mixer will make this easier.
2. Fold in the cornflour, vanilla, and vinegar. The vinegar will stiffen the mixture.
3. Preheat the air fryer to 110C//230F.
4. Scoop your meringue mixture into a mound on a sheet of baking paper and place in the air fryer.
5. Cook at 110C//230F for 40 minutes until the mixture has dried out.
6. Allow to cool, then serve with whipped cream and berries.

Nutritional Information per Serving:

SERVES –8 | CALORIES –105KCAL | PROTEIN –1.8G | CARBOHYDRATES –25.4G | FAT –0G

SWEET POTATO DESSERT FRIES

INGREDIENTS

- 2 sweet potatoes, peeled and cut into skinny fries
- 15g//0.5oz of melted butter
- Another 1 teaspoon butter, melted kept to one side
- 30g//1oz of sugar
- 1/2 teaspoon of cinnamon

METHOD

1. Preheat the air fryer to 195C//380F.
2. In a bowl, toss the skinny fries with the melted butter until coated.
3. Put in the air fryer and cook for 15–18 minutes at 195C//380F.
4. Combine the remaining melted butter with the sugar and cinnamon in a bowl and toss in the fries to thoroughly coat.
5. Enjoy immediately.

Nutritional Information per Serving:

SERVES –4 | CALORIES –110KCAL | PROTEIN –1G | CARBOHYDRATES –18G | FAT –4G

MERINGUE NESTS

INGREDIENTS

- 3 egg whites
- 200g//7oz of caster sugar
- 150 ml cream whipped
- 70g//2.5oz of winter berries compote

METHOD

1. Preheat the oven to 120C//250F and line a baking sheet with baking paper.
2. Whisk the egg whites in a bowl until it forms stiff peaks. An electric mixer will make this easier.
3. Gradually add the sugar until the mixture is thick and glossy.
4. Using a piping bag, or scoop with a tablespoon, place 6 meringue nests onto the prepared baking sheet, making sure they do not touch one another and place in the air fryer.
5. Cook for about 20 minutes at 120C//250F until the meringues are firm to touch, but softer in the middle.
6. Allow to cool in the air fryer before lifting out and removing the meringues from the baking paper.
7. Whip the cream and berry compote together in a small bowl.
8. Serve the meringues topped with berry cream! Enjoy!

Nutritional Information per Serving:

SERVES –5 | CALORIES –218KCAL | PROTEIN –3G | CARBOHYDRATES –50.5G | FAT –1.4G

FRUIT SPONGE PUDDING
• •

INGREDIENTS

For the Topping:

- 85g//3oz of plain flour
- 60g//2oz of sugar
- 1 egg
- 30ml of milk
- 60g//2oz of soft butter
- 1/2 teaspoon of baking powder

For the Filling:

- Canned fruit to serve

METHOD

1. Preheat the air fryer to 160C//320F.
2. Beat the flour, sugar, egg, milk butter and baking powder together in a bowl until the mixture is creamy and soft.
3. Grease a baking dish and pour in about ¾ of the batter mix. Place the canned fruit over the top, then finish with the remaining batter mix. Level to a smooth surface.
4. Cook at 160C//320F for about 25–30 minutes until golden brown.
5. Serve with custard.

Nutritional Information per Serving:

SERVES –4 | CALORIES –319KCAL | PROTEIN –5G | CARBOHYDRATES –47G | FAT –13G

VANILLA CAKE
• •

INGREDIENTS

- 230g//8oz of butter, room temperature
- 230g//8oz of brown sugar
- 2 eggs
- 1 teaspoon of vanilla extract
- 190ml of sour cream
- 300g//10.6oz of plain flour
- 1 teaspoon of baking powder

For the Brown Sugar Topping:

- 120g//4.2oz of plain flour
- 165g//6oz of brown sugar
- 1 teaspoon of ground cinnamon
- 90g//3.2oz of melted butter

METHOD

1. Grease your air fryer safe cake tin ready for the cake mixture.
2. Beat the butter and brown sugar together in a bowl until creamy, then gradually mix in the eggs, vanilla extract, sour cream, flour, and baking powder until well combined.
3. Pour your cake batter into the prepared, greased cake tin.
4. In a separate small bowl, mix the topping by combining the flour, brown sugar, ground cinnamon, and melted butter. Sprinkle over your cake batter mix.
5. Put the pan in the air fryer and cook for about 12 minutes at 155C//320F. Add a few minutes onto the cooking time if it's not quite cooked after the 12 minutes is up.
6. Remove from the air fryer and allow to cool before serving.

Nutritional Information per Serving:

SERVES −6 | CALORIES −959 KCAL | PROTEIN −10.8G | CARBOHYDRATES −111.6G | FAT −53

Disclaimer

This book contains opinions and ideas of the author and is meant to teach the reader informative and helpful knowledge while due care should be taken by the user in the application of the information provided. The instructions and strategies are possibly not right for every reader and there is no guarantee that they work for everyone. Using this book and implementing the information/recipes therein contained is explicitly your own responsibility and risk. This work with all its contents, does not guarantee correctness, completion, quality or correctness of the provided information. Misinformation or misprints cannot be completely eliminated.

EXCLUSIVE BONUS

40 Weight Loss Recipes

&

14 Days Meal Plan

Scan the QR-Code and receive
the FREE download:

Printed in Great Britain
by Amazon

10114368R00125